ANTIQUE
IRON

ANTIQUE IRON

Survey of American and
English forms

fifteenth through nineteenth centuries

by Herbert, Peter, and Nancy Schiffer

77 Lower Valley Road, Atglen, PA 19310

Acknowledgments

We appreciate the help of so many people whose interest in this project has encouraged us to completion. Their enthusiasm for particular objects has been infectious, causing us to want to include every example. Hopefully our selection will prove to be satisfying to them, and instructive to the general audience. Not mentioned by name are several people who prefer to remain anonymous. They are silently but equally gratefully acknowledged along with these friends and staffs of the institutions. H. Perrott Bacot, Anglo American Art Museum, Baton Rouge, Louisiana;   Ann M. Baker, Hall of Records, Dover, Delaware; Lu D. Bartlett; Fred R. Bell, National Park Service picture library, Washington, D.C.; Marylou Birchmore, Essex Institute, Salem, Massachusetts; Philip Bradley, Downingtown, Pennsylvania; Diane E. Chalcoat, The Baltimore Museum of Art; Elizabeth E. Disrude, Hopewell Village, Elverson, Pa.; Charles Dorman, Independence National Historic Park, Philadelphia; Nancy Goyne Evans, Winterthur Museum, Winterthur, Delaware; Conover Fitch, Jr., Perry, Dean, Stahl and Rogers, Boston, Massachusetts; Debra J. Force, Insurance Company of North America museum, Philadelphia, Pennsylvania; Audrie Furcron, Carnegie Library of Pittsburgh; Philippa Glanville, The Museum of London; Katherine B. Hagler, Greenfield Village and The Henry Ford Museum, Dearborn, Michigan; Henry J. Harlow, Old Sturbridge Village, Sturbridge, Massachusetts; Nancy Hazlett; Walter Himmelreich; Carroll J. Hopf, Pennsylvania Farm Museum of Landis Valley; Frank L. Horton, Museum of Early Southern Decorative Arts, Winston-Salem, North Carolina; Phillip Johnston, Wadsworth Atheneum, Hartford, Connecticut; Mary Alice Kennedy, The New York Historical Society, New York City; Joe Kindig 3rd, York, Pennsylvania; Norman Litman, Oceanside, New York; Gordon M. Marshall, The Library Company of Philadelphia; Tyrone G. Martin, Captain, USS *Constitution;* Richard Merrill, photographer, Saugus, Massachusetts; Mr. and Mrs. Karl E. Miller, Chestertown, Maryland; Janice B. Newman, Pennsylvania State Library, Harrisburg, Pennsylvania; Migs Nutt; Carolyn B. Owen, Old Colony Historical Society, Taunton, Massachusetts; Cynthia G. Pollack, Saugus Iron Works, National Historic Site, Saugus, Massachusetts; Brad Rauschenberg, Museum of Early Southern Decorative Arts; Albert Sack, Israel Sack, Inc., New York City; Carol Schmiegle, Winterthur Museum, Winterthur, Delaware; Dr. Donald Shelly, The Historical Society of York County, York, Pennsylvania; Bruce Smith; Jane Smith, historian of Laurel Hill Cemetery, Philadelphia; Frank H. Sommer, Winterthur Museum, Winterthur, Delaware; James C. Sorber, West Chester, Pennsylvania; Lina Steele, Index of American Design, National Gallery of Art; Ruth Troiani, Pound Ridge, New York; Ria Warihay; Deborah D. Waters, Decorative Arts Photographic Collection, Winterthur Museum, Winterthur, Delaware; Carol Wojtowicz, The Philadelphia Contributionship. Thank you.

Published by Schiffer Publishing, Ltd.
77 Lower Valley Road
Atglen, PA 19310
Please write for a free catalog.
This book may be purchased from the publisher.
Please include $2.95 postage.
Try your bookstore first.

We are interested in hearing from authors
with book ideas on related subjects.

Table of Contents

Introduction

From a reconstruction of a Roman blacksmith's shop now installed in the Museum of London of the type originally in Londinium, the first century settlement that is London today, it can be seen that there has been remarkably little change in the iron making process since its earliest beginnings from Chinese antiquity to the European Iron Age to the present.

German craftsmen had achieved a high level of competence in working iron by the medieval era when armour was a nobleman's security. The mining and processing of ore into useable metal was also well developed elsewhere in Northern Europe at this time. By the eighteenth century superior manufacturing processes and qualities of ore had made Sweden famous for quality.

Problems with inflation affected every generation. A fourteenth century written complaint about the cost of spurs in London notes that:

A pair of spurs shall be sold for 6d, and a better pair for 8d, and the best at 10d or 12d, at the very highest.[1]

English government regulations made in 1350 fixing maximum wages and prices were an attempt to control rising costs that resulted from a shortage of skilled craftsmen after the great plague of 1348-9.[2]

Small forges were scattered around London, sometimes in unsuitable locations. In 1377, an armourer was taken to court by his neighbors in Watlin St. who complained that:

The blows of the great hammers shake the walls of their houses and disturb the rest of them and their servants, day and night, and spoil the wine and ale in their cellar, and the stench of the smoke from the sea-coal used in the forge penetrates their hall and chambers.[3]

Industries gradually moved out of London's walls to Southward and other surrounding industrial areas. Henry VIII set up an armory at Greenwich Palace with German craftsmen imported for the purpose. Even though an increasing use of guns made heavily armoured knights less effective by this time, armour remained popular as protection in hand-to-hand combat and as a status symbol for noblemen. The workshop at Greenwhich continued to produce suits of armour until the English Civil War in the mid-seventeenth century.

Guns were imported to England from Germany and Italy after King Henry VIII dissolved the church properties. The scrap metal from several London churches was available for sale between 1530 and 1550. English workmen were skilled enough to re-cast the scrap into cannons. King Henry VIII incorporated the first professional gunners into the Fraternity of Artillery in 1537 and gave them a firing range.[4] By 1600, London was by far the largest industrial center in England, making a wide range of items for sale both at home and abroad.

Deforestation was a tremendous problem all during European history. In 1354, Windsor Castle's accounts refer to over 3,000 oaks being cut. In 1361, another 2,000 were cut. At the time of Charles I, the Forest of Dean was estimated to contain 105,000 trees; by the restoration approximately 30 years later this figure had declined to 30,000 trees. The Forest of Arden disappeared between the reigns of Elizabeth I and William III, a period of about 90 years.[5]

Abraham Darby, Sr., who moved his iron works from Bristol to Coalbrookdale in 1709, changed the charcoal furnace that had been in existence since 1638 to a coke fired furnace to smelt iron. It took until 1750 before the English caught up with him and until 1840 for the Americans to use coke predominantly, even though a few charcoal furnaces survived the American Civil War.

In the New World, evidence of iron-making is no less prevalent than in Europe. The Norsemen probably smelted the first iron in Greenland. Aztecs, Mayas and Incas were using some iron when Cortez arrived. This iron was meteoric and had not been smelted.[6] Even the Cherokees in North Carolina were using crude furnaces at an early date.

Both the French and English explorers of North America, who were officially looking for gold, were also searching for iron. Forests were vitally important to these European countries where too much timber had been cut to make charcoal. Frequent changes in elevation in America gave the abundant water power to run the machinery.

The explorer, Jacques Cartier, noted in 1541 that in Canada limestone was "a goodly-Myne of the best yron in the world".[7]

In the early seventeenth century, Champlain mentioned that his "miner" claimed iron deposits that would yield 50% metal. When the iron was taken home, it was found to be not nearly that good.

The earliest indication of serious interest in discovering commercial iron in the limits of the United States comes from Harriot's *A Report on Virginia* of 1587, which noted:

> In two places of the countrey specially, one about fourescore, & the other six score miles from the fort or place where we dwelt, we found nere the water side the ground to be rocky, which by the triall of a Minerall man was found to holde iron richly. It is found in many places of the country els: I know nothing to the contrary, but that it may be allowed for a good merchantable commodity, considering there the small charge for the labour & feeding of the men, the infinite store of wood, the want of wood & deerenesse thereof in England and the necessity of ballasting of ships.[8]

Data on the first attempts to date iron ore from Virginia are fragmentary. In an appendix to *A True and Sincere declaration for the purpose and ends of the Plantation begun in Virginia,* of 1609, is a list of artisans required for Virginia. Among them are ten iron men for the furnace and two "minerall men".[9] These are also listed in *A Publication by the Counsell of Virginia touching the Plantation There* of 1610.[10]

John Smith, writing about his trip to settle Virginia in 1614, claimed that one of the reasons for settlement was the hope of preventing England from being too dependent on iron and rope from Sweden and Russia.

Virginia had three early projects to make iron, but these failed before 1621 due partly to illness among the iron workers as well as Indian massacres.

In 1612, John Smith suggested that iron works be built at the future site of Richmond and made copious notes about the possibilities for iron manufacturing. Richmond has one of the best industrial sites in America at a falls line (for water power) on navigable water. An iron works was started here but ended with the Indian massacre of March 22, 1622.

There were many attempts to organize iron works in Virginia after this, but a long time elapsed before one was financially successful.

This Iron Works at Saugus, Massachusetts was America's first and one of the most sophisticated *integrated iron and brass works of its time in the world. Richard Merrill, photographer*

A foundry from which workable iron could be extracted from natural ore ideally would be located near the ore deposits, running water, and a vertical drop in terrain. Nearby it was necessary to have timber in large supply for fuel and some type of natural lime for flux. Therefore, foundries are typically found along streams in forests with limestone or sea shells nearby.

Iron ore can be mined in various methods. In Europe, shaft mining is common. Shaft mining was an expensive process that requires blasting powder which was expensive and hard to obtain. In America pits 20 to 40 feet deep sometimes were dug. Ore also can be extracted from iron-rich bogs and marshes. "Bog iron" was a typical early source of iron in both Europe and America.

Bog iron is formed by a natural chemical action caused by decayed vegetable matter upon iron salts in some stream beds. When there is a strata of greensands or marls which carry a soluble iron, under the soil, water seeps through the marls causing the iron in solution to rise to the surface of the water where it oxidizes. The oxide is deposited along the banks of the stream. The deposits mix with mud and turn into thick red and rocky masses of ore. This is the ore that was used in early furnaces. Theoretically, an ore bed will renew itself in about twenty years.

Timber was cut from nearby forests and converted to charcoal by men called colliers. About twelve colliers were needed to keep a single furnace of average size going.

Workmen digging ore from an open pit.
Richard Merrill, photographer

Colliers cutting and stacking trees to make charcoal.
Richard Merrill, photographer

To make charcoal, a level spot was selected, and trees were cut into lengths and bundled into cords. This wood was then stacked around a primitive wooden chimney. Most charcoal piles were about 25′ in diameter at the base. Over this "coal" of wood, damp leaves, earth or turf were stacked. Flammable material such as wood chips were placed in the chimney which was partly closed at the top. Air vents were cut into the sides of the pile. Once the pile was ignited, it took from three to ten days to become charcoal, according to the nature of the wood. While the wood was charring in piles, it had to be watched steadily. Charcoal was always in danger of spontaneous combustion and was transported in small lots to the charcoal house near the forge. Hickory was the best wood for charring, although black oak was more available and more generally used. The production of charcoal was a laborious, lonely, dirty, unpleasant job.

The Oley Furnace in Pennsylvania used 840 bushels of charcoal every twenty-four hours in 1783. This represents about twenty cords of wood. It is known that this furnace made about two tons of iron a day, thus about 400 bushels of charcoal were required for one ton of iron.

Records exist of carters fined for loading charcoal too hot and burning up their carts. There are also numerous records of fires at foundries caused by charcoal that had not cooled sufficiently before it was transported to storage. A dozen colliers at the Hopewell Furnace in Pennsylvania annually converted 5,000 cords of wood into charcoal.

A flux of lime based stone or seashells was dug from deposits near each foundry and stored for later use in the smelting process.

The charcoal was made by stacking cut wood, covering it with leaves, and cutting air vent holes into the sides. Richard Merrill, photographer

In New England where limestone was not readily available, sea shells provided the lime flux that was combined with ore and charcoal. Richard Merrill, photographer

At the two story furnace, a walkway was usually constructed from a high elevation. At the top of the chimney men crossed the walkway to dump ore, fuel and flux into the furnace stack. This dumping process was known as "charging the furnace."

During Henry VII's reign, blast furnaces were known to be in England. The earliest one was a Spanish type that had a low, stocky furnace but, by the eighteenth century, blast furnaces were close to 30' high.

Charcoal was carried in carts containing these baskets from the charcoal storage house and the baskets were dumped into the furnace as one part of "charging" the furnace.
National Park Service, Hopewell Village

A workman is charging the furnace with charcoal. Richard Merrill, photographer

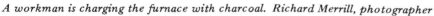

Here the fires burned with air forced in through water driven bellows and an iron air tube called a "tuyere". About once a day red hot molten iron was tapped from the bottom of the furnace. The molten iron was ladled and cast into sand molds on the furnace floor. Pots, firebacks, weights and other small solid iron objects were cast as well as irregular bars. These bars, called pigs, were sold directly to foundries for further manufacture. Iron carriers were men who moved these heavy bars from sand casts to horseback or wagons for transport away from the furnace.

A view of Hopewell furnace showing the waterwheel bellows which send air into the furnace.
Richard Merrill, photographer

Foundrymen pour molten iron into molds for three legged pots at Saugus in sand below the furnace. One pot has just been removed.
National Park Service, Hopewell Village

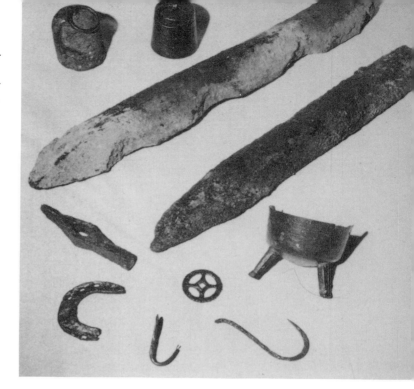

Here are actual objects removed from the site of Saugus Iron Works before the re-building program: weights, possibly for scales or clock jacks, pigs of cast iron, a pick head, a wheel, a 3-legged pot not complete, a horse shoe and two hooks, Richard Merrill, photographer.

This is an iron pig marked from the ISABELLA furnace in Southeastern Pennsylvania. Courtesy, Pennsylvania Farm Museum of Landis Valley.

Very few photographs exist showing the iron pigs broken off from their channels. Rugged men carried these pigs away from the sand beds. The men shown here were known as Iron Carriers. Their job was to remove the pieces of pig iron from the sand. The photograph of the pig iron in the sand was taken at Pittsburgh's Eliza Blast Furnace in the 1880's. Courtesy Carnegie Library, Pittsburgh.

A foundryman prepares a mold for pouring. His flasks for holding the sand and pattern, handles for crucibles, screen for sifting sand, mallets and other tools are ready for use. National Park Service, Hopewell Village.

The foundryman is blowing extra sand off his flasks which contain an upper and a lower side of a mold. The wooden block is holding the flue hole open and will be removed.
National Park Service, Hopewell Village

Foundrymen prepare to pour molten metal into a mold. The plug has been removed. This mold has had a pattern pressed into the sand. The pattern is then removed, the top side of the mold pressed, and the two halves put together.
National Park Service, Hopewell Village

At a forge, pig iron was made into wrought iron. Large hammers, run by water power, struck reheated cast iron to make it malleable and ready for rolling or slitting. National Park Service, Hopewell Village

At the forge, cast iron pigs were reheated and forged by a huge hammer that beat the fibers into conformity. This process resulted in iron bars with greatly increased strength and malleability. The hammer used for this process was probably made at the foundry, and was usually driven by a water powered wheel. The hammer beat continously during production. The noise of the hammer's pound deafened many of the forge workers. These bars of wrought iron were usually sold to blacksmiths.

This is the actual hammer used at the Saugus Iron Works and found during the excavations of the site. This large water-driven hammer could do the work of many men. The noise must have been appalling. Richard Merrill, photographer

A further process was sometimes available for converting the wrought iron bars into flats and rods. This conversion took place at a rolling and slitting mill where wrought iron bars were rolled into flats and the flats slit into rods. These rods could then be cut, often into nails.

Theophile Cazenove, a Frenchman, toured a New Jersey iron works in 1794 and made the following notes:

> The forge for making iron bars is double; a fire and two hammers. Bellows [are] of new construction, kinds of iron boilers whose lids are pushed by pistons up to the further end, and from there the air passes through tin pipes into an iron pipe, which conducts the air into the fire. In another workshop the bars are made red hot and pass through a roller that flattens them and from there they pass through another roller where the plates are cut into rods suitable to make nails.[11]

At the Saugus Iron Works in Massachusetts, two water wheels were used at the slitting mill for this process, one to power the rollers and the other for the slitting machine.

Some iron laborers were free servants whose wages, transportation, food and lodging was guaranteed by the iron company.

Individual agreements were made between the companies and suppliers of certain services such as the following examples:

> Agreement with John Shaw July 23rd, 1761 to stock (with charcoal) the upper forge, and at any time to assist in stocking at any of the other two forges when he has not stocking to do at the said upper forge. The said Shaw is to be paid for the faithful performance of the above agreement eighteen pounds and a pair of shoes, and if he does not get drunk above once in three months, a pair of stockings and his diet.[12]

> Oct. 6th, 1762 Agreement between John Boyer and Patton and Bird to drive team one whole year from the date hereof, for the due performance of which said Patton promises to pay him the sum of twenty-six pounds and two pairs of shoes.[13]

There were also bond servants who were indentured for a period of years without pay.

Some iron works also used European prisoners who had been captured and exiled, and bond servants who were indentured for a period of years without pay. In all, it was usually a rough group of people. Not many Indians are recorded as iron workers in America.

At a slitting mill, water-powered machinery turned wrought iron bars into nails and strips of iron which the blacksmith could use.
Richard Merrill, photographer

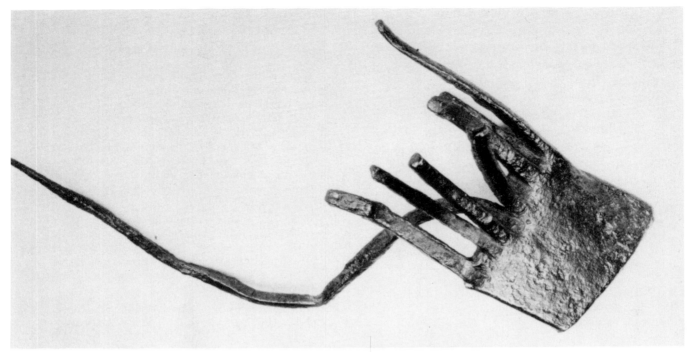

This piece of partially slit wrought iron was found during excavations at the Saugus, Massachusetts Iron Works site. Richard Merrill, photographer.

This group of nails and large bolt were found at the Saugus Iron Works site during excavations and presumably were made there. Richard Merrill, photographer.

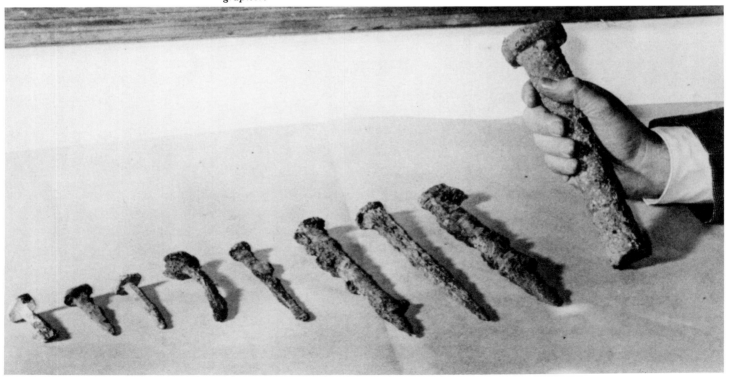

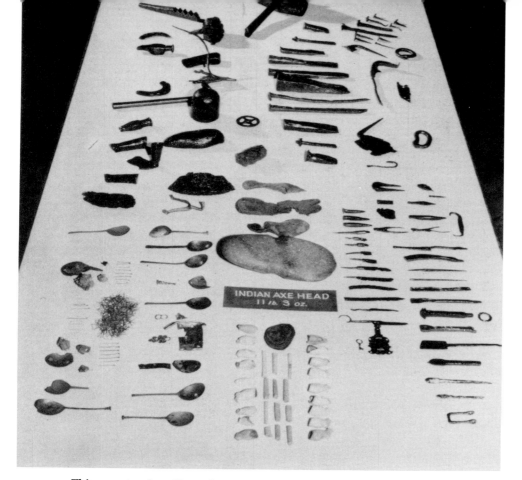

This group of artifacts found during excavations at the Saugus Iron Works indicate both the products of the iron works, and items for daily life, including spoons, nails, chisels, and wedges. Richard Merrill, photographer.

Because the blast furnaces ran steadily once started, the workers had two twelve-hour shifts, lived very near the furnace, had very few days off and were dependent on the company store for practically all their goods. Pay was generally issued as credit at the company store.

Most of the furnaces shut down for a few days during the winter months when the water supply froze. This period of inactivity provided the time necessary for routine repairs, relining of the furnace, and for any men not involved with repair work to help the wood choppers replenish the wood supply. Therefore, year round employment was insured for all who became involved in these iron producing communities.

In America, most furnaces and forges were situated on large tracts of land because a tremendous amount of wood was needed for fuel and good farmland was needed for food for the workers. In Pennsylvania, the Elizabeth Furnace had 10,124 acres; Reading Furnace had 5,600 acres; Colebrook Furnace had 7,684 acres, and Cornwall and Hopewell Furnaces 9,669 acres.

So many workers were needed to furnish the raw materials at a foundry that there was ample room for ineffective management. Generations of the same families in America managed a number of furnaces on the east coast from the seventeenth through nineteenth centuries. The industry staggered along between periods of greater demand to provide an impressive quantity and variety of iron goods. Wars, of course, stimulated iron production for cannons, hand armament, chains, wagon wheel rims, etc. When the railroads were developed, iron was needed for the building of trains and tracks, and the railroads provided a superior means of transportation for finished iron products.

As migrants pushed westward, the iron industry moved and grew to provide tools and materials needed to cultivate, build and civilize the land. Pennsylvania iron works were kept busy as so many people moved through the state to the West.

Low wages gave little incentive to laborers and slim **profits** gave little prospect to investors. Nevertheless, some prominent individuals invested in early furnaces. In the eighteenth century, those who fostered the iron works in Pennsylvania and New Jersey included Anthony Morris, Robert Ellis and Daniel Drinker, all vital members of their business communities.

Varying conditions of iron works can be compared by the operations of works of different times and places. The Saugus, Massachusetts works of the seventeenth century; Batsto, New Jersey, works of the eighteenth century; and Hopewell, Pennsylvania, works of the nineteenth century illustrate conditions of varying natures.

The iron works at Saugus, Massachusetts dates from the seventeenth century, and has been fully excavated and restored by the American steel industries. It is now under the auspices of the National Park Service and open to the public. Therefore, it is possible to closely study the operation of this iron works.

The General Court of Massachusetts passed an ordinance in 1641 entitled "Encouragement to discovery of mines, &c." The measure itself went as follows:

> For the encouragement of such as will adventure for the discovery of mines, it is ordered, that whosoever shall be at the charge for discovery of any mine within this jurisdiction shall enjoy the same, with a fit portion of land to the same, for 21 years to their proper use; and after that time expired, this court shall have the power to allot so much of the benefit thereof to public use as they shall think equal, and that such persons shall have liberty hereby to purchase the interest of any of the Indians in such lands where such mines shall be found, provided that they shall not enter any man's property without the owner's leave.[14]

This ordinance was sparked by the interest of one man in particular, John Winthrop, Jr., the son of the governor of Massachusetts. John Winthrop, Jr. was born at his family home, Groton Manor, England in 1606. After attending Trinity College, Dublin, he studied law in London and took a grand tour of Europe. In 1631, he joined his father in Massachusetts. He seems to have been one of the most scientific men of his day, as an inspection of his library housed now at the

New York State Historical Society can verify. He was admitted to the Royal Society and displayed far-sighted liberalism for a Puritan. His interest in promoting the development of an iron industry in Massachusetts to provide the much needed commodity led him to head back to London in 1641 to raise funds necessary to promote his idea. In a year and a half, by 1643, he had convinced 24 people, including a few in Massachusetts, to risk investment in his idea and formed the Company of Undertakers of Iron Works in New England. That year Winthrop visited Agamenticus, Maine, in search of bog iron and a suitable site for an iron works. There he met Joseph Jenks, who was running a blacksmith shop.

King Charles I imported skilled German cutlers in 1629 to oversee English craftsmen in the sword industry in England. Benjamin Stone, who had a sword factory in Hounslow, employed some of these Germans. A broad sword, 38″ long, survives inscribed "Ioseph Ienckes" (Joseph Jenks). This sword would have been made by Jenks at this forge from metal supplied by the master Benjamin Stone, and ground and polished at Stone's Mill.[15]

In the autumn of 1643, John Winthrop and the group of men he had gathered for his project arrived in Massachusetts from England. They set out to build the iron works at the edge of the Saugus River near Lynn, Massachusetts. Here they built a foundry, forge and slitting mill as modern as any in Europe. Colonists from nearby communities were hired for unskilled work in the building of the iron works and for its early operation.

In 1645, Joseph Jenks and one of the shareholders of the Company of Undertakers petitioned the Massachusetts general court for the right to establish a plantation at Nashaway where Winthrop had found bog iron. Neither this plantation, nor the Nashaway site for an iron works, was ever built. However, in May of 1646, Jenks petitioned the general court stating that "the Lord hath been pleased to give mee knowledg in Makeing, and Erecting of Engines of Mills to goe by water for the speedy dispatch of much worke with few mens labour in little tyme". Jenks requested the exclusive privilege of setting up mills to make scythes and other edged tools, together with a "new Invented Saw Mill" for the term of fourteen years."[16]

The court agreed. Even though water powered scythe mills had been known in England as early as 1614, this was a new venture for America.

By 1648, John Winthrop was succeeded as agent for the Company of Undertakers by Richard Leader. Leader was one of America's first practical engineers and he is responsible for building a number of industrial works from sawmills to the most sophisticated iron machinery of his day, the iron works at Saugus. This year Jenks agreed with Leader to "build and erect a mill or hammer for the forging of sithes or any other iron ware by water."[17] This site was connected to the spillways of the Saugus Iron Works. He apparently also made brass items here, as several brass pins have been found at the site through excavation.

This is the actual remains of one of the water-wheels at the Saugus Iron Works as it was being excavated. Richard Merrill, photographer

This overview shows part of the excavations at Saugus, including a mill race and the remains of a waterwheel and shaft. Richard Merrill, photographer

Leader was to supply Jenks with the bar and cast iron needed for its construction at no cost to Jenks, if the forge was erected within five months. Jenks' forge had three water wheels, a hearth, and possibly a water powered hammer. It is logical to assume that the grindstones were run by water power. Jenks must have learned a great deal about steel as a sword maker because among the jobs he was paid for in 1653 included making and setting saws, making a broadaxe, repairing iron fixtures for the company's boat and steeling axes. For this work Jenks got £18 and 10 shillings over 5 years.[18] Jenks employed his son and at least one apprentice.

Jenks frequently petitioned the court for monopoly for the manufacture of various machines such as "that engine the said Jenks hath proposed . . . for the more speeding cutting of grasse."[19]

Jenks succeeded in drawing wire but the general court refused his petition for "encouragement" of that trade. In fact the court bought wire drawing tools and distributed them to those who could make the best use of them. Pins and cards (for carding flax and wool) were very much needed in the Bay Colony. During archeological excavations at the site of the Jenks forge, many pins were found so it seems probable that he did manufacture them. Jenks was succeeded by his son and then his grandson, who later became a Governor of Massachusetts.

In 1651, a shareholder of the Company bought 62 Scotsmen prisoners in England who had been captured by Cromwell at the Battle of Dunbar in the autumn of 1650. By 1653, thirty-five of these men were still on the company's books working at the Saugus forge in Massachusetts. There are numerous records of personal disagreements between the Massachusetts Puritan colonists and these laboring Scotsmen from the iron works. Living and working conditions were very hard. The laborers were rebellious sorts who were found guilty of swearing, cursing and assault. The intemperate use of liquor seems to have been the cause of much misery. The Puritans were also annoyed by the laborers missing church. Nevertheless, gradually the two groups mingled, as records of marriages indicate, and the Scotsmen eventually were absorbed into the Puritan society.

The iron works at Saugus failed ultimately due to several factors. Management was extremely difficult for so ambitious a project with such diverse personnel and conditions. The price of iron was fixed at £20 per ton, and there was constant competition from imported iron. Eventually the Saugus works could not return a profit to the shareholders, and they refused to advance more capital. By 1654, the project was disbanded.

After the failure of Saugus, the workmen, with encouragement from other colonies moved to Connecticut and other places in Massachusetts. An iron works was built at Taunton in 1652, where the members of that town invited the Leonard family formerly of Saugus to join with some of the local workers in building an iron making furnace. Eight iron making plants were established and running by 1700, as far south as Rhode Island and New Jersey.

The Leonard family also dispersed to central southern New Jersey. Here the pine barrens region furnished the necessary raw materials and conditions for iron making. The Leonards settled near Red Bank, Shrewsbury in Monmouth County, where they are believed to have built a foundry at Tinton Falls about 1675 on 1,170 acres purchased from the Indians.[20] Although bog iron was plentiful then as it is now, today this ore is not used.

The Pine Barrens region of New Jersey had been settled in the early 1700's by lumbermen who were attracted by the natural water power and abundant forest. Here saw mills were built and lumber was shipped down the Mullica River to Philadelphia for sale. The area has had numerous paper mills, saw mills, glass and brickmaking establishments, as well as iron works. The center of the area is the town of Batsto.

The Leonard's iron works at Tinton Falls failed, but their interests extended to additional sites.

About 1720, James Leonard, a son of the second James bought land in what is now Easton, and built still another forge and put it in the charge of his son Eliphalet. Originally named Brummagem, it was more commonly referred to as Eliphalet Leonard's forge. His son, and namesake, is thought to have made steel at Easton prior to 1771, and his son, Jonathan Leonard, set up steel furnaces in

This restored kitchen at the Saugus iron master's house shows a clock jack, spit, andirons with spit hooks, fire back, trammels, three-legged pots, and tongs all in use. Richard Merrill, photographer

1787 and 1808. Another son, a third Eliphalet, established a forge, trip hammer, and nailer's shop in 1790 which went bankrupt by 1801, but became, along with other properties of the Easton Leonards, the basis of the subsequently prosperous Ames enterprises. [21]

Real success for New Jersey iron works began with the discovery of large bog iron deposits near the Mullica and Wading Rivers around Batsto. No limestone was available for flux in New Jersey, so oyster and clam shells were used there instead. As demand for iron products was created by the French and Indian War and American Revolution, New Jersey iron works furnished enough products to make the trade profitable.

Charles Read realized the potential for profit and by 1768 had built the Etna, Taunton, Atsion and Batsto furnaces. Read, born in 1715, had no formal legal training but worked as a lawyer and politician. He worked at a number of jobs in New Jersey variously as "clerk of the circuits, Surrogate of the Prerogative Court, Indian Commissioner, Deputy Secretary of the Province, Member of the Assembly, Member of the Governor's Council, Associate Justice of the Supreme Court, and for a short period, Chief Justice of that tribunal. [22]

Charles Read's hostile biographer, Aaron Leaming said:

> No man knew so well as he how to riggle himself into office, nor keep it so long, nor make so much of it. [23]

At the age of fifty-one, Charles Read had decided to go into the iron business. The Batsto Furnace was started in 1766 along with two glass factories, a brick-making establishment, two saw mills, and a gristmill. Before his iron furnaces were in full production, Read sold the Batsto Furnace and eventually fled the country to escape his creditors. While he was active, though, he was extremely vital. He petitioned the New Jersey legislature in 1765 for permission to build a dam across Batsto Creek to furnish water for his iron works. At that time he apparently enjoyed a fairly good reputation. The petition reads in part:

> And whereas the Honourable Charles Read, Esq., by his humble petition, set forth that he hath proved to demonstration good Merchantable Bar-Iron may be drawn from such Ore as may be found in plenty in the Bogs and . . . in such parts of this Province which are too poor for cultivation, which he conceived will be a public emolument; and that

This English trade card of the 18th century mentions steel trusses and braces as products of the Holmes and Laurie Company. Museum of London.

in order to erect the necessary Works, he had lately purchased a considerable Tract of Land lying on both sides of Batsto Creek near Little Egg Harbour in the County of Burlington; praying the aid of the Legislature to enable him to erect a Dam across the said Creek for the use of an Iron works; and in order to remove every objection against the Prayer of his Petition hath produced a certificate from Joseph Burr, is and for several years past hath been in possession of Saw-Mill at the head of Batstow [sic] Creek aforesaid, from whence Boards only have been floated down but attended with such Expence as to afford a probability that the said Creek will not be hereafter used for the like purpose; hence the said Burr alledges that the Dam over the said Creek as petitioned for by the said Charles Read, cannot be of any public or private detriment, but on the contrary greatly advantageous.[24]

Read left Batsto furnace to his partners before construction was completed. Thereafter, its ownership passed through many hands including those of men with enormous wealth and political importance. In 1770, Charles Thompson who became Secretary of the Continental Congress, co-owned Batsto Furnace with John Cox. The furnace at that time produced small iron goods in increasing quantity and variety. The Pennsylvania Gazette of June 7, 1775, carried the following advertisement:

MANUFACTURED AT BATSTO FURNACE in West New Jersey, and to be sold either at the works or by the subscriber, in Philadelphia, a great variety of iron pots, kettles, Dutch ovens and oval fish kettles, either with or without covers, skillets of different sizes, being much lighter, neater and superior in quality to any imported from Great Britain; Potash, and other large kettles from 30 to 125 gallons, sugar mill Gudgeons, neatly rounded and polished at the ends; grating-bars of different lengths, grist-mill rounds; weights of all sizes, from 7 to 56 lb.; Fullers plates; open and close stoves, of different sizes; rag-wheel irons for saw-mills; pestles and mortars, sash weights and forge hammers of the best quality. Also Batsto Pig-Iron as usual, the quality of which is too well known to need any recommendation.

JOHN COX[25]

Cox was a patriot in the American Revolution and by 1778 was made Assistant Quartermaster General. Therefore, his interest in Batsto Furnace was served well by Army contracts. Cox was commissioned by the Pennsylvania Council of Safety to provide a large

number of cannon balls to be made at Batsto. Cox organized the running of supplies past the British to Valley Forge. His account of one of the trips reveals the desperate situation he faced obtaining transport:

Six waggons [sic] are now loaded and ready to start, and I expect will be at Cooper's Ferry [Camden] by tomorrow evening. My manager sent off three loads this morning, and I am in hopes that my Overseer, who is gone in Quest of Teams, will return sometime tomorrow with a sufficient number of waggons to take the remainder of the Committee's Order up in the course of next week. You judged well in sending Teams from Philadelphia, it being almost impossible to procure them here at this season of the year, most of the Farmers being busily engaged in planting, and those who make carting a business, all employed in transporting goods from hence to Philada., Brunswick and New York.
P.S.   All the shot ordered by the Committee is cast.[26]

Colonel Cox received 2,481 pounds for this shipment. The importance of the Batsto and Mt. Holly Iron Works to the American Revolution can not be overstated. The state had granted iron workers exemptions from military service to insure production of iron supplies. Therefore, the following advertisement in the *Pennsylvania Evening Post* of June 26, 1777, was probably answered by many seeking employment:

Wanted at Batsto and Mount Holly iron works a number of labourers, colliers, nailores, and two or three experienced forgemen to whom constant employ and the best wages will be given four shillings per cord will be paid for cutting pine and maple wood. For further information apply at Colonial Cox's counting house on Arch Street, Philadelphia, to Mr. Joseph Ball, manager, at Batsto, or to the subscriber at Mount Holly.
RICHARD PRICE
N.B. The workmen at these works are by law of this State exempt from military duty.[27]

In 1779, Cox sold Batsto Furnace to his manager, Joseph Ball, also a revolutionary patriot. Ball was then 32. Curing the five years he owned the furnace, he built the forge and slitting and rolling mill. The forge had a reported capacity of 200 tons of bar iron a year, and the mill turned out sheet iron, nails and wheel tires. All during this period Batsto was a tremendously profitable furnace.

Ball sold the furnace to William Richards,

a man of experience with iron, who had been sent to Coventry Forge in Pennsylvania to learn the iron trade. Richards married the daughter of the manager at Coventry Forge, became manager of Batsto, and then joined the army during the Revolution. During this period, the agent in Philadelphia for Batsto furnace was Charles Pettit. He sold four firebacks to George Washington with the initials G.W. on them. Two of these are exhibited at Mount Vernon today.

Richards improved many features of the iron making process, including extending the integrated plantation-like organization of the workers which he had experienced in Pennsylvania. Both Richards and his son, Jesse, were quite successful running Batsto. When Jesse noticed that local bog iron was not sufficient to meet his demands, he contracted to bring iron to Batsto from other areas. As well as running Batsto furnace, he developed a shipping fleet, introduced the cranberry culture to New Jersey, made his own bricks, and sold finished wooden products as well as raw wood from his landing on the Mullica River. Some of Jesse Richards' ships exported charcoal and iron pipe to Philadelphia, New York, and Albany as well as kettles to Portland, Maine. An ornamental iron fence which was made at Batsto furnace subsequently enclosed the yard of Independence Hall. During Jesse Richards' ownership, the steam cylinder for John Fitch's fourth steamboat was made at Batsto Furnace. These products indicate America's changing economy during the early nineteenth century. When Jesse Richards died in 1854, his son assumed direction at the furnace, but the end of the furnace was near. A disastrous fire in 1874 crippled the business, and by 1876 foreclosure proceedings closed the business.

There was a close family as well as business relationship between the Batsto and Coventry Forge furnaces which represents the similarity between the New Jersey and Pennsylvania iron communities. The National Park Service has restored the furnace and community at Hopewell Village, Pennsylvania. It is now possible to study the iron-making process and the living conditions of the iron workers there during its years of operation from 1771 to 1883. Many small iron furnaces throughout the Delaware Valley were operating. At first, the eastern foundries were sending iron west. The developing ability to produce coke from coal enabled furnaces in Western Pennsylvania to assume much of the American iron business in the late 19th century. Much research needs to be done on other furnaces before Hopewell can be termed an average type, but since it is fairly well documented and restored today, it serves as an adequate example for this study.

Hopewell Furnace was begun in south Berks County, Pennsylvania by Mark Bird in about 1770 or 1771 on land he apparently acquired for the purpose. Early records are very vague, but evidence contributes to suggest this time as the probable start. Mark Bird had inherited significant land and money when his father died in 1761, and was apparently familiar with the process of smelting iron since his various financial interests included other foundries. In Pennsylvania, iron ore was mined near the surface of the earth, not in bogs as in New Jersey. At Hopewell, existing woodland provided an abundant supply of wood for charcoal, a sufficient supply of limestone was present for flux, and the French Creek supplied water power. The terrain was sufficiently hilly for access to the furnace stack, and at the markets in nearby Philadelphia, the product could be sold and transported. It seemed to Bird that a viable business could be started at Hopewell.

When smelting began in 1770 or 1771, Bird was apparently an owner in absence for he rented the furnace to William Hays early in the 1779's and Hays acted as manager. Bird is listed as a resident of Philadelphia through this period, and served there on the Committee on Observation and the Committee of Correspondence and in 1775 was chosen for the Provincial Conference. During the Revolution, he served first as Lieutenant Colonel and later as Colonel of the Second Battalion of Berks County militia, provided uniforms, tents and provisions for 300 men from his personal funds, served in the Pennsylvania Assembly, Provincial Convention of 1776, and was judge of the Berks County Court.[28] He was instrumental in having barrels of flour sent to Washington's army at Valley Forge in February, 1778. When the war ended he was owed money by the new

nation. Perhaps to satisfy this debt, or for the large amount of iron, he asked to be given the chain that had been made to cross the Hudson River to repel the English forces, but this request was denied. His financial position, interests in five different forges and military experience ranked him among

This is a view of the Hopewell furnace site before restoration. The building at center front is the wheelwright shop, behind which is the casting house. The roof line, upper left is the bridge house. The charcoal house is located slightly to the right of center, and the ore roaster is the peaked roof structure on the right.

The Hopewell furnace buildings have now been restored.

the leading citizens of Berks County at that time. He even had an interest in the ship, *United States,* which was among the first American ships to trade with China. Apparently all these activities and postwar inflation were taking a toll. In 1784, he asked that the taxes on Hopewell be lowered. He was certainly not alone in this dilemna, for the entire American iron industry was then suffering from a surplus of iron aggravated by imports. Floods in the fall of 1786, further cut into his property. The Hopewell property was unsuccessfully offered for sale in 1786. Creditors pressed for a sheriff's sale, and in 1788, Cadwallader Morris and James Old bought the furnace and over 5,000 acres of land. For the next few years, ownership changed hands often with frequent periods of absentee owners.

In 1790-91, Cadwallader Morris' brother, Benjamin Morris became owner. Two years later, however, James Old bought the furnace again, but this time as its sole owner. Old then sold it to James Wilson who leased

Hopewell to a group of businessmen. In 1797, a sheriff's sale put Hopewell in the hands of James Old for a third time. Again, however, Hopewell was the subject of financial problems and was offered at another sheriff's sale in 1800. Once more, Benjamin Morris purchased the furnace and land, but sold it the same year to Daniel Buckley and his brothers-in-law, Thomas and Mathew Brooke. Hopewell stayed in these families and their descendents until it was sold to the United States Government in the 1930's.

The Brooke and Buckley partnership of owners changed the history of financial instability at Hopewell, gradually turning it into a prosperous business as family members lived and worked at Hopewell. Upon possession, the Brookes and Buckleys made many significant improvements in the furnace operations, rebuilt old buildings and added new ones. The furnace was in operation with limited success for eight years, then shut down between 1808 and 1816. During this period the facility was maintained, but was

Bread making in the 18th century manner is still carried on at the restored Hopewell Village

using authentic methods and iron tools.
National Park Service, Hopewell Village

not active. From 1805, a stamping mill crushed pieces of the slag waste to recover beads of iron. These beads were sold to nearby furnaces that used them to improve their iron. It is certainly unfortunate that during a period of great demand for iron, the War of 1812, Hopewell was inactive. Numerous legal problems, however, prevented its activity. By 1816, the disputes were sufficiently satisfied for business to begin again at Hopewell.

Under Clement Brooke's shrewd management, Hopewell prospered. New markets were found, transportation improved and new products were created. By 1825, canals were used for transport, and by 1838, railroads were linked to distant points and created a new market for iron. Stove casting became the primary product at Hopewell after 1820 and was very successful. The period from 1830 to 1836 was the most productive from every standpoint. Another depression began in 1837, caused by President Jackson's destruction of Nicholas Biddle's bank. By 1840, coke

from coal had proved far superior than charcoal as a smelting agent.

At Hopewell, the decline was gradual but steady until 1844, when stove casting was halted. After that pig iron was again the primary product for the next 40 years. In 1883, the last blast was made at Hopewell. Thereafter, sporadic sales of lumber, charcoal, farm animals and stone are recorded.

It is not unfair to call the financial history of these iron furnaces unstable and inefficient, as most of them operated for only short periods under a variety of owners and managers. A tremendous amount of money was involved in starting up the furnaces. The furnace structures, workers' houses, mines, farmlands, timber lands, skilled workers and laborers were all expensive to coordinate. It was difficult to convince investors of the benefits of the industry.

Small iron implements were usually made by local blacksmiths. Blacksmiths were essential parts of each community. making tools household items, horseshoes, straps for bar-

A blacksmith is surrounded by his tools and products. The water barrel is for quenching — or hardening metal. The assorted tongs on the back rock are for gripping differently shaped iron. Some of the *short strips of iron will become horse shoes. The anivl and hammer are the blacksmith's principle tools. National Park Service, Hopewell Village*

rels, swords, axes, hammers, spears and armour, and iron items for the home. Working independently often in remote areas, the blacksmiths coped with a wide variety of repairs, often having to devise their own methods for improvements. The rural blacksmith has produced ornamental iron of traditional design for generations, making accurate dating of these items often impossible.

Having bought bars of wrought iron from the forge, the blacksmith worked in a dimly lit shop where he judged the temperature of molten iron by its color. Here the iron was heated and hammered successively into desired shapes.

Biringuccion, while writing in 1540, summed up the rigors of the blacksmith's day as follows:

> The task of the smith who works in iron is very laborious . . . For he . . . handles heavy weights continually, and stands constantly erect before the fire of the forge, since the hardness of the iron cannot be softened except by means of heating and boiling it well. In this place he continually moves his body, now thrusting the iron into the heart of the fire with large thick tongs, now removing it to look at it and to put sand, tuff, or other earth over it, now putting on fresh charcoal, now moistening and slowing down the fire, and now cleaning it . . . Finally, while the iron is hot he strikes with powerful mallets and heavy hammers, as you see, and brings it to whatever end he wishes to make of the work. As you can understand, the unhappy workmen are never able to enjoy any quiet except in the evening when they are exhausted by the laborious and long day that began from them with the crowing of the cock. Sometimes they even fall asleep without bothering about supper.[29]

The fine blacksmith would finish ornaments by tapering and drawing down edges of implements to save iron, and give a more finished look. Some blacksmiths developed into waftsmen whose products were not only useful but artistically beautiful as well.

By the mid-nineteenth century, items formerly made by blacksmiths began to be produced in factories. Gradually hand forging of iron became restricted to shoeing horses and making small repairs. An account of a blacksmith shop in 1856 lists:

To 12 links & a ring in halter chains	.25
To 10 nails & dress up two pair of hinges for gates	.25
To 1 remove	.08
To sharp 2 shovels, 2 rivets in a cornrake & lay a prong for a plow	.41 [30]

Large steel companies took over the majority of iron manufacturing during the last decades of the nineteenth century when mechanized methods became perfected. Small operations were absorbed or abandoned, and the village blacksmith became a memory.

This study covers the hand and early machine made iron items that people used everyday at home and in small businesses. Most of these examples were common when they were made, but have become interesting and rare as their numbers grow fewer. Worn out and rusted, many of the old iron implements have been discarded. It will take a study of the survivors to refresh appreciation for the iron industry, the blacksmith and his products in today's people.

A-B. Group of wrought iron hardware, English, 18th century, James C. Sorber.

These pieces of hardware were recently raised from the wreck of a ship that sank in the Delaware River between Pennsylvania and New Jersey in 1760. These fragments show what was being shipped from England to America at that date. Even though similar items were made in America, these indicate that the quality and price of English hardware still made trade in iron attractive to the American buying public.

Included in the larger group are a sickle blade, a pair of H-hinges, two padlocks, a scythe blade, and a carpenter's hand saw blade. In the smaller group are a mattock and part of a lumberman's saw. It is a matter of speculation as to whether wooden handles were sold with these items and have deteriorated under water, or if they were sold as we see them now. James C. Sorber Collection.

[1] Fourteenth century quote on label at the Museum of London.

[2] Label at the Museum of London.

[3] Ibid.

[4] Ibid.

[5] Michael Owen, *Antique Cast Iron,* (Poole, Dorset: Blandford Press Ltd., 1977), p. 5.

[6] E. N. Hartley, *Ironworks on Saugus,* (Norman: University of Oklahoma Press, 1971), pp. 23-24.

[7] *The Voyages of Jacques Cartier,* ed. H. P. Bigger, (Ottowa: 1924), p. 255.

[8] Richard Hakluyt, *The Principal Navigations, Voyages, Traffiques and Discoveries of the English Nation,* (reprint ed., Glasgow: 1903-05), VIII, p. 356.

[9] *The Genesis of the United States,* ed. Alexander Brown, (Boston and New York: 1891), I, p. 353.

[10] Ibid., p. 356.

[11] Arthur D. Pierce, *Iron in the Pines,* (New Jersey: Rutgers University Press, 1957), p. 14.

[12] Arthur Cecil Bining, *Pennsylvania Iron Manufacture in the Eighteenth Century,* (Harrisburg: Pennsylvania Historical Commission, 1938), IV, p. 118.

[13] New Pine Forge Ledgers.

[14] Massachusetts Records, I, p. 327.

[15] Stephen P. Carlson, *Joseph Jenks: Colonial Toolmaker and Inventor,* (Saugus Iron Works, revised 1975), p. 3; *Dictionary of National Biography,* XVIII, p. 1294; Meredith Bright Colker, *Jenks Family of England,* pp. 7-8.

[16] Meredith Bright Colker, *Jenks Family in America,* p. xvi.

[17] Ibid., p. 6.

[18] Ibid., p. 8

[19] Ibid., p. 10; Browne, *Jenks Family in America,* p. xvii; Wallace Nutting, *Early American Ironwork,* (1919), p. 1.

[20] E.N. Hartley, *Ironworks on the Saugus,* (Norman: University of Oklahoma Press, 1971), p. 300.

[21] Ibid., pp. 275-76.

[22] Arthur D. Pierce, *Iron in the Pines,* (New Jersey: Rutgers University Press, 1957), p. 22.

[23] Ibid.

[24] Ibid., p. 119

[25] Ibid., p. 122.

[26] Ibid., p. 123.

[27] Ibid., p. 126.

[28] Joseph E. Walker, *Hopewell Village, The Dynamics of a Nineteenth Century Iron-Making Community,* (Philadelphia: University of Pennsylvania Press, 1974) p. 28.

[29] Biringuccion, *Pirotechnia,* pp. 369-70.

[30] Ibid., p. 9.

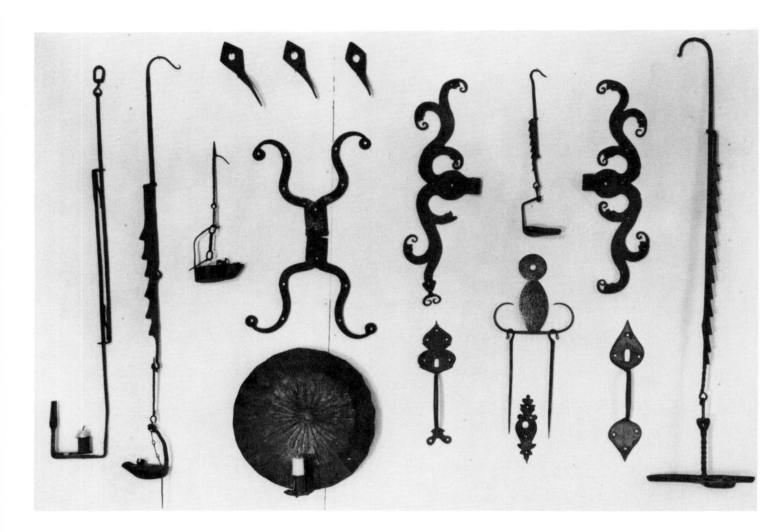

CHAPTER 1
Architectural Hardware

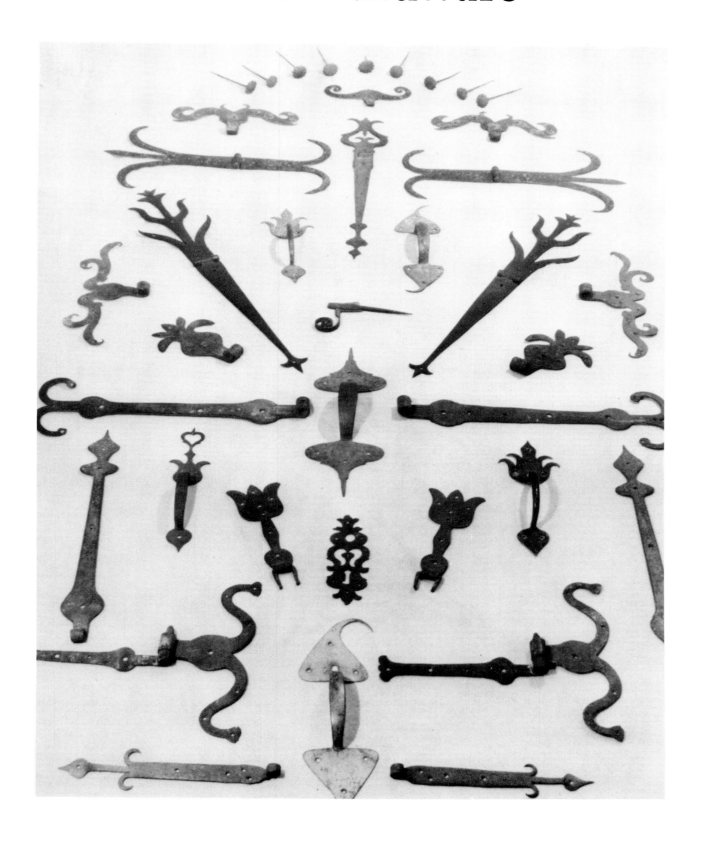

A.

Bolts were used on doors and on furniture (cupboard doors), although the furniture bolts are usually smaller. This kind of bolt has been produced from the Middle Ages to modern times.

A. Bolt, wrought iron, 18th c., American, Wallace Nutting collection, Wadsworth Atheneum.

B. Bolt, wrought iron, late 18th or early 19th c., American, Wallace Nutting collection, Wadsworth Atheneum.

C. Bolt, wrought iron, mid-18th c., American, 17 1/4" high.

D. Door bolt, wrought iron, 18th c., American or possibly European.

The form of this rather charming bolt suggests a craftsman of Germanic origin as its maker, possibly a Pennsylvania German.

B.

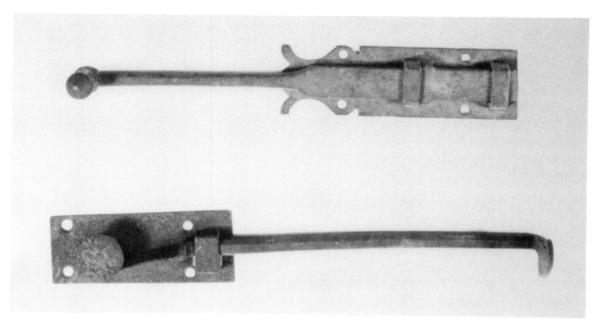

C.

D.

A. Boot scraper, wrought iron, 18th c., American, Philip Bradley Antiques.

Boot scrapers have always been an essential of country living. The roads were so appalling in the eighteenth and nineteenth centuries, that even in the cities these were a necessary part of life. This boot scraper is mounted in a marble slab for stability. The iron bolt is secured in the hole by molten lead poured in to seal the joint.

B. Boot scraper, wrought iron, American, Wallace Nutting collection, Wadsworth Atheneum.

The L-shaped projections on this boot scraper suggest that it may have been suspended from a wall or board.

C. Boot scraper, wrought iron, probably 18th c., American, Philip Bradley Antiques.

Graceful curls at the top of the posts distinguish this boot scraper.

D. Boot scraper, wrought iron, 18th or 19th c., American, Wallace Nutting collection, Wadsworth Atheneum.

Boot scrapers like this were attached to upright posts.

E. Boot scraper, wrought iron, late 18th c., American, Wallace Nutting collection, Wadsworth Atheneum.

This attractive boot scraper with key-hole cutouts was fastened to a wooden floor.

A.

B.

C.

E.

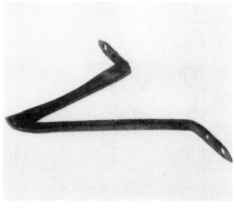

D.

A.

B.

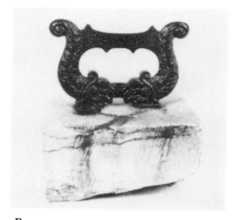

C.

D.

A. Boot scraper, wrought iron, early 19th c., American, Philip Bradley Antiques.

Although it shows signs of obvious wear, this boot scraper retains a marvelous curving form and spiral curls.

B. Boot scraper, cast iron, c. 1815-1830, American, Philip Bradley Antiques.

Cast iron boot scrapers appear in more elaborate forms than their hand wrought counterparts. Cornucopia and flowers, motifs shown here in cast form, were also widely used as carved ornament on furniture of the Empire period.

C. Boot scraper, wrought iron, late 18th c., American, Wallace Nutting collection, Wadsworth Atheneum.

This elaborately scrolled boot scraper was undoubtedly set in stone.

D. Boot scraper, wrought iron, probably mid-19th c., American, 10 3/4" by 10 1/4".

Boldly executed volutes surmount this scraper with cut-out cross plate.

E. Boot scraper, wrought iron, 18th or 19th c., American, Old Sturbridge Village.

Stamped by its maker, J. Winkley, this boot scraper follows a traditional form.

E.

A.

A. *Boot scraper, wrought iron, early 19th c.,*
American, Old Sturbridge Village.

P. W. Flynn, the maker, stamped this boot
scraper that was designed to be fastened down
on a wooden floor.

B. Bracket, wrought iron, 18th c., European,
National Gallery of Art, Index of American
Design.

This bracket was supported by a pole. The
top element surrounds the pole, while the
brace below bolts to it. The naturalistic and
circular geometric ornaments are an eye-catching
design.

B.

A.

B.

A. Bracket, wrought iron, c. 1700, English, Victoria and Albert Museum.

Attached to a building, these brackets held inn or shop signs. The fanciful foliate scroll design here suggests a French Huguenot influence.

B. Bracket, wrought iron, late 17th or early 18th c., English, Victoria and Albert Museum.

C. Bracket, wrought iron, probably early 18th c., English, Victoria and Albert Museum.

A charming whimsey, this sprightly fox surmounted the sign for the Fox Inn in Huntington, England. The very essence of the animal is captured and interpreted with the simplicity of a line drawing.

C.

A.

A. Plaster casts from door panels, originally wood with wrought iron scroll work, 13th c., Doors of Aumbry, Chester Cathedral, England; Victoria and Albert Museum.

The symmetrical stylized foliate design and contrasts of dark and light typify medieval tracery.

C. Dungeon doors, wrought iron, 17th and 18th c., English, from Newgate Prison, courtesy Museum of London.

A network of locks and grills arranged in a simple geometric pattern forms a formidable barricade for the seventeenth century prison door on the left, while the suggestion of paneling on the eighteenth century door at the right gives it a slightly more conventional appearance.

B. Door with hinges, pull and escutcheon, wrought iron, on oak door, 14th c., England, Victoria and Albert Museum.

The design inspiration for these hinges derived from the Romanesque and extends to the Gothic period. The simplified stylized plant forms also resemble Pennsylvania German motifs of the eighteenth and nineteenth centuries.

D. Body cage, wrought iron, 17th c., English, Museum of the City of London.

Shown amid elements of old Newgate Prison is this body cage, an exhibition cage in which the bodies of traitors or other wrong-doers were suspended in prominent places for public viewing.

B.

C.   *D.*

A.

C.

A. Keyhole escutcheon, wrought iron, late 18th c., American, William Penn Memorial Museum, Harrisburg.

Probably made by a Pennsylvania German craftsman. This charming figure depicts a Hessian soldier.

B. Escutcheon, wrought iron, late eighteenth century, American, James C. Sorber.

These groups of escutcheons were found on various American pieces of furniture. The birds' heads on some of them are noteworthy.

B.

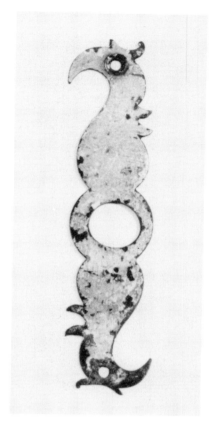

B.

A.

C.

D.

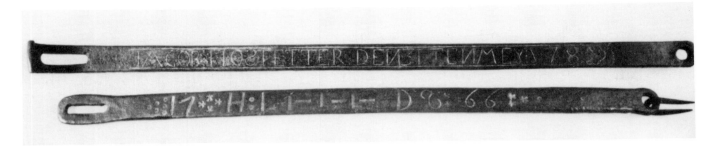

A.

A. Stable door hasps, wrought iron, Lancaster County, Pennsylvania, top one marked "Jacob Hostetter, 1785", 46" long; bottom one marked "H. I. D. S. 1766", 43 1/2" long.

Traditionally on the Pennsylvania German farm the horse stable door had a hasp and lock, whereas the cow stable door often did not.

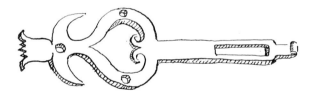

B. Hasp, wrought iron, early 19th c., Pennsylvania, Pennsylvania Farm Museum of Landis Valley.

This unusual hasp has been decorated on the neck of the hook.

B.

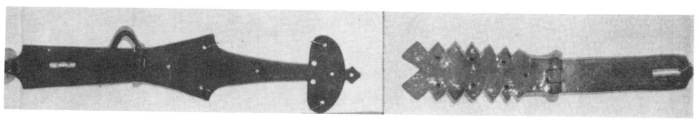

C.

C. Two hasps, American, 18th c., wrought iron, W. Himmelreich.

The most attractive and decorative hasps were used on Conestoga Wagon Boxes such as the examples shown on the opposite page. Hasps on houses, barns, and out buildings were usually quite dull like the ones shown on this page. These are all unquestionably American. The simple ones are plentiful and cheap, the finest almost impossible to obtain.

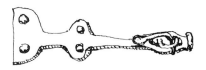

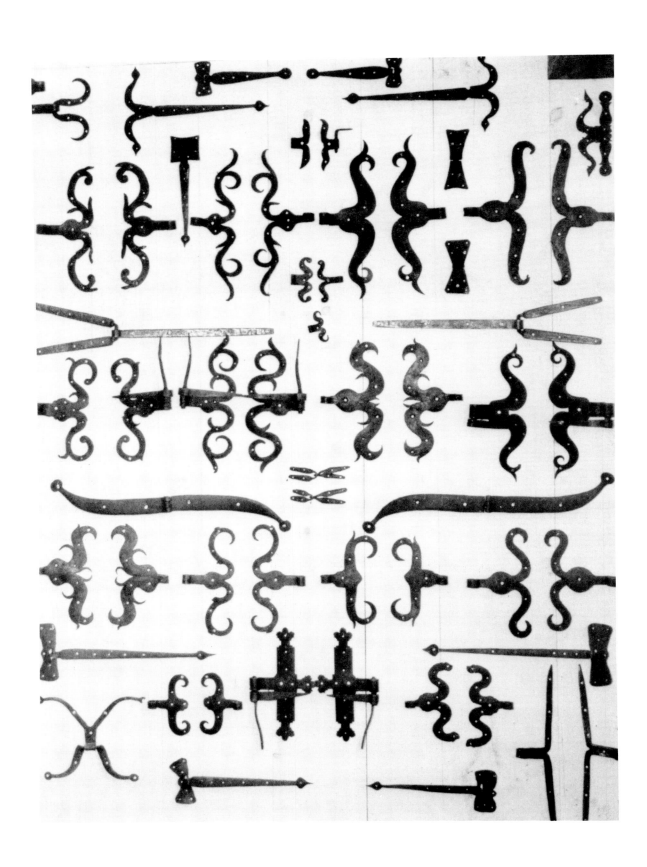

A.

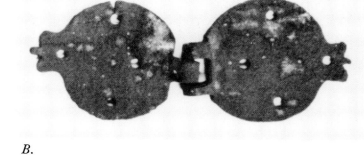

B.

Four butterfly hinges, wrought iron, 17th or 18th c., English or American, W. Himmelreich.

Butterfly hinges are found as original hardware on seventeenth and early eighteenth century American and English furniture. They definitely were made in both places and probably throughout most of central and northern Europe as well.

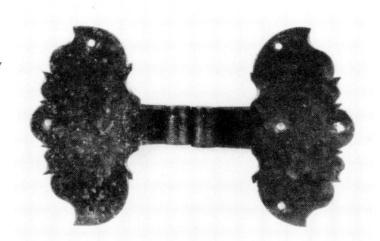

C.

D.

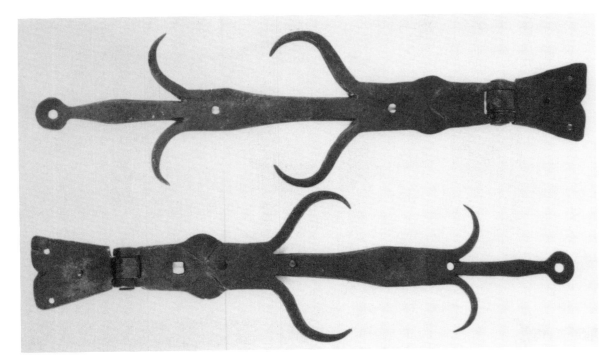

A.

A-C. Butterfly and strap hinges, wrought iron, early 18th c., probably Pennsylvania, Wallace Nutting collection, Wadsworth Atheneum.

This rare group of hinges have a butterfly on one side and a strap on the other.

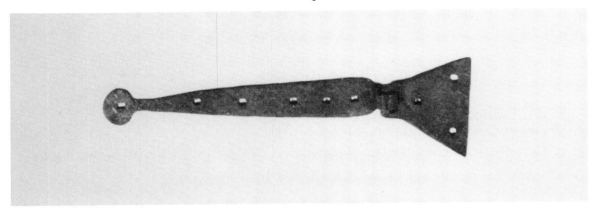

B.

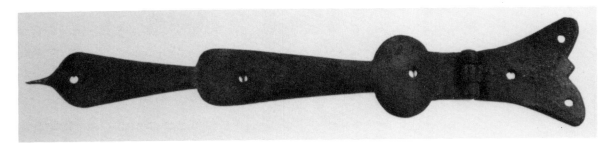

C.

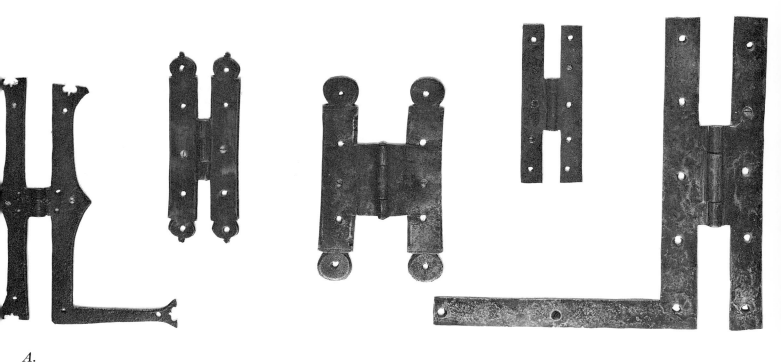

A.

A. Hinges, wrought iron, 17th and 18th c., English, Victoria and Albert Museum.

This group of hinges shows styles that have been considered as American as 'Ma's apple Pie': crowned top H, and HL hinges. There are examples in use at Kensington Palace in England designed by Sir Christopher Wren, that can be assumed to have been made in England. Bills exist among American family papers for enormous amounts of architectural hardware being imported to America in the eighteenth century.

B. Hinge, wrought iron, 18th or 19th century, American, Library of Congress.

This is a drawing of the crowned-H hinge found on the second floor, west room, entry door of the Col. Paul Wentworth House, Salmon Falls, Strafford County, New Hampshire.

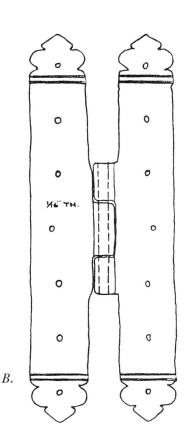

B.

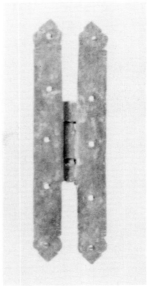

A.

B.

A. Crown topped H-hinges, wrought iron, late 17th to early 18th c., American, English or Continental, Wallace Nutting collection, Wadsworth Atheneum.

While these hinges survive as original hardware on American furniture and houses, they also occur in such buildings in England as Kensington Palace, built in the seventeenth century by Sir Christopher Wren. They probably were made all over the American Colonies and Europe. They are a more elegant and early form of the H-hinge.

C. "HL" or "Holy Lord" hinges, wrought iron, early 18th c., English and American, Wallace Nutting collection, Wadsworth Atheneum.

Because some of these hinges were found on churches and ministry houses, the "Holy Lord" ecclesiastic name developed. They are not necessarily religious in use, but are a version of an H-hinge.

Hinges were usually painted the color of the walls. A set bought in Dublin on Mount Joy Square had many layers of paint matching the wood work from which they were removed. Outlining hardware in black may be a twentieth century idea to accentuate early hinges of which collectors are so proud.

Similar hinges have been found in thousands of American houses. Some were imported, while others were made in America. Hinges similar to this were found and drawn by the Historic American Building Survey Team in the Amos Seavey House, Rye, New Hampshire.

B. Crown Topped H-Hinge with Strap, Wrought iron, late 17th or early 18th c., probably American, possibly English or Continental.

This is a rare variation of the crowned H-hinge.

C.

D.

D. Double L-hinges, wrought iron, 18th c., American or Continental.

The double L is a rare, but practical, version of the HL hinge. The door surround must be wide enough to accommodate the bottom of the "L".

DOOR AND CUPBOARD HINGES.
ENGLISH; 16ᵀᴴ AND 17ᵀᴴ CENTURIES.

A.

A. Group of ram's horn hinges, wrought iron, English, 16th and 17th c., Victoria and Albert Museum.

The top row of hinges date from the sixteenth century, while the lower two rows date from the seventeenth century. This type of ram's horn hinge has generally been considered of German, Swiss or Pennsylvania German origin only.

A. Ram's horn hinge, wrought iron, American or European, Wallace Nutting collection, Wadsworth Atheneum.

This is the classic ram's horn hinge. It could be of European origin, although a few like it were made in America.

B-D. *Three pairs of ram's horn hinges, wrought iron, possibly Pennsylvania, late 18th c.,*
B. 6 3/4" long, 5" wide, W. Himmelreich.
C. 10" long, 12" wide, W. Himmelreich.
D. Wadsworth Atheneum.

There is a good chance that German and Swiss trained blacksmiths and apprentices made simpler versions of ram's horn hinges in America. These are more in the American taste than the European taste as they lack the details usually found on European iron.

E. Double split hinges, wrought iron, 18th c., American and European, W. Himmelreich.

This group varies in size from very long to very short. The ones with the hearts are the rarest.

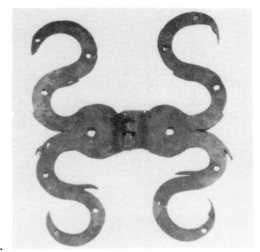

A.

B.

D.

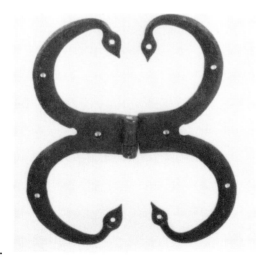

C.

E.

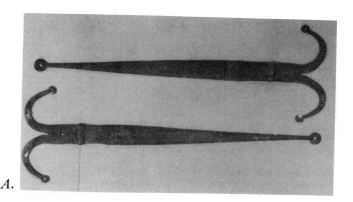

A.

B.

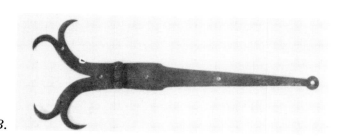

C.

A. Ram's horn and strap hinge, wrought iron, late 18th and early 19th c., American, W. Himmelreich.

The first example is a fairly standard pair of bean end, split strap hinge. The next pair is longer than the first. The third pair have split ends with a more sophisticated strap and a very interesting end. The split ends are pointed and sometimes called "tulip ends."

B. Split end and strap hinge, wrought iron, c. 1760, American or European.

This fine split-end and strap hinge has a suggestion of leaves in the splits, while the end of the strap is shaped like a bean.

C. Split end and strap hinge, wrought iron, c. 1760, American or European, Wallace Nutting collection, Wadsworth Atheneum.

This split end and strap hinge has an additional small split at the end, suggesting the beginning of the ram's horn style. The split end is short to fit on the surround of a door or window.

D. Split end and strap hinge, wrought iron, early 19th or late 18th c., American, 22" long, 14 1/2" wide, W. Himmelreich.

Combinations of tulip bud and tulip ends are rare and desirable.

D.

A. Ram's horn and strap hinge, wrought iron, late 18th c., European, 24 3/4" long.

Many pairs of ram's horn hinges found on American made furniture and architectural elements actually come from Europe. Switzerland, Germany, Holland, and Denmark all used ram's horn hinges in some combination.

B. Hinge, wrought iron, late 18th or early 19th c., Pennsylvania, Wallace Nutting collection, Wadsworth Atheneum.

Tulip ends on strap hinges are very rare. The split ends terminate in "beans".

C. Split end and strap hinges, wrought iron, late 18th c., Pennsylvania, Pennsylvania Farm Museum of Landis Valley.

These split end and strap hinges have a large stylistic tulip on one end and bean ends on the short split sides.

D. Split end and strap hinges, wrought iron, late 18th or early 19th c., Pennsylvania, 23 5/8" long.

The stylized tulip at the end of the strap is a unique interpretation.

A.

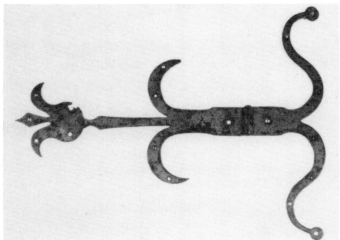

B.

C.

D.

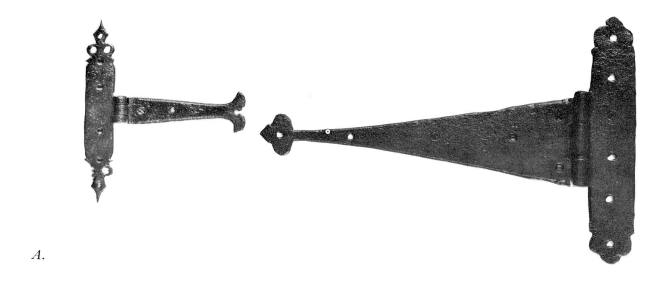

A.

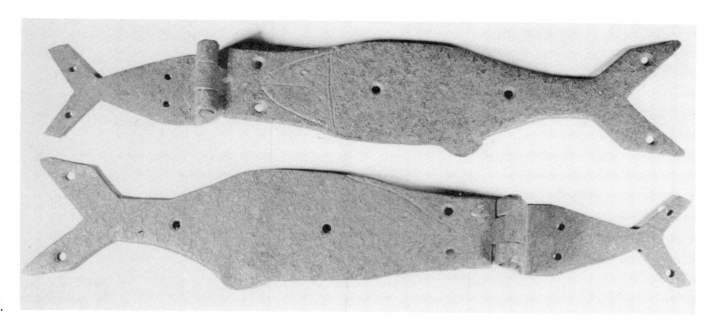

B.

A. Strap hinges, wrought iron, 16th c., English, Victoria and Albert Museum.

B. Split end and strap hinges, wrought iron, early 19th c., American, Pennsylvania Farm Museum of Landis Valley.

These split end and strap hinges were designed to resemble large fish eating small fish. The details of the fish heads and eyes are stamped into the metal.

A.

B.

A-B.Two pairs of double strap hinges, wrought iron, late 18th or early 19th c., American or European, Wadsworth Atheneum.

Here are two variations of double strap hinges. The top one is the simplest. The bottom one is beautifully designed. This type of hinge was useful on a small door within a larger door, a design often used on barns. The small door was easier to open and allowed less heat to escape.

C. Double strap hinge, wrought iron, late 18th or early 19th c., American or European, Wadsworth Atheneum.

Here is a charming curved bean end variation on the double strap hinge.

D. Hinges, American, Wallace Nutting collection, Wadsworth Atheneum.

Here are strap hinges with a horse shoe end and a bar end. Both variations are rare.

E. Bar and strap hinges, wrought iron, 18th c., American or European, 9 1/2" long, 17" wide, W. Himmelreich.

These are another unusual variation of the strap hinge. Some collectors look only for the unusual examples, while some prefer to find fine examples of standard types.

C.

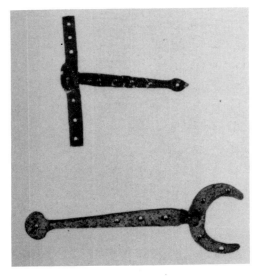

D.

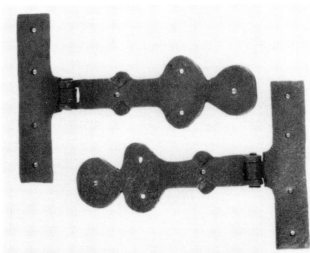

E.

A.

A. Hinges, wrought iron, late 18th and early 19th c., Pennsylvania, W. Himmelreich.

This has been considered one of the most vigorous and well designed pair of Pennsylvania German hinges. They are great masterpieces of the blacksmith's art.

B. Split end and strap hinges, wrought iron, late 18th and early 19th c., American.

Three slightly different pairs of hinges, are shown here; one with a bean, split end and strap; another with tulip bud ends; and a pair of split end with a more sophisticated strap with an interesting end and pointed split ends.

C. Hinge, wrought iron, 18th c., W. Himmelreich.

B.

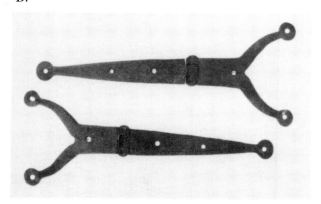

C.

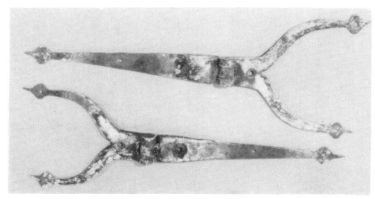

A.

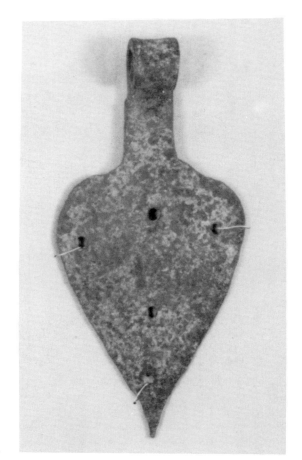

A-D. Hinges, wrought iron, 18th c., American.

Here are four noteworthy short hinges made
to fit on pintles. The designs include birds,
tulips, leaves, and circles.

*C. Hinges, 18th c., 6" long, 4 1/2" wide, W.
Himmelreich.*

B.

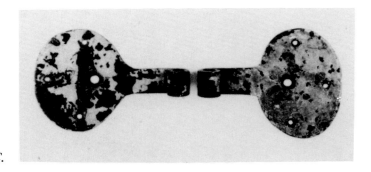

C.

D.

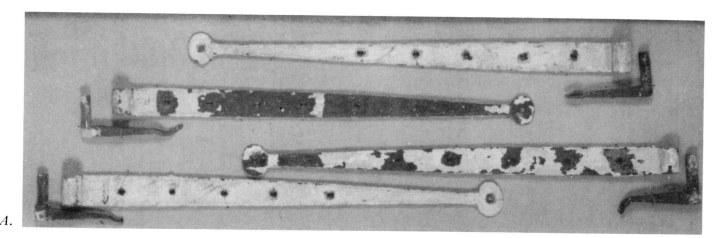

A.

B.

*A-C. Strap hinges, wrought iron, late 18th c.,
American.*

Many strap hinges rested on pintles making it
possible to lift the door up if necessary. These
are some of the more interesting examples
of the type. The straps terminate in beans,
tulips, birds, curved leaves, and mushrooms,
as well as other variations. Many imaginative
varieties of common items were possible
when they were hand made.

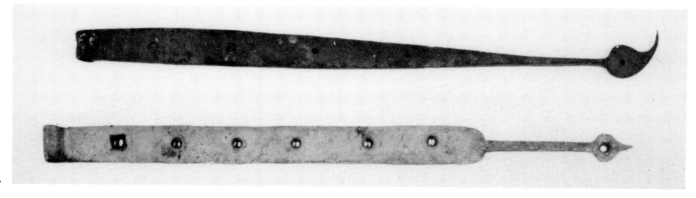

C.

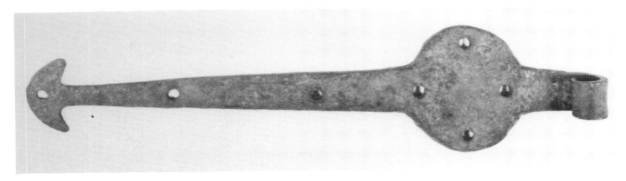

A.

B.

A-C. Strap hinges, wrought iron, 18th or 19th century, American.

C.

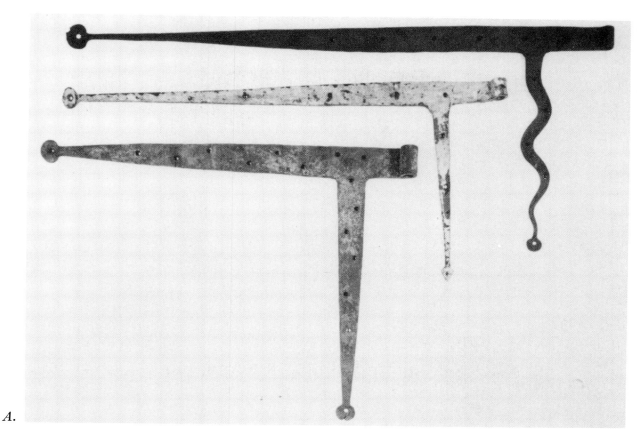

A.

A. Supported strap hinges hung on pintles, wrought iron, 18th and 19th c., American, Wallace Nutting collection, Wadsworth Atheneum.

Supported strap hinges are rare, but very functional as they greatly strengthened large doors.

B. Strap hinges, wrought iron, late 18th to early 19th c., American.

C. Strap hinge for pintle, wrought iron, American, late 18th c.

Another rare variation is the split strap hinge.

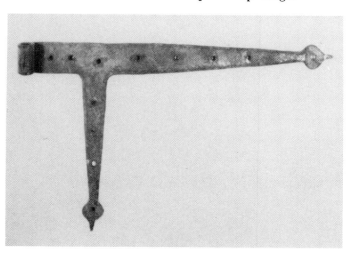

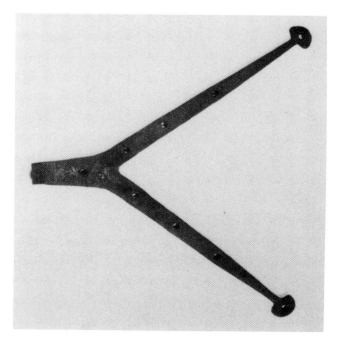

B.

C.

A.

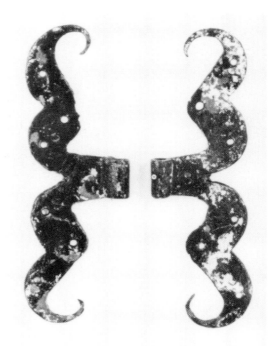

A-D. Group of hinges for pintles, wrought iron, mid-18th c., American and European, W. Himmelreich.

Ram's horn hinges on pintles included some of the most beautiful and intricate designs found. A few fit rattail pintles.

Many of these hinges are Dutch or German. It is practically impossible to distinguish a hinge definitely made in America unless it is signed. The blacksmiths of European origin brought these styles with them to America and changed little during the first half of the eighteenth century.

B.

C.   D.

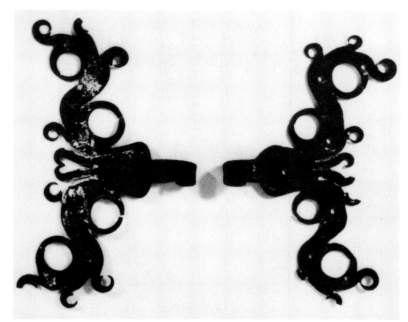

A.

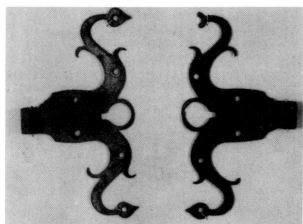

C.

B.

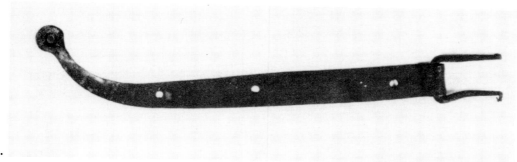

A.

*A. B. Brad and strap hinge, wrought iron, late
18th or early 19th c., American.*

Some hinges hung on staples. Here are two of
these rare types.

*C. Strap hinges for pintles, wrought iron, late
18th or early 19th c., American.*

*D. Butterfly hinges, wrought iron, 18th c.,
American.*

A double butterfly hinge with a pintle instead
of a center hinge is a very unusual piece.

*Opposite: American wrought iron hinge with
pintle, eighteenth century.*

B.

C.

D.

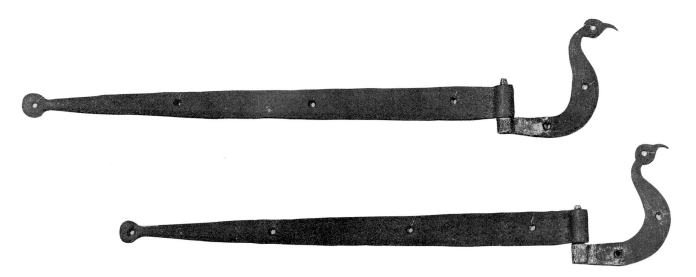

A.

A. Strap hinge and pintle, wrought iron, 19th c., American, W. Himmelreich.

A pintle with a bird's head end is a pleasant and unusual combination.

B. Rat-tail hinge for pintle.

A strange variation of the rattail hinge is shown here.

C. Hinge and pintle, W. Himmelreich.

B.

C.

A.

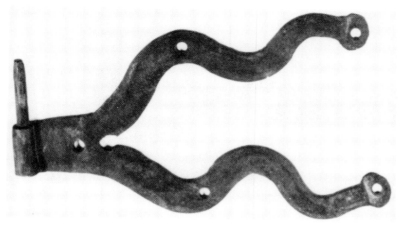

A. Pintle, wrought iron, 18th c., American, Wallace Nutting collection, Wadsworth Atheneum.

A wavey 'V' pintle is most unusual.

B. Pair of pintles, wrought iron, American, 4 1/2" high, 5 1/8" wide.

Double rattail pintles are an interesting variation.

C. Pintles, wrought iron, 18th c., American, W. Himmelreich.

Leaf shaped pintles provide another variation.

D. Pintle, wrought iron, 18th c., American.

This is a primitive rattail type pintle.

E. Double pintle, wrought iron, late 18th or early 19th c., American, James C. Sorber.

This rare double pintle would be useful on many farm gates today.

B.

C.

E.

D.

A. Hook, wrought iron, 17th, 18th or 19th c., 9" high.

Here is the most common of hooks found in America and Europe on cranes in fireplaces for a myriad of purposes, principly to hold pots.

B. Hook, wrought iron, 17th, 18th or early 19th c., American or European.

This type of hook is often associated with betty lamps.

C. Hook, wrought iron, possibly American, 18th c., 11" high.

This exquisitely made hook secured into a ceiling.

D. Engraving by Thomas Birch of a market in Philadelphia with hooks for displaying meat 1800.

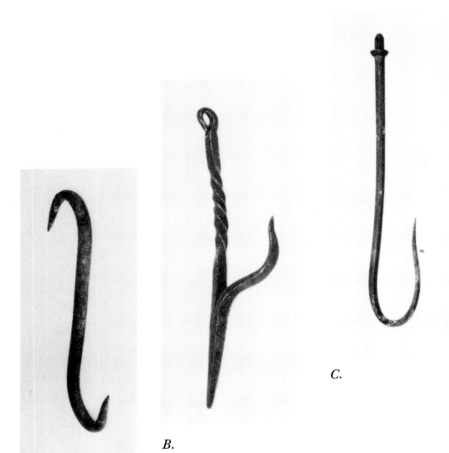

C.

B.

A.

D.

A.

C.

B.

A. Set of hooks, wrought iron, probably 18th c., European.

Series of hooks were hung on walls and have been found frequently in Holland and England. They may have been useful for fireplace or kitchen tools, or possibly to hang keys.

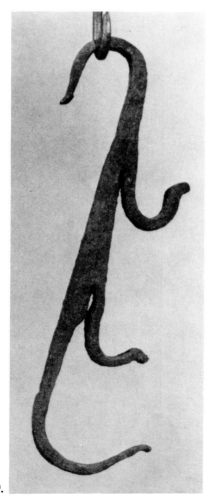

D.

B. Hook, wrought iron, probably 18th c., American, 15" high.

This is a true "whatsit?" No one has been able to give me a satisfactory explanation of its use. It was carefully designed and beautifully made.

C. Hook, wrought iron, probably 18th c., American, Old Sturbridge Village.

D. Hook, wrought iron, 18th c., American or European, Old Sturbridge Village.

This interesting hook may have hung on a trammel or fireplace crane.

A.

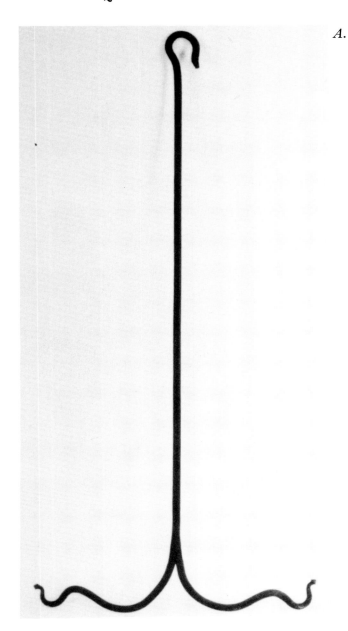

B.

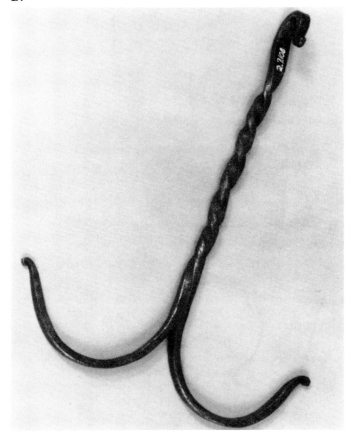

A. Double hook, wrought iron, late 18th or early 19th century, American, James C. Sorber.

The refinement of upsetting the ends and the double curved design changes this pair of hooks from the purely functional to the decorative.

B. Double hook, wrought iron, probably late 18th c., American or European, Old Sturbridge Village.

Hooks of this type can be used for hanging bridles to clean. Note the little curls at each extremity, a nicety of blacksmithing. The twisted shaft is another example of embellishment without loss of function.

Early keys are generally heavy, thick, ornately turned, and should have quite of bit of wear. Keys B and C date from the first half of the eighteenth century. A small hole is often found at each end of the key shaft. This mark was made by the lathe bit when the shaft was turned. Key D was made for a carpenter lock about 1830. Key E was found with a late Victorian lock.

A.

Chatelaine and keys, steel and wrought iron, 18th c., European, James C. Sorber.

This chatelaine was worn on a waist band. The keys have elaborate notching.

B.

C.

E.

D.

A.

The earliest door knockers were wrought iron. In the nineteenth century, cast iron knockers appeared.

B.

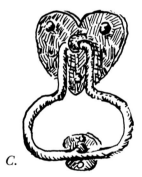

C.

E.

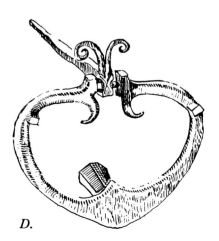

D.

E. Eagle door knocker, cast iron, c. 1820, American, Metropolitan Museum of Art, Rogers Fund, 1924.

This American symbol is similar to designs shown in English catalogs. American hardware manufacturers competed with the English technologically superior and larger iron industry.

Thumb latch, wrought iron, late 18th or early 19th c., W. Himmelreich.

This latch shows all the associated working parts of door hardware. They include the handle with thumb-piece, the latch bar, the staple and the keeper. The staple limits the movement of the latch bar as it engages the keeper on the door jamb.

Interior Locking Device of a Thumb Latch

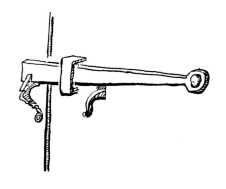

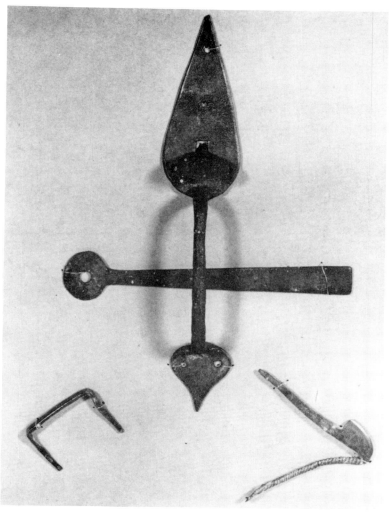

A.

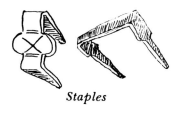

Nail

Latch Bar

Staples

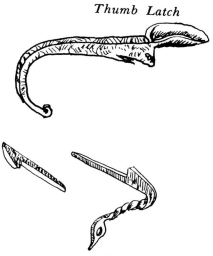

Thumb Latch

Keepers

A. Thumb latch, wrought iron, late 18th c., American, James C. Sorber.

One of the most unusual, interesting and desirable of thumb latches is shown here.

B-D. Three thumb latches, wrought iron, 18th or early 19th c., American

From the purely functional bean or diamond end to fanciful tulips and birds' heads — thumb latches have an interesting design range. Some are delightful whimseys, some generally well designed, and others merely crude and functional. They are very much collected and sometimes used at new residences to recall the day of handmade individuality.

B.

D.

C.

A.

A.

B.

C.

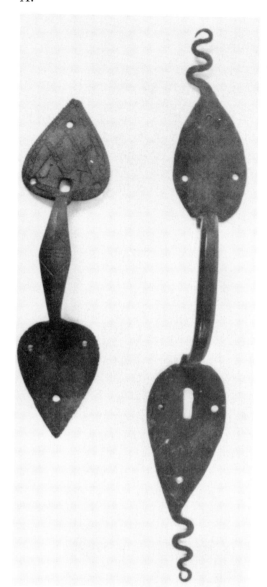

A. Two thumb latches, wrought iron, late 18th c., American, James C. Sorber.

Two utterly different, but very dynamic, thumb latches are shown here. The snakes at the top and bottom of one are quite developed. The other has masonic devices stamped into the surface.

B. Thumb latch, wrought iron, late 19th c., English, 9 3/4" high, Victoria and Albert Museum.

Some people assume that all thumb latches are American. This latch disproves the theory as it comes from the Three Horse Shoes Inn, Harston, near Cambridge. Note the chamfering at the top and bottom and the carefully punched design on the handle.

C. Door latch, wrought iron, American, 19" high.

This enormous latch was probably made for a barn door.

A.

B.

C.

A. Thumb latch, wrought iron, late 18th c., American, National Gallery of Art, Index of American Design.

The lower element of the handle is turned up, an unusual variation.

B.   Thumb latch, wrought iron, American, 11 3/4" long, W. Himmelreich.

This is sometimes called a curled leaf latch. It is a very boldly designed one.

C. Latch, wrought iron, 14" long, W. Himmelreich.

Each of the following latches have artistic merit and extra interest. The one marked I.S. is a rare example of a signed thumb latch. I.S. may be the mark of Joseph Stumb, whose name is also on a grab lock in another section of this book.

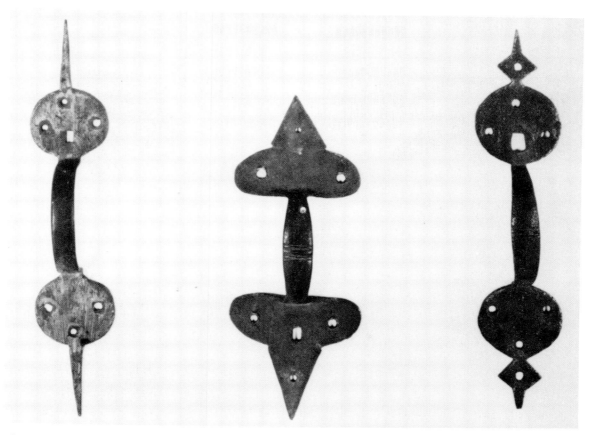

A.

A. Three handles from thumb latches, wrought iron, late 18th c., American, Wadsworth Atheneum.

These are better-than-usual, New England thumb latches.

B. Thumb latch, wrought iron, late 18th c., Pennsylvania, W. Himmelreich.

This excellent thumb latch features a tulip variation.

B.

A. Thumb latch, wrought iron, 18th c., American, 11 1/8" high.

The beautifully scalloped edges of the handle determine this to be a good quality thumb latch.

B. Thumb latches, wrought iron, late 18th c., New England.

An interesting group, including some very sophisticated latches.

A.

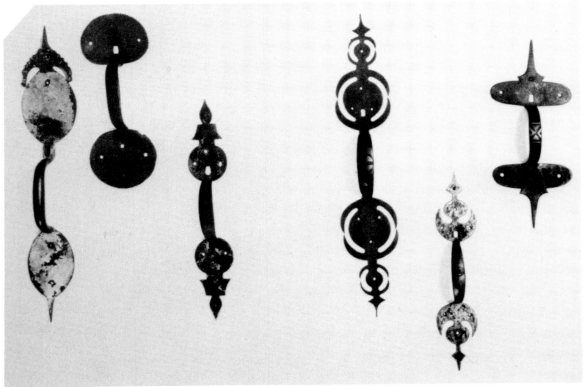

B.

A-B. Thumb latches, wrought iron, late 18th c., Pennsylvania and New England, Wadsworth Atheneum, W. Himmelreich collection.

Note that these two latches have balanced top and bottom elements.

C. Thumb latch, wrought iron, late 18th or early 19th century, American, Wallace Nutting Collection, Wadsworth Atheneum, Hartford.

Flat handles and round handles were used simultaneously. The latch with the hearts is the most desirable.

A.

B.

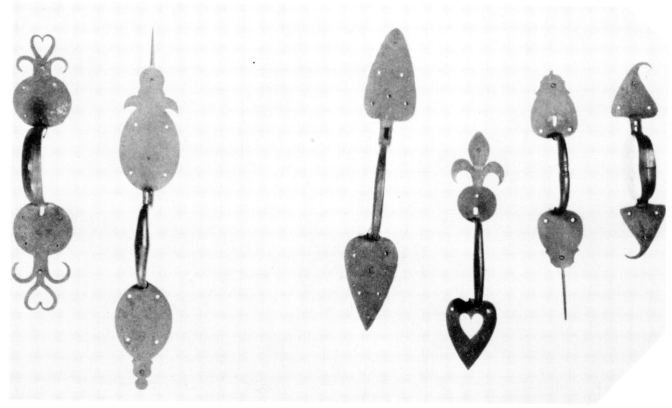

C.

A-C. Thumb latches, wrought iron, 18th c.,
American.

The group of round handled latches are all
of above average quality. The lower element
of the handle is usually greatly reduced in size
and important to the total design. The handles
have been decorated on a swedge block in most
cases.

B. Thumb latch, wrought iron, 18th c., Ameri-
can.

The combination of the two roosting birds on
the top element and the heart on the lower
make this latch one of the most charming.

A.

B.

C.

A-C.Thumb latches.

The following group of very refined thumb latches have one characteristic in common — the handle has been struck into a swedge (see example) giving it the appearance of a turned piece of wood. The first example was struck lightly into a poorly defined block, while some of the later ones have beautifully defined swellings.

B.

A.

C.

D. Swedge block, American, 5" high, Pennsylvania Farm Museum of Landis Valley.

A mass of metal is gathered into a crude blob on a rod, then the rod is heated and struck against the swedge to take on the shape of the impression. Then the rod is heated, turned, struck against the swedge several more times, eventually taking on an appearance, like turnings on furniture. The swedge block when in use fits into a hole on top of the anvil. The handles of these round handled locks have been decorated this way.

D.

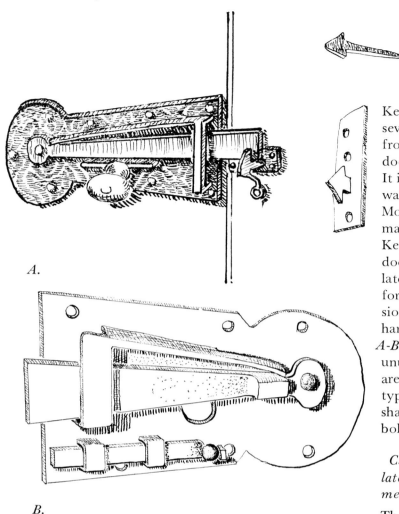

A.

B.

Keyhole plate latches date from the end of the seventeenth century to about 1820, and vary from three to thirteen inches in length. Early door hardware was painted to match the door. It is a fairly modern tradition to show the hardware in black paint or brushed and oiled steel. Most of the latches taken from old houses have many layers of paint matching the room colors. Keyhole latches were primarily found on interior doors, closets and doors to stairs. Most of these latches are of English origin. Bills and ledgers for some of the most important American mansions include enormous amounts of English hardware.

A-B. Example A is a keyhole latch with a fairly unusual keeper. More usual types of keepers are shown at the right. Example B is an early type of keyhole plate latch without its cam, shaft, or knobs, but with an early type of night bolt. The night bolt knob is solid wrought iron.

C. Morvanian latch, wrought iron and brass, late 18th and early 19th c., American, W. Himmelreich.

The interesting curvilinear outline of the back plate marks this as a Moravian latch. The outline is somewhat similar to that of Moravian locks.

C.

Square plate latches were made from about 1730 to 1830 primarily in England for use on interior doors. Some were beautifully champhered whil others were quite crude.

Like keyhole plate latches, square plate latches have been found with brass stirrup pulls on early examples, and oval or round knobs on later ones. The average size is three to four inches long. Brass knobs on night latches add refinement.

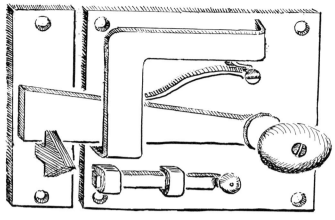

A.

B. Advertisement for Lock Manufactory, 1826, Carnegie Library of Pittsburgh.

In this 1826 Pittsburgh advertisement a lock manufacturer offers everything from Norfolk latches to jail and bank latches.

Lock Manufactory.

J. & J. PATTERSON, Jr.

BIRMINGHAM, near Pittsburgh,

Take this method to inform the public, that their LOCK MANUFACTORY is in full and active operation,

WHERE ARE MANUFACTURED

Knob, Rim, Fine Plate and Bambury Stock Locks, from 6 to 12 inches.

ALSO

Best Norfolk Thumb Latches and Bolts,

Of a quality equal, if not superior, to any imported, which will be disposed of as low as can be brought from any of the eastern cities.

ALL orders for any of the above articles, addressed to the Manufactory—to *George Cochran,* Agent of the Pittsburgh Manufacturing Association, or to *Benjamin Darlington,* Market street, Pittsburgh, will be thankfully received, and promptly attended to.

Birmingham, June 1, 1826.

N. B. Large Locks for Banks or Prisons, made to any pattern.

B.

A.

B.

C.

E.

D.

F.

A-C. Three Norfolk latches, wrought iron, late 18th and 19th c., American and English, National Gallery of Art.

Norfolk latches were first used in the early eighteenth century, but most date from the mid-nineteenth century. They were made both in England and America.

D-F. Norfolk latches, wrought iron, late 18th c., American, Wallace Nutting collection, Wadsworth Atheneum.

Here is a collection of three very unusual Norfolk latches.

A.

B.

C.

A-C. Latches, 18th c., American, Wallace Nutting collection, Wadsworth Atheneum.

These three rare beautiful latches only required a keeper to function.

D. Latch, 18th c., American, 10" long, W. Himmelreich.

This latch bar for a sliding latch is very unusual with its stamped decoration.

D.

A.

Box locks were made from the 1720's to the
1820's of wrought iron, and after about 1820
of cast iron. Oval, round and stirrup knobs are
found. The stirrups are by far the rarest and
possibly earliest. This type of lock is found in
both formal and informal rooms. The size ranges
from 3″ by 4″ to 9″ by 12″ with the smallest
sizes being the most common. Most box locks
were made in England, yet after the American
Revolution some were made in America.
Drawing "B" shows the back view of an early
box lock. Note the small keyhole plate and
visible works. In Victorian times the entire back
was covered. Drawing "C" is the same lock with
the keyhole plate, latch and lock bars removed.

*A. Lock, wrought iron and steel, early 16th
c., English, Victoria and Albert Museum.*

This very early lock — the Beddington lock
from Beddington House — can be dated from
the Royal crest on the center panel. Money
chests with this type of lock have concealed
key holes which are revealed only when one
of the applied elements is swung aside.

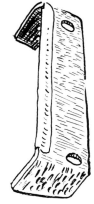

A.

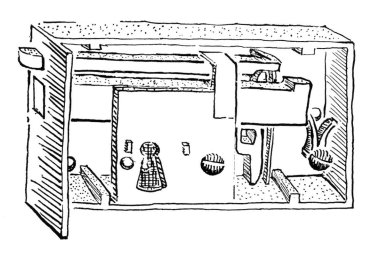

B.

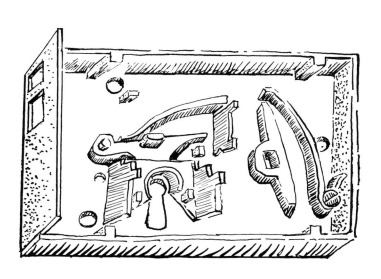

C.

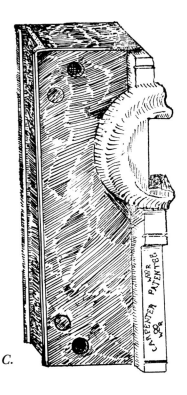

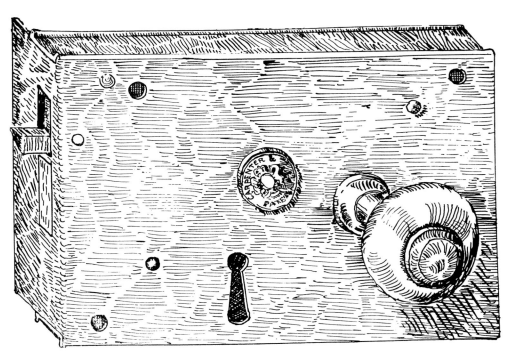

A.

A. Box lock, wrought iron, late 18th c., American.

This lock was on the Columbia County jail. The key only works from the outside.

B.

"Carpenter" locks were devised by a man named Carpenter who patented their design in the early nineteenth century in England. Instead of moving horizontally as on the earlier types of locks, the latch on a Carpenter lock is raised by turning the knob. These were widely used in America in the mid-nineteenth century and were made by a variety of makers who often identified their work by small round brass placques bearing their name. Some of these makers were W. Badger and Company, Carpenter, Carpenter and Tildesley, John Povey, S. Smith, James Tildesley, Walker, and Young. Like other Victorian locks, the Carpenter group have solid back plates.

B-C. Example B has an exposed mechanism, while example C has a covering plate.

C.

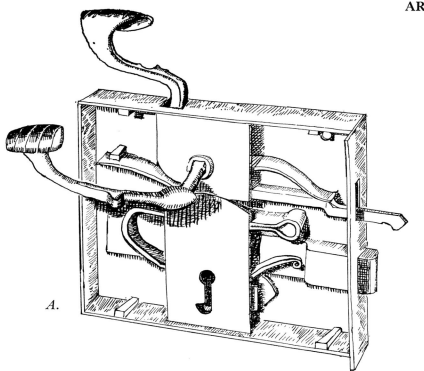

A.

B.

Dutch elbow locks were made in the eighteenth and nineteenth centuries in Europe and probably also in America in German-settled areas. The latch is raised by pushing down the handles on either side of the door with your elbow or hand.

C. Dutch elbow lock, iron and brass, Pennsylvania, made by D. Rohrer, 1822.

Few Dutch elbow locks are signed, and this may be a unique example with engraved brass plate. The mechanism inside is made of iron and steel.

C.

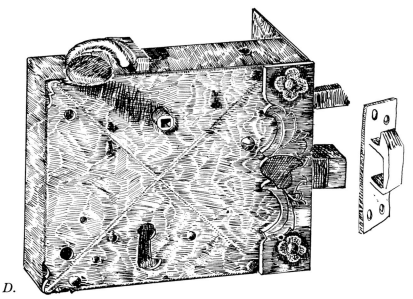

D.

A-E.Moravian locks, wrought iron, late 18th and early 19th c., Pennsylvania.

The outlines of the back plate of Moravian locks show an infinite variation of attractive curves. These locks were painted the color of the woodwork.

Moravian locks were first used in the areas settled by Moravians, but soon found their way around most of the Pennsylvania Dutch areas. Henry J. Kauffman's discovery of a Moravian lock signed "Rohrer" for the Rohrer family of Lebanon, Pennsylvania, proves they were made in America. Locks of this type were also made in Switzerland, Germany, and other countries. There is little difference between the known American locks and the Continental locks although some of the Continental locks have finer decoration.

On the back side of a Moravian lock, the flat plate fits against the inside of the door.

A.

B.

C.

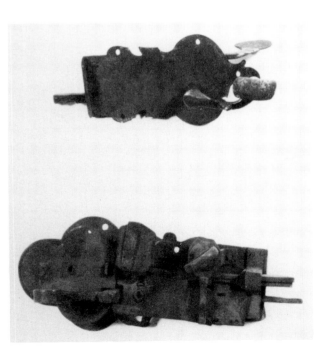

D.

E.

A. Grab lock, wrought iron, late 18th c., Pennsylvania, The Henry Francis du Pont Winterthur Museum.

This grab lock is signed by its maker, Joseph Stumb, and was found on a Pennsylvania German blanket chest. Grab locks are found on chests of the eighteenth century. By the second quarter of the nineteenth century locks were mounted flat to the inside of chests.

B. Lock picks, wrought iron, 18th c., probably English, James C. Sorber.

This group of lock picks probably belonged to an eighteenth century locksmith or burglar. These are very useful to open accidentally locked early locks and are a great rarity.

A.

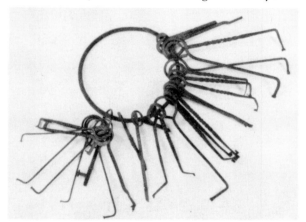

B.

C. Three padlocks, wrought iron, 19th c., American, Pennsylvania Farm Museum of Landis Valley.

The center padlock is probably the earliest, possibly dating from the first quarter of the nineteenth century. The padlock without a key was probably made in the mid-nineteenth century. The one with a key dates from the late nineteenth century.

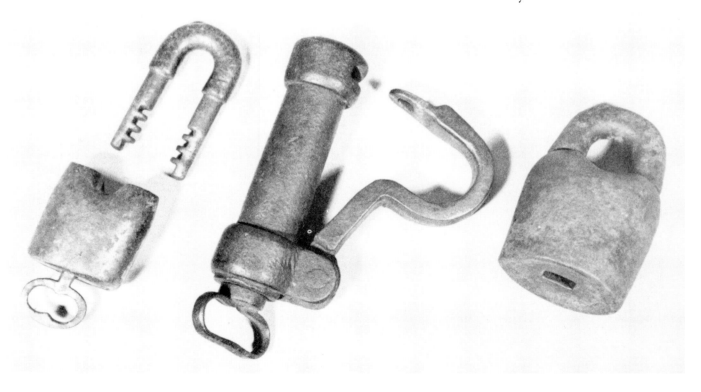

C.

A.

A. Numerals from a Dutch house front in New
Castle, Delaware, wrought iron, 1687, American,
National Gallery of Art, Index of American
Design.

Water color paintings of the old Dutch house
in New Castle exist showing how the numbers
were used. In a mistaken effort of urban renewal
in the late nineteenth century, this house was
torn down. With its stepped gable end the house
would have looked completely authentic in
Holland.

B. Roof ornament, wrought iron, 1778, American, James C. Sorber.

This is a rare type of gable ornament — actually
one of a kind. Two iron loops held this to
the walls at the corner of a building.

B.

A.

A. *Engraving of a scene in Philadelphia in 1800 by Thomas Birch.*

This type of pump was operated by an iron handle and had an iron spout support.

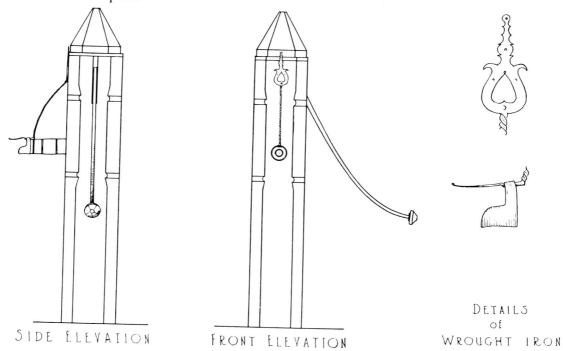

SIDE ELEVATION

FRONT ELEVATION

DETAILS
of
WROUGHT IRON

B. *Drawing of an 18th century pump found in Lancaster County, Pennsylvania.*

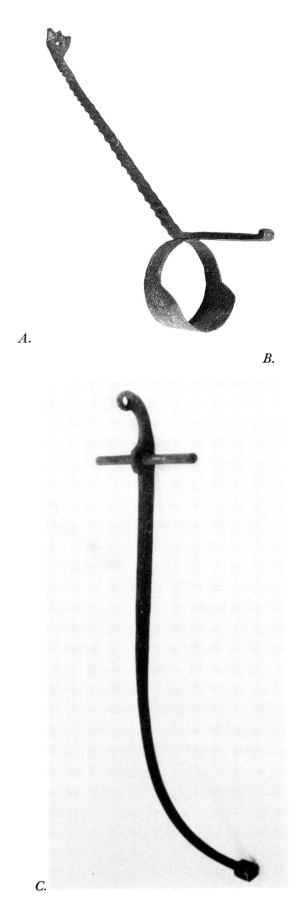

A.

B.

A-B. Two pump spout supports, wrought iron, 18th c., Pennsylvania, 2 1/2" high, Pennsylvania Farm Museum of Landis Valley.

These pump spout supports have a bar to hold the pail handle while the pail is being filled. Many wooden pumps and spouts have rotted leaving the iron spout supports. One of these has a "tulip bud" end, while the other sports a tulip.

C-D. Pump handle, wrought iron, l858, Pennsylvania, James. C. Sorber.
The pump handle shown here is a standard shape. Of interest is the stamped design and the date of 1858. This type of pump handle was also made during the late 18th century.

C.

D.

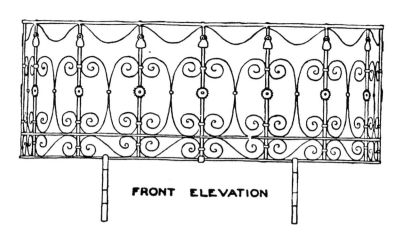

FRONT ELEVATION

A.

A. *Balcony, wrought iron, 19th century, American, Library of Congress.*

This is one of the balconies at the Governor Levi Woodbury Mansion in Portsmouth, New Hampshire.

B. *Section of balcony, wrought iron, mid-18th c., American, New York Historical Society.*

This is one of America's most historic railings, on Federal Hall, New York, where George Washington stood during his first inauguration. Even if it weren't of historical importance it would still be admired as a work of art.

B.

A. Balcony, early 19th c., Regency period, English, Victoria and Albert Museum.

The anthemion and the wave pattern are constantly repeated in the English Regency style which corresponds to the American Empire period.

B. Panel from balcony front, cast iron, 1830, Gordon Square, London, English, Victoria and Albert Museum.

At the end of the Regency period the designs are a little heavier and the flowers foreshadow the roses and grapes that will be seen in much of the Victorian designs.

C. Balcony, columns and rilaing, cast iron, first quarter of

This Regency balcony uses the same motifs as the American Empire metal work of the same or slightly later years.

B.

A.

C.

A. Balcony, columns and railing, cast iron, first quarter of the 19th c., American, New York City, National Gallery of Art.

If this iron were English, it would be called Regency in design. It is American in a transitional style between Classical and Empire. The anthemion design is the latest feature, and would have been seen in England ten years earlier.

A.

B. Porch railing and detail, cast iron, 19th c., southern United States, National Gallery of Art, Index of American Design.

Cast iron was a suitable material for porches and balconies in the South. Besides allowing for a open flow of air, it was not subject to termites and rot.

B.

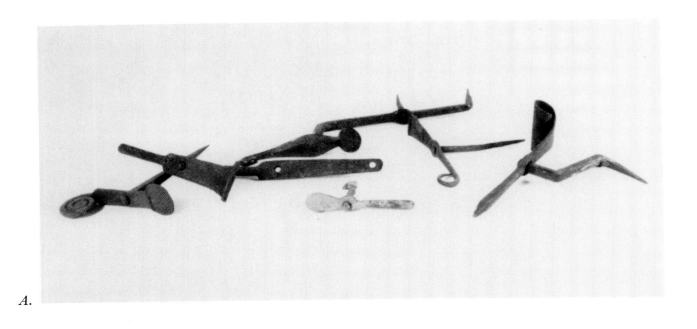

A.

*A-B.Group of shutter fasteners, wrought iron,
18th c., American, Wallace Nutting collection,
Wadsworth Atheneum.*

Again, it is very difficult to date these closely,
as styles did not change significantly from the
mid-eighteenth century to early nineteenth
century. Many original ones have survived on
old buildings.

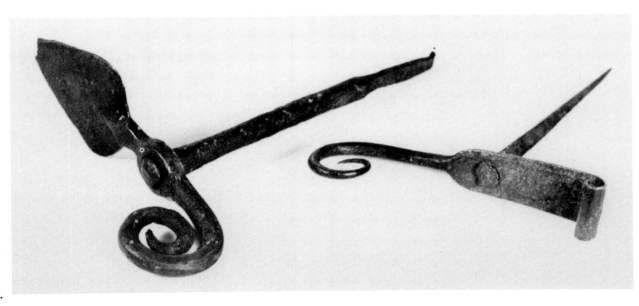

B.

There are many varieties of shutter fasteners dating from the eighteenth century. The earliest were wrought into shape, later they were cast with designs like stars and grapes.

Most shutter fasteners attach to buildings by shafts from which the shutter catch pivots. Common designs are shown as figures A, B, and C. Figure D pivots within a keeper. Figure E rotates in two fixed shafts.

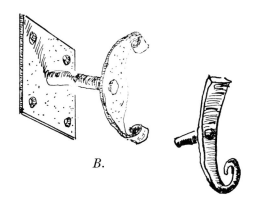

A.

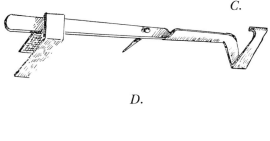

B.

C.

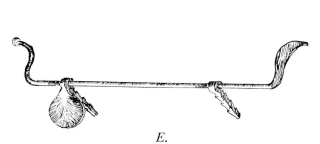

D.

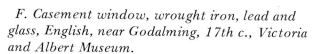

E.

F. Casement window, wrought iron, lead and glass, English, near Godalming, 17th c., Victoria and Albert Museum.

This casement window of iron has iron stiffening bars and lead cams. Lead is so soft that without iron stiffeners the windows would blow in a storm. American casement windows had iron bars, but usually oak frames. The latch and handle would have been less elaborate on an American window.

F.

A.

B.

A. Cellar grill, cast iron, early 19th c., Montgomery, Alabama, Library of Congress.

Again the anthemion in its infinite variation occurs on this cellar grill.

B. Cellar grill, cast iron, mid-19th c., Montgomery, Alabama, Library of Congress.

Here is a variation of the grape pattern.

C. Yoke for bell, wrought iron, 1840-1855, Louisiana, Museum of Rural Life, Louisiana State University.

While the bronze bell was made by C. W. Coffin and Company at the Buckeye Foundry in Cincinnati, Ohio; the yoke was made by a local Louisiana blacksmith.

CHAPTER 2
Armament

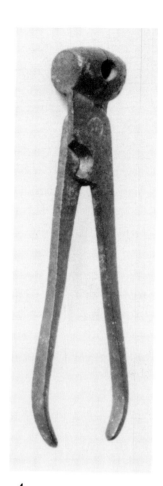

A. Bullet mold, cast iron, 18th or 19th century, European or American.

Bullet molds were a necessity when wild game and hostile people threatened. These molds were common, and therefore quite a few have survived.

B. Ladle, wrought iron, and bullet molds, cast iron, 19th century, probably American, Old Sturbridge Village.

A pouring ladle, two bullet molds and their products are shown here. Any metal with a low melting point is suitable to make bullets. The bullets with the pointed ends are pewter or lead. Round bullets changed little in design from the seventeenth to the early nineteenth century.

A.

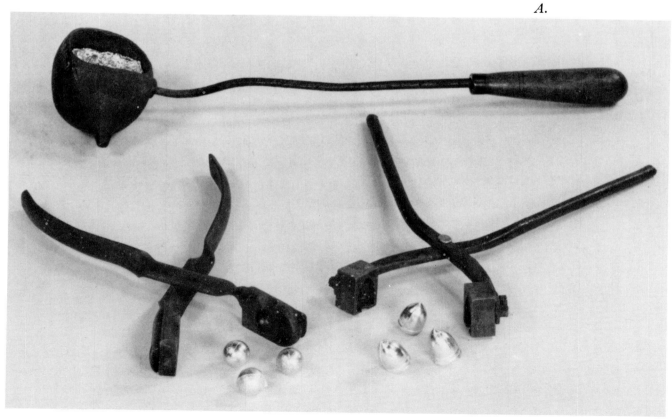

B.

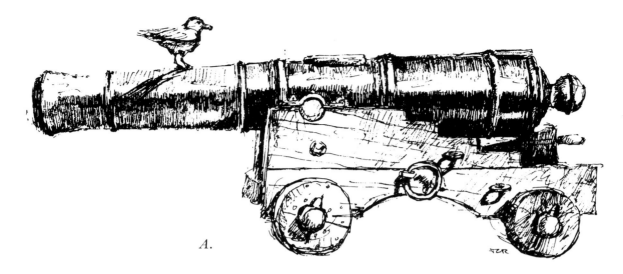

A.

*A. Long guns on the U.S. frigate Constitution,
built 1794. Courtesy, U.S. Navy.*

Original gun contracts were let with Cecil
Iron Works, Baltimore, and Hope Furnace,
Rhode Island, but these were not fulfilled in
time for the ships in 1797, and several expedi-
ents were used. Eighteen of *Constitution's*
24-pounder battery came from purchases in
England, while the 18-pounder long guns
which made up her spar deck battery were
borrowed from the Commonwealth of
Massachusetts. Subsequently, her batteries
changed many times — always iron guns —
18-, 24- and 32-pounder long guns; 32- and
42-pounder carronades; and 68-pounder Paix-
hans guns, in general terms.

*B. Cannon, National Park Service, Hope-
well Village.*

This cannon was probably cast at Warwick
Furnace in Pennsylvania as it was found in a
meadow below the furnace.

B.

A.

A. Mold, National Park Service, Hopewell Village.

This cannonball mold and cannonball were used at foundries like Hopewell Village. The two parts of the mold flank a six and a 12 pound shot.

B. Helmet, steel, 17th c., English, Museum of London.

A closed helmet like this was recently discovered by the eminent archeologist Ivor Nöel-Hume of Colonial Williamsburg at the Carters Grove site of an early fort. This is the earliest type of helmet found in English settled North America.

B.

A.

A. Hunting knives, steel and wood, 19th c., American, lengths 16 1/2" and 15 1/2", Pennsylvania Museum of Landis Valley.

Both of these knives could be called "Bowie knives". Knives like these were standard equipment for hunters and foot soldiers through the Civil War. The blacksmiths that made them were experts at tempering.

B. Three swords, English (center) with Italian blade by Antonio Picinio, 17th c., Victoria and Albert Museum.

Sword hilts were often the finest work of the sword makers of this day, but the finest swords still used blades by Italian masters like Antonio Picinio whose name can be read on the center blade. The Damascene work on these hilts in silver and gold is exceptionally fine quality.

B.

A.

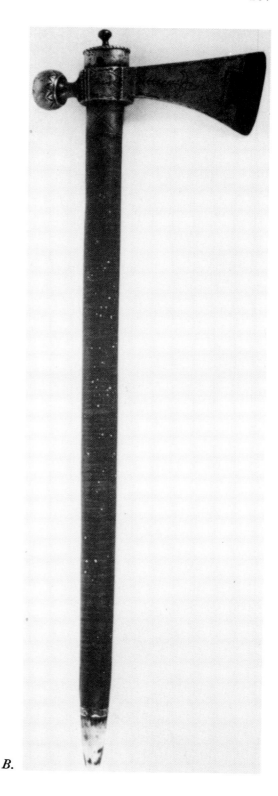

B.

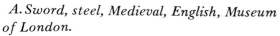

A. Sword, steel, Medieval, English, Museum of London.

Many of the best iron workers were armorers and later clock makers and blacksmiths.

B. Tomahawk, steel blade and brass head, striped maple handle, late 18th century, 18½ inches long, Walter O'Connor.

The steel blade holds a sharp edge while the brass head is decoratively engraved.

A.

B.

C.

CHAPTER 3
Boxes

A. *Chest, iron , 1776, Elliston and Perot, Philadelphia, The Philadelphia Contributionship.*

The Philadelphia Contributionship insurance company ordered this chest made on July 2, 1776 to deposit valuable papers belonging to the company for hasty removal in the event they were threatened by enemy British troops. Almost a hundred years later, on July 3, 1863, the company called a meeting at which the treasurer was authorized to remove the company books and papers to a safe place because Rebels (Southern troops) had invaded Pennsylvania.

B. *Box, damascened, steel with gold and silver, 1590, English, Victoria and Albert Museum.*

The decoration of this box suggests Spanish origin with Moorish influence.

C. *Coffer, steel, velvet and brass, 1690, English, 9 1/2" high by 18 1/2" wide, Victoria and Albert Museum.*

This exquisite coffer was the jewel chest of Queen Mary II of England. It is a steel box covered in velvet and decorated with embellished studs, ornate handles and escutcheons.

D. *Carrying handle, wrought iron, mid- to late 18th c., Pennsylvania.*

Carrying handles of this and other shapes were found at the ends of blanket chests. Most of the carrying handles were on walnut chests of the early type with long hinges and grab locks.

E. *Blanket chest, wood and wrought iron, 18th c., Pennsylvania.*

The iron handles on this Pennsylvania blanket chest are typical of the early German influenced iron work. The escutcheon is especially fine. Early chests like this tend to have long strap hinges. As the chests date closer to 1800, the straps on the hinges get shorter, and by the mid-nineteenth century, butt hinges were usual.

D.

E.

A.

A. Tobacco box, cast iron, 1792, English.

This carefully cast tobacco box has on the opposite side raised figures playing checkers, smoking, playing musical instruments, and playing backgammon.

B-C. Box, tin with black japanning, 19th c., American.

Tin boxes were made for many purposes. This sort was used for fishing tackle, tea and spices, and a paint set.

B.

C.

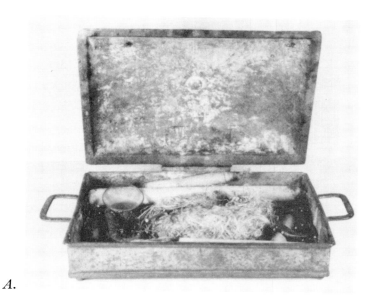

A.

A-B. *Candle box with domed lid, rolled sheet iron, early nineteenth century,shown with the old candle, straw kindling and lighter.*

C. *Candle box, tinned iron, early 19th c., American, Walter Himmelreich.*

Tin candle boxes of this shape are quite rare. The raised ribbed decoration can be made by pulling tin through shaped rollers, or by the use of a swedging hammer.

B.

C.

A.

B.

C.

A. Box, rolled and tinned iron, early 19th c., American, W. Himmelreich.

The feet give this box a certain charm. This type of box has been called a "deed" box because it has a hasp that can be locked.

B. Box, tinned iron, 19th c., American, W. Himmelreich.

The repousse flowers decorating the top were probably hammered into a wooden mold.

C. Box, tinned iron, late 19th c., American.

Little boxes like this held shot, powder, patches, medicines, etc.

A.

A. Candle box, rolled, tinned and japanned iron, early 18th c., American, 13 1/2" long, 4" diameter, W. Himmelreich.

Punched tin candle boxes are incredibly rare. This one has two Indians on each side facing a circle enclosing a flower.

B. Candle box, rolled, tinned and japanned iron, late 18th or early 19th c., American, National Gallery of Art, Index of American Design.

The English made these candle boxes also and they are very similar. Sometimes they are called document boxes.

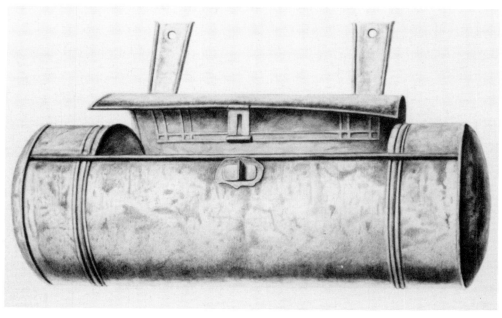

B.

A.

B.

A. Hanging box, tinned iron, 19th c., American, 5" high, 4 1/2" wide, 2 5/8" long.

Too short for documents or candles — the purpose is uncertain; possibly for matches or spills.

B. Hanging match box, cast iron, late 19th c., American, National Gallery of Art, Index of American Design.

Many small cast iron decorative objects were made.

CHAPTER 4
Conestoga Wagon

A.

B.

A. Conestoga wagon, Pennsylvania, 19th century, Pennsylvania Farm Museum of Landis Valley.

Conestoga wagons were an important means of transportation around farms and for migration to the West. The iron parts and tools are shown individually in this chapter.

B. Wheel brake, wrought iron, late 18th or early 19th c., American, James C. Sorber.

These pieces of metal were chained on two back wheels to act as additional braking.

A.

A. *Three Conestoga wagon boxes, wrought iron, wood and old blue paint, 18th c., Pennsylvania, James C. Sorber.*

The hinges, hoops, and bindings on Conestoga wagon boxes represent some of the most charming and innovative wrought iron made in Pennsylvania. While most of the iron survives, very few of the boxes do.

B. *Conestoga wagon box hasp, wrought iron, early 19th century, Wadsworth Atheneum.*

C. *Conestoga wagon box lid showing hinges and hasp, wrought iron and wood, late 18th c., American, National Gallery of Art, Index of American Design;*

Conestoga wagon boxes show some of the most imaginative of the Pennsylvania wrought iron hinges and hasps.

D. *Conestoga Wagon box hasp, wrought iron, early 19th c., Pennsylvania, W. Himmelreich.*

B.

C.

D.

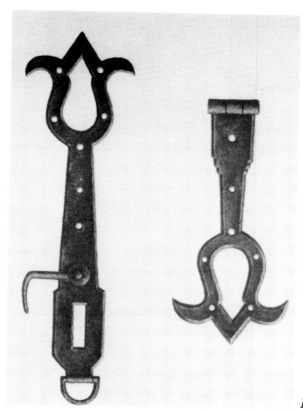

A.

B.

C.

A. Conestoga wagon hasp and hinge, National Gallery of Art, Index of American Design.

B. Conestoga wagon box hasp, wrought iron, Pennsylvania, late 18th or early 19th c.

This hasp shows the popular Pennsylvania Dutch motif of the tulip.

C. Conestoga wagon box hasp, wrought iron, early 19th century, Wadsworth Atheneum.
The stamped design and split leaf ends make these hasps noteworthy.

D. Conestoga wagon tool box hasp, mid-19th c., 7 1/2" long, 5 1/2" long (hasp proper), Pennsylvania Farm Museum of Landis Valley.

E. Hasp, first half of the 19th c., 7 1/4" long, Pennsylvania Farm Museum of Landis Valley.

D.

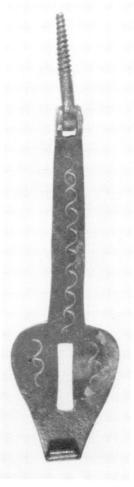

E.

A.

B.

C.

D.

Double tree, wrought iron, late 18th c., Pennsylvania, James C. Sorber.

This rare double tree has the terminations of the trace holders shaped into snakes' heads. A double tree takes the traces from each side of the horse corral and converts the pull into one line.

B. Conestoga wagon double tree hasp, wrought iron, 1837, Pennsylvania, 10 1/4" long, Pennsylvania Farm Museum of Landis Valley.

The double tree hasp was fastened to the rear end of the wagon tongue to help provide stronger support against the full pull of the double tree. This example is dated 1837 and numbered 137. The stamped name is illegible.

C. Conestoga wagon coupling pole pin, 19th c., 9" long, Pennsylvania Farm Museum of Landis Valley.

This heart shaped Conestoga wagon coupling pin is an example of a combination of functional design and art.

D. Conestoga wagon hardware, wrought iron, late 18th or early 19th century, signed D. Miller, Pennsylvania, James C. Sorber.

This carefully designed and signed piece of iron connects the front and back wheels of a Conestoga wagon. A metal hammer was put through the hole to act as a pin. The sunburst design was made on the corner of the anvil.

A.

B.

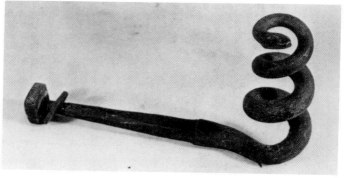

C.

A. Rein guard, wrought iron, early 19th c., American, James C. Sorber.
This beautifully proportioned piece of iron is decorated with punched decoration. It was fastened to the front of a sled to guide the reins.

B. Ax carrier, wrought iron, end of the 18th and beginning of the 19th c., American.

C. Conestoga wagon stay chain holder, early 19th c., Lancaster and York County, 8 1/4" long, Pennsylvania Farm Museum of Landis Valley.
The snake is a frequent ornamentation of Conestoga wagon stay chain holders.

D. Conestoga wagon equipment, wrought iron, American, Walter Himmelreich.

D.

A.

C.

B.

A. Conestoga wagon axe holders, wrought iron, late 18th and early 19th c., Pennsylvania, James C. Sorber.

These interesting axe holders were fastened to the wagon and have a hook and bar to keep the axe from being jolted loose.

B. Conestoga wagon hub band, wrought iron, late 18th or early 19th c., American, James C. Sorber.

This wagon hub band was decorated with punched designs done while hot with a curved chisel. This band strengthened the wooden hub.

C. Wagon jack, dated "1865", initialed "C.B.," 20 1/2" high, Pennsylvania Museum of Landis Valley.

A traditional form of wagon jack utilizing a wrought iron lifting mechanism mounted in a large wooden black. This example is dated 1865 and with intials C B. The wooden block retains much of its original red paint.

CHAPTER 5
Decorated Tin

A.

As tinsmiths went from Europe to America, they set up the guild system in some of the major cities, except in Connecticut and Maine. The early tinsmiths made all sorts of useful articles and in the cities congregated in groups at Tin Pan Alley, New York; Mechanics Alley, Baltimore and Brazier's Alley, Philadelphia.

Some of their signs still exist, such as the Julius Mickey's enormous coffee pot at Winston-Salem, which is close to 8 feet tall (and is shown in this book).

The painting was done on a production basis, so each design was simplified to a few brush strokes that could be painted fast and well. The background was very thin.

Today, some decorators' work can be recognized. There are a few signed pieces, but unfortunately much has to be attributed.

A. Pair of book ends, rolled and tinned iron, 19th c., American.

B. Decorated tin box, cream pitcher and tea caddy, painted, tinned and japanned iron, 19th c.

B.

A.

B.

A-B. Two coffee pots, rolled and tinned iron, nineteenth century, American.

C. Tray, rolled, tinned and japanned iron, early 19th c., National Gallery of Art, Index of American Design.

C.

A.

B.

A-D. Four serving trays, rolled and tinned iron, painted decorations, early nineteenth century, English.

C.

D.

A-C. Three coffee pots, rolled and tinned iron, early 19th c., American.

Punched tin decoration is very rare. Two with "J. Ubele, 1834" stamped on the handle have remained intact. Eagles, American flags, and baskets of flowers are the most usual decoration. These were probably presentation pieces as the many hours required to manufacture them would preclude commercial manufacture.

A.

B.

C.

CHAPTER 6
Fireplace Equipment

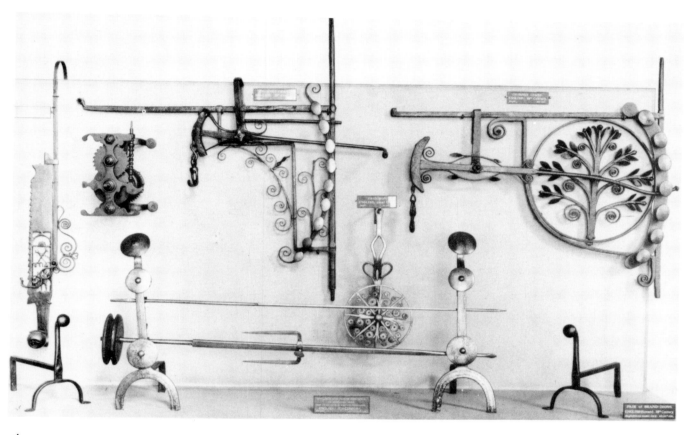

A.

A. Group of iron fireplace accompaniments, wrought iron, 17th and 18th c., English, Victoria and Albert Museum.

On the far left is a complicated trammel with pierced decoration of a blacksmith's tools, a hammer and tongs. trammels of this quality were of English or Continental manufacture while American trammels and fireplace cranes are very simple. The elaborate cranes were made in England sometime during the eighteenth century. The gridiron and clock jack are standard English examples. The andirons with the spit hooks and spit are seventeenth century, English; while the smaller ball topped andirons are English of the early eighteenth century.

A.

B.

A. *Andirons, wrought iron and brass, c. 1680, English and American, 28" high, Peter Hempson.*

Because houses were dark, an extra light re-flection was welcomed. Embellishing andirons with brass was elegant, so brass decorated andirons are usually finer in design than their plain iron counterparts.

The stamped decoration is a traditional design dating back to the Middle Ages, and continued to the nineteenth century in folk cultures like the Pennsylvania German.

The second group, as the legs arch higher and higher, are eighteenth century.

The andirons with urn, lemon top, or knife blades are often after the Revolution.

B. *Andiron, brass and iron, 17th c., north-ern European, 35 1/4" high.*

The scrolled base indicates the seventeenth century date.

C. *Andiron, iron and brass, late 17th c. to early 18th c., English.*

The scrolled base and spit hooks indicate an early date.

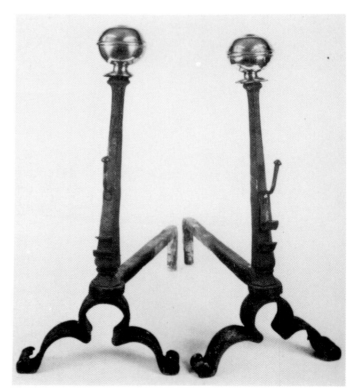

C.

The flat based andirons originated around 1700 and later the foot gradually rose higher. These three examples could be of English or American origin.

B. Andiron, brass and iron, c. 1700, English or American, 17" high, Bowers collection.

C. Andiron, brass and iron, probably American, c. 1710.

D. Andiron, brass and iron, c. 1710, probably American, Jesse Pavey.

A.

A. Andiron, brass and iron, late 17th c., European, 19 1/2" high.

Bold brass finials and the brass face decorations are elegant features of this early pair of andirons.

B.

C.

D.

A.

B.

C.

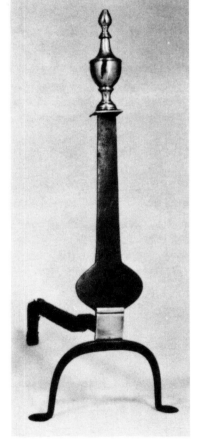

D.

E.

A. Andirons, brass and iron, mid-18th c., Penn
sylvania, Bihler and Coger Antiques.

These fine brass ornamented iron andirons are
American and were probably made in Philadelphia. The chamfered ball and flame finial appea
often in more sophisticated brass andirons.

B. Andirons, brass and iron, third quarter
of the 18th c., American, 17 1/2" high, Bowers
collection.

This example has an early chamfered finial
with a ball top, but a flat knife blade plinth,
typical of the later part of the eighteenth
century.

C. Andirons, brass and iron, late 18th c.,
American, 14 1/4" high.

These andirons have acorn finials, a rare variatio
of the ball finial of this period.

D. Andiron, brass and iron, late 18th c.,
American, Bowers collection.

E. Andirons, brass and iron, late 18th c.,
24" high, Bowers collection.

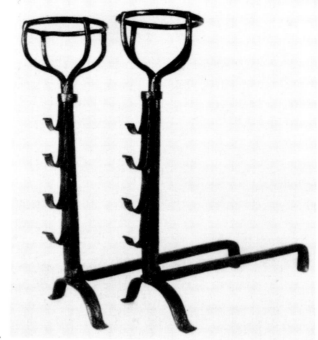

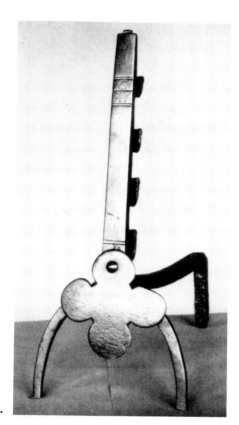

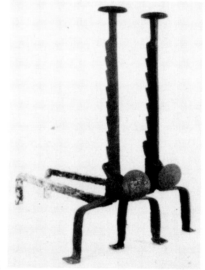

B.

C.

A.

A. Andirons, wrought iron, late 17th c., English, Victoria and Albert Museum.

This is a rare, early type of andiron, with spit hooks and a cypher H^{C}M.

B. Andirons, probably 16th c., European, 17 1/2" high, 5 1/8" wide.

This type of spit hook andiron with a support for a bowl was used in the medieval and Renaissance times and up to the mid-seventeenth century.

C. Andirons, 17th c., probably European, 20 1/2" high.

The design of adjustable spit heights using a ratchet back is extremely practical.

D. Andirons, wrought iron, late 17th c., American.

Ball topped andirons are found in England and America making it very difficult to know exactly where they were made.

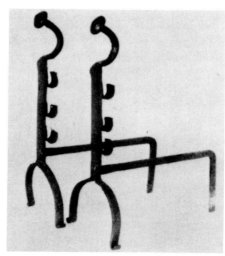

D.

A.

B.

A. Andirons, wrought iron, late 17th or early 18th c., American, Wallace Nutting collection, Wadsworth Atheneum.

This pair of andirons have the same early flat feet. The scrolled top is a feature that extends over a 150 year period.

B. Andirons, wrought iron, early 18th c., American, National Gallery of Art, Index of American Design.

This later variation of the scroll top andiron shows the higher legs found at the beginning of the eighteenth century.

C. Andiron, late 18th c., American, Wallace Nutting collection, Index of American Design.

Here is the latest and most sophisticated version of the scroll type andiron. The widened, flattened area above the junction of the log supports and legs is a late eighteenth century feature.

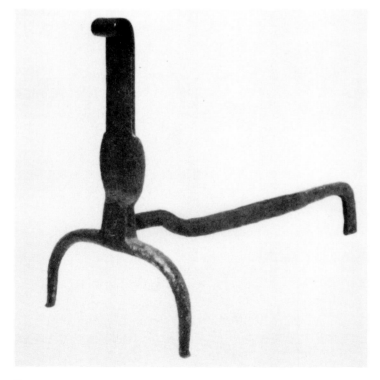

C.

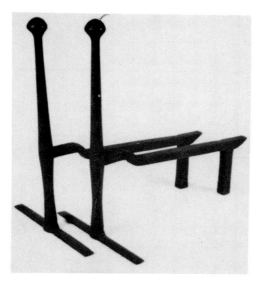

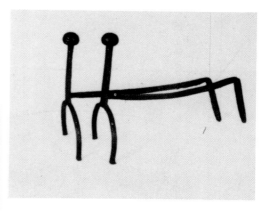

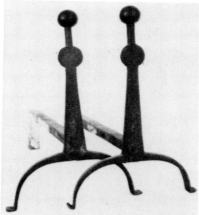

C.

A.

B.

D.

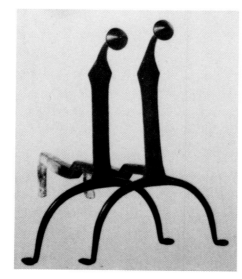

E.

A. *Andirons, 17th c., probably English or American.*

The flat base dates these about 1700.

B. *Andirons, wrought iron, late 18th c., American, 14 1/4" high, 9 1/2" wide, 16" long, Philip Bradley Antiques.*

This highly sophisticated and unusual pair of American andirons has flat swelling below the top knobs that is usually much lower on the shaft.

C. *Andirons, wrought iron, 18th c., American.*

This charming small early pair of round topped andirons was possibly made for a Franklin Stove.

D. *Andirons, wrought iron, English or American, 14" high, 10 1/2" wide, 18" long, Philip Bradley Antiques.*

This round headed goose-necked pair of andirons has large penny feet and a spreading shaft.

E. *Andirons, wrought iron, English or American, 18 3/4" high, 13" wide, 19" long, Philip Bradley Antiques.*

This unusual variation has great refinement.

A.

A. Sleepers and snakes, wrought iron, 18th and early 19th c., American, James C. Sorber.

Sleepers or very small andirons were made to support kindling. Most were made of brass, which would have been impractical. The larger ones (over 6") may have been fire tool rests. Mr. Sorber believes the smallest ones were toys for children or samples for the blacksmith to show a potential customer. These are very rare and collectable. The largest pair, and probably the latest, were made about 1790. The two smallest are mid-eighteenth century.

The snakes are either toys for children, or made for practical jokers. This type of iron work takes great skill.

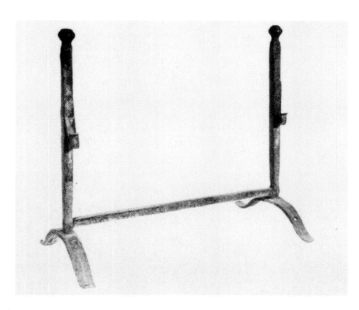

B.

B. Two pairs of andirons, wrought iron, the samller pair possibly 15th c., the larger 16th c., European, James C. Sorber.

Early pictures of great halls with a fire pit and a hole in the roof show this type of andiron. The wood was stoked in from both sides.

C. Andirons, wrought iron, c. 1700, English, 21 1/2" high, 23" wide.

This arrangement for holding a spit probably stood in front of conventional andirons or a grate, and wood may have been laid across the central bar.

C.

A.

B.

A-B. Andirons, early 18th c., signed B. Varanne, possibly French or French Canadian, Museum of Early Southern Decorative Arts.

These are handsome and unusual andirons which are not in the Anglo-American tradition.

C. Grate, late 17th or early 18th c., American or French Canadian, 7 1/2" high, 26 1/4" wide, 17" long, Philip Bradley Antiques.

C.

A. Andirons, wrought iron, early 18th c., probably American, 18" high, 5" wide, 19 1/2" long, Philip Bradley Antiques.

Straight chamfered headed andirons are rare. The short legs on these are unusual.

B. Andirons, wrought iron, early 18th c., American, 12 1/2" high.

These three pairs illustrate the development of the style from weak to sophisticated. These are very small for chamfered headed andirons.

C. Andirons, wrought iron, 18th c., American, 15" high, 10 1/2" wide, 15" long, Philip Bradley Antiques.

D. Andirons, wrought iron, probably mid-18th c., American.

Goose necked chamfered headed andirons are usually vigorous and handsome. This pair has an extra widening below the middle that adds to their interest.

A.

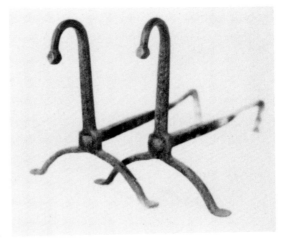

B.

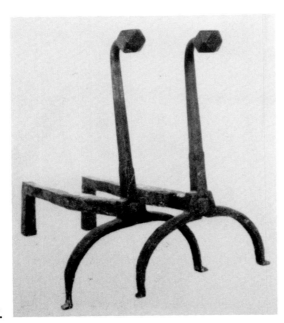

C.

D.

A.

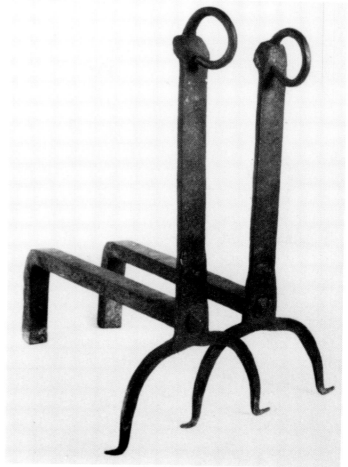

A. Andirons, wrought iron, mid-18th c.,
American, Wallace Nutting collection, Wadsworth Atheneum.

The rings may have had some function on this
variation of the scroll top andirons.

B. Andirons, wrought iron, 18th c., American.

This taller version of the pig tail andirons
sometimes has a reverse curve at the lower
end of the pig tail.

B.

C.

C. Andirons, wrought iron, c.1700, American, Walter Himmelreich.
Pig tail andirons are most probably all of American origin.

A.

A. Andirons, 11 1/4" high, 9" wide, 15" long, Philip Bradley Antiques.

Here is an unusual way to make a decorative top for andirons.

B. Andiron, wrought iron, late 18th c., American, Wallace Nutting collection, Wadsworth Atheneum.
Another version of the ring topped andirons but taller and later.

C. Andirons, wrought iron, 1845-1860, Louisiana, 12" high, Museum of Rural Life, Louisiana State University.

Duck headed andirons are incredibly rare.

B.

C.

A.

A. Andirons, cast iron, 16th and 17th c., Victoria and Albert museum.

These four pairs of early cast iron andirons are Renaissance in feeling and were made all over Europe. We show an early fireback decorated with a pair of this type of andiron with a raised design.

B. Andirons, cast iron, c. 1765-1793, American Mount Etna Furnace, Frederick County, Maryland, 22 1/2" high, 25 1/2" long, bequest of John Glenn, Baltimore Museum of Art.

The small faces at the tops of these andirons are a charming bit of whimsy. Note the suggested gadrooning and fluting making these andirons of very strong design.

B.

A.

B.

A. *Andirons, probably early 19th c., American, Old Sturbridge Village.*

It is difficult to date these cast iron andirons.

B. *Andirons, cast iron, mid-19th c., American, 14 1/2" high, 7 1/2" wide, 15 1/2" long, Philip Bradley Antiques.*

This is a more elaborately decorated type.

C. *Andirons, cast iron, 1825-1844, New York, 14" high, Museum of Rural Life, Louisiana State University.*

These dolphin andirons have a great similarity to the carving on Empire furniture of that area.

C.

A. Andirons, cast iron, 19th c., American, Old Sturbridge Village.

These cast iron ladies are concealing a raised date on their stomachs of 1774. The date is not correct for their manufacture.

B. Andirons, cast iron, 19th c., American, Old Sturbridge Village.

These charming cast iron andirons of ladies have a repair to one of the log supports. Log supports often burned through, usually the entire log support is then replaced. Many repaired ones survive.

A.

B.

C. Andiron, cast iron, American, nineteenth century.
These have charming heads in the tops and were found in Ohio.

C.

A.

A. Andirons, cast iron, American, Metropolitan Museum of Art, Gift of Mrs. Russell Sage, 1909.

There is some debate about the dating of these andirons between mid-eighteenth century and mid-nineteenth century.

B. Andirons, cast iron, log supports — wrought iron, early to mid-19th c., American, Old Sturbridge Village.

The popular notion that is widely spread that these were cast from the iron of cannons captured form the English is a fallacy. They represent Hessian soldiers in America. There are infinite variations of the "Hessian" andirons group.

B.

C.

C. Andiron, cast iron,American, probably nineteenth century.

The enthusiasm for George Washington in the early nineteenth century affected even andiron designs. These are particularly noteworthy, however, because of their construction. They are bolted together. Eighteenth century andirons have the upright shaft pierced to receive the end of the log support which is then peaned over and welded.

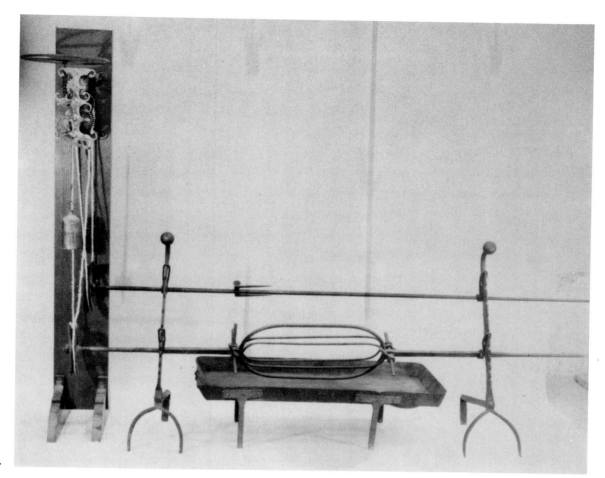

A.

A. Clock jack, iron and brass, English, 18th c. Andirons, spits, and pan, iron, English, 18th c.

The clock jack is properly rigged with a weight to turn two spits which rest on andirons with adjustable hooks. There was little change in the design of spits from the Middle Ages to the mid-nineteenth century. A painting in Her Majesty The Queen's collection of a rural house by John Wilke, dated 1841, shows a clock jack and spits in use. Here the basket spit would hold meat that cannot be skewered while the spear spit can get a firm hold on either a solid piece of meat or meat already secured with skewers. The pan beneath the spits is by far the rarest part of this assembly. It is raised on legs to allow a well beneath for basting.

B. Clock jack, wrought iron and brass, English, late 17th or 18th c., Herbert Schiffer Antiques.

This clock jack has a three-armed fly wheel governor with brass heart shaped ends. Note the care lavished on the large nuts at the top and bottom of the face.

B.

A.

A. Clockjack, steel, late 17th or early 18th century, English.
The steel front plate of this clockjack is brilliantly engraved with masks, floral design, and "Br. Dicks in y upper ground." This is one of the finest early clockjacks known to the authors. Another of the period was made by Isaac Pierson, Bristol.

A.

B.

A. Clock jack, iron and wood, c. 1700, English, 15" high, 7" wide, 9 5/8" long, Herbert Schiffer Antiques.

The fly wheel or governing device at the top of this clock jack is the most usual type.

B. Clock jack, wrought iron and wood, c. 1700, English.

This clock jack originally had four arms for goveners — two are missing now. The bell signals that the weight has reached the bottom and it is time to rewind the rope.

A.

Firebacks served the dual purpose of protecting fragile brick at the backs of fireplaces and reflecting heat into rooms.

The earliest fireback that Doctor Henry Mercer, author of *The Bible in Iron,* saw during his research was dated 1548. Not long before then fires tended to be placed in the middles of halls with roof holes above. Firebacks were not necessary until fires were moved to chimneys.

A. Fireback, cast iron, 16th c., English, 25 1/2" high, 40 1/2" long, Victoria and Albert Museum.

The straight angular rope edges and small seals make this a very interesting and early fireback.

B. Fireback, cast iron, dated 1586, English, 25 1/2" high, 27 1/2" wide, Victoria and Albert Museum.

Noteworthy because of its early date, this Elizabethan fireback is interesting for its architectural feeling. The brass founder reversed a letter of the owners' name on his wooden pattern.

B.

A.

A. Fireback, cast iron, second half of the 16th c., English, 19" high, 36 1/2" wide, Victoria and Albert Museum.

The shape and placement of the Heraldic arms of William Aylopp of Hornchurch, Essex impaling those of Jane Sulyard suggests an early date as are our other "rope" edged examples.

B. Fireback, cast iron, 16th c., English, 20" high, 30" wide, Victoria and Albert Museum.

The andirons depicted on the front of this fireback are similar to andirons of the sixteenth century shown in this book. The "rope" edge appears in other sixteenth century firebacks in this section.

B.

A.

A. Fireback, *cast iron, 16th c., English, 25"*
high, Victoria and Albert Museum.
The pattern on this fireback suggests early Elizabethan needlework designs, thus pointing to a
date in that period of time.

B. Fireback, *1600, English, 25 1/2" high,*
32 3/4" wide, Victoria and Albert Museum.
Bearing the arms of the Earl of Devonshire, this
fireback was made in the last year of Queen
Elizabeth I's reign. The costumes of the supporters are of far earlier fashion styles.

B.

A.

A. Fireback, cast iron, dated 1604, English, 23" high, 30 1/2" wide.

I. R. — the initials of King James the First and the date 1604 confirm this to be an important fireback. The design shows the monarch's coat of arms, the motto of the order of the garter "on y soit qui mal y pense", and the royal motto "dieu et mon droit".

B. Fireback, cast iron, dated 1606, English, 29 1/8" high, 26" wide, Victoria and Albert Museum.

The unusual round shouldered shape, the complicated mantling, the coat of arms, plus the early date, combine to make this a very important fireback.

B.

A.

A. Fireback, cast iron, 17th c., English, Victoria and Albert Museum.

The Boscane oak where Charles the First hid is shown here bearing three crowns uneasily. They are the crowns of England, Ireland and Scotland. The C. R. dates the fireback after Charles The First's execution and Cromwell's political ascendancy. One would have been courageous indeed to have had such a fireback cast. It is amazing that this one survived the Commonwealth — unless it was cast at the time of the Restoration (which we believe) to show an old adherance to the Stewarts. If so, it probably should have had C. R. II in raised letters. This design also occurs on English delftware plates of the late seventeenth century.

B.

B. Fireback, cast iron, dated 1650, English, 17 1/2" high, 17 1/2" wide.

The date cast in the fireback alone would make this an important example, but the use of the Tudor rose is interesting because it was long out of date. Elizabeth I was the last Tudor monarch. The Stewarts had come to power after Elizabeth's death more than 40 years before. Perhaps the Tudor rose was non-political by this time and used merely as a decorative device.

A.

A. *Fireback, cast iron, dated 1660, Massachusetts, The Essex Institute, Salem, Massachusetts.*

The great bosses and split spindles on this New England fireback resemble the applied ornamentation on court cupboards of the period.

Doctor Henry Mercer has written in *The Bible in Iron* that this fireback was obtained from Mr. John Pickering of The Pickering House at 18 Broad Street, Salem, built 1659-1660. The pattern, undoubtedly cast from an imported English mold or one carved in New England by an English mold carver, shows scroll work of Elizabethan style. It is dated 1660, and has initials I A P standing for John and Ann Pickering, original settlers. The form of the vertical spindle-shaped ornaments resemble one of the designs illustrated by Starkie Gardener in *Iron-casting in the Weald*, Archaelogia, second series, volume 5, page 158, figure 24. These were cast at English furnaces in the so called "Weald district" of Kent. According to a tradition in Mr. Pickering's family, this one was cast by the founder, Joseph Jenks, at the Old Lynn or Braintree, Massachusetts. This was founded in 1645 and in blast in 1660.

B. *Fireback, cast iron, dated 1687, English, Victoria and Albert Museum.*

The use of swords on this crest indicates a style dating back to the Middle Ages.

B.

A.

*A. Fireback, cast iron, late 17th c., English,
18 1/4" high, 21 3/4" long, Victoria and Albert
Museum.*

The Royal Navy fireback has the Navy emblem
of the "Fouled Anchor" — PROBAST I ME.

*B. Fireback, cast iron, 17th c., English cast
from a Dutch model, Victoria and Albert Museum.*

This elaborately designed fireback is typical of
the best German, Dutch and Danish designs
of the Renaissance type. The Victoria and Albert Museum has several English firebacks that were
cast from Dutch patterns.

B.

A.

A. Fireback, cast iron, late 17th c., English, Sussex, Victoria and Albert Museum.

Saint Paul is shown shaking the viper into a fire (Acts 23, 3-6). Pennsylvania Germans often used Biblical subjects on stone plates and firebacks in the nineteenth century.

B Fireback, cast iron, mid-18th century, marked Aetna Furnace, Burlington, New Jersey, The Metropolitan Museum of Art, Rogers Fund, 1936.

Surviving American firebacks are rare. This is one of the most beautiful with Chippendale scrolls. The design resembles decoration on great Philadelphia furniture of the mid-eighteenth century.

B.

A.

B.

A. Fireback, cast iron, c. 1760, American,
48 3/4" high, 23 3/8" wide.

Possibly the greatest of American heroes was
General Wolfe, whose victory ended the War
of 1760 between the French and English. After
this battle many Americans no longer tolerated
British troops in America as the border with
Canada was secure. Their anger for having to
pay for the British troops helped lead to the
American Revolution. This fireback design is
one of the most sought after.

B. Fireback, cast iron, dated 1758, American,
31 1/2" high, 29" wide.

This fireback is American. It shows the English
royal coat of arms, but was cast at Oxford Furnace, Warren Country, New Jersey between
1745 and 1758.

    In *The Bible in Iron*, Henry Mercer shows
two slightly different versions of this design.
Note Oxford in raised capitals across the bottom
of this fireback. The Oxford furnace was founded
in 1742 and abandoned in 1822.

C. Fireback, cast iron, dated 1763, American,
Colebrookdale Furnace, The National Gallery
of Art, Index of American Design.

This fireback has Pennsylvania German decorative motifs of tulips and hearts. According to
the records of the iron master Thomas Potts,
of Pottstown, Pennsylvania, Colebrookdale
furnace made five-plate stoves.

    There was another Colebrook furnace in
Lebanon County, Pennsylvania, built by Robert
Coleman in 1791.

C.

A.

A. Fireback, cast iron, mid-18th c., Isaac Zane, Jr., Virginia, 34" high, 31 3/4" wide, Museum of Early Southern Decorative Arts.

This large cast iron fireback is one of the finest existing examples of American decorative cast iron. It bears the arms of the Fairfax family (note the early spelling, "FARE FAC", on the ribbon at the bottom). The pattern for this may have been a custom order for George William Fairfax, the Virginia agent of the five-million acre Fairfax land holdings in the Northern Neck of that state.

The fireback is one of the very few armorial types cast in this country, this form being more popular in Europe. This one was cast at the Marlboro Furnace in Frederick County, Virginia, near the present site of Stevens City in the upper Shenandoah Valley. The proprietor of the furnace was Isaac Zane, Jr., formerly of Philadelphia, and scion of a prominent Quaker merchant family there. Zane had bought into the iron manufacturing trade late in the 1760's, and before the Revolution he was one of the more successful ironmasters in the colonies, owning a large estate at the site of the furnace.

The Fairfax fireback is particularly interesting in that records exist which establish the origin of the pattern:

"Red[c] 12mo[th] 1770 of John Pemberton
Eight pounds for the carving the Arms of
Earl of Farifax for a Pattern for the Back
of Chimney sent Isaac Zane jr."[31]

The document is signed by the firm of Bernard and Jugiez of Philadelphia, which contracted carving and guilding for cabinetmakers and house builders.[32]

The formal Chippendale-Georgian design of the pattern, with its bead-and-reel border, tight acanthus scrolls, and realistic portrayal of the animals recalls the great carved "Aesop's fables" case pieces of Philadelphia some of which may have been carved by this firm.

[31] *Seaport in Virginia: George Washington's Alexandria,* by G. M. Moore. (Richmond: Garrett and Massie, 1949), pp. 77-80.

[32] Winterthur *Newsletter,* Vol. V, No. 9, Nov. 27, 1959. John Pemberton evidently was a factor for several of the large furnaces in Pennsylvania and Virginia, and sold their ware in Philadelphia.

A.

*A. Fireback, cast iron, c. 1770, American,
Valley of Virginia, 22" high, 27 1/4" wide,
Museum of Early Southern Decorative Arts.*

This fireback (decorated in the Chinese Chippendale manner) is one of three such castings that
have been found in the upper Valley of Virginia.
Since the design has not turned up elsewhere,
it has been attributed to Isaac Zane at the Marlboro Furnace in that area.

The Chippendale carved leaves, were executed
by a fine wood carver of the Philadelphia school.

*B. Miniature fireback, cast iron 1714-1760,
4" high, 5" long, 1/4" thick, Victoria and Albert Museum.*

Since this shows the coats of arms of both Kings
George I and George II, it could have been made
from 1714 to 1760. Was this a sample to show
a client, a present or a whimsy?

B.

A. Fireback, English or Dutch, Essex Institute, Salem, Massachusetts.

Although this fireback now is at the Saugus Iron Works in Massachusetts, it may be an English or Dutch production. The tulip design is probably a Dutch design.

B. Fireback, dated 1781, 29 3/16" overall height, 27 1/16" overall width, The Henry Francis du Pont Winterthur Museum.

This fireback from Boston has leaves and a tree of the Chippendale rather than the Classical period. The mold was probably earlier than the date here and had the date added when the cast was actually made.

B.

C. Fireback, cast iron, dated 1767, American, 32" high, 21" wide, Metropolitan Museum of Art, Rogers Fund, 1916.

This fireback is known as the Highlander. The figure wears a British army uniform of a Scottish regiment of the eighteenth century. The inscription "New York" suggests that this was cast in that city, yet no foundry records on Manhattan have been found for this date. Doctor Henry Mercer has suggested that it may have been cast at the Sterling Iron Works of Orange County. This foundry was started in 1751 by men named Ward and Colton. Before the Revolution the foundry was owned by Peter Townsend. At that time the land was owned by William Alexander, known as Lord Sterling for his claim to be the heir of the Earl of Sterling in Scotland. The initials at the top of the fireback "A T" may stand for Alexander Townsend.

A.

B.

A. Fireback, c. 1840, American, Charleston, South Carolina, 23 1/4" high, 23 3/4" wide, Museum of Early Southern Decorative Arts.

This is an important fireback. The eagle and leaves are typical Classical motifs found frequently in the early nineteenth century. The Charleston Iron Foundry was first advertised in the *Charleston Times* in 1808 with John Johnson, Jr., proprietor. The *Charleston Directory* lists Johnson by name with no trade in 1802, as a blacksmith with shop and counting house in 1803, and as a blacksmith at one address, "or at his foundry" in 1806.

B. Fireback, cast iron, 19th c., English or Welsh, 22 1/4" high, 20 3/8" wide, Victoria and Albert Museum.

By this period most people of wealth and status in England were buring coal in grates, so there are few late firebacks. This is a very high quality example bearing arms and supporters of Conroy of Llanbrynmair, Montgomeryshire, with the mottoes: 'Fideliter et constanter' and 'L'antiquite ne peut pas l'abolir'.

A.

A. Fire blower, rolled and cast iron, 18th c., American.

The fire blower was the precursor of the eighteenth and nineteenth centuries household bellows.
It is effective in starting a fire and works on the same principle as a breath blow torch for pewter and other delicate metal repair work.

B. Shovel, wrought iron, 18th or 19th c., American.

This shovel was made for a specialized purpose. Its depth suggests it could have been used for fire carrying.

C. Fire carrier, rolled iron, late 18th c., American.

Carriers such as this were used to transport embers from one fireplace to another.

B.

C.

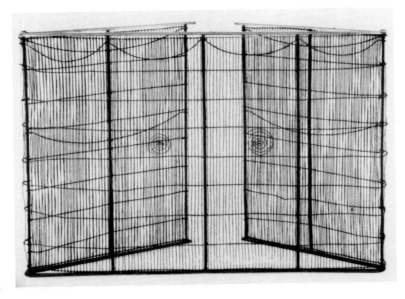

A.

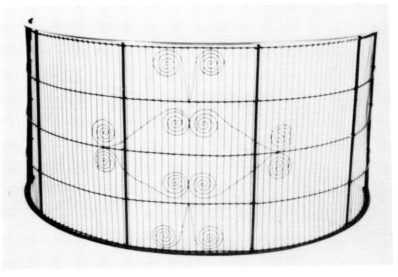

B.

A. *Folding fire screen, iron wire and brass, English or American, late 18th or early 19th century.*
The flexibility of this style makes it suitable for fireplaces of varying size. Examples are found on both sides of the Atlantic Ocean dating from the twenty year period around 1800.

B. *Nursery fender, iron wire and brass. English, late 18th or early 19th century. Philip Bradley Antiques.*
The extra height and depth of this style makes it perfectly suited for a nursery's heating fireplace. This example is also embellished with interesting wire work decoration.

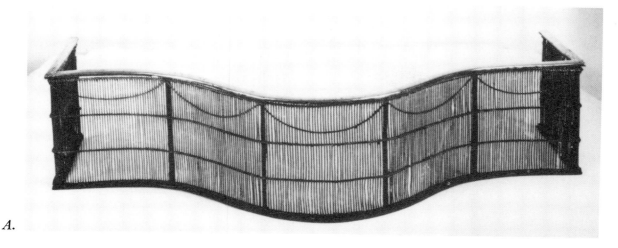

A.

B.

A. *Fender, iron wire and brass,*
English or American, late l8th or
early l9th century, 36½" wide.
The serpentine outline of this
fender is a carryover from earlier
all-brass fenders of serpentine shape.

B. *Fender, iron wire and brass,*
English or American, early l9th century.
The bottom brass edge (and the ball

finials) indicate an early l9th century
date for this fender. Fire tools sometimes accompanied a fender with
matching finials.
C. *Fender, sheet iron and brass.*
English or American, early l9th century.
The pierced pattern has been cut out of
a sheet of iron and mounted between
brass bands. The small ball feet indicate an early l9th century date.

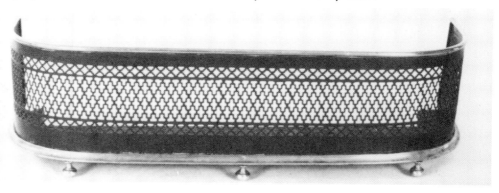

C.

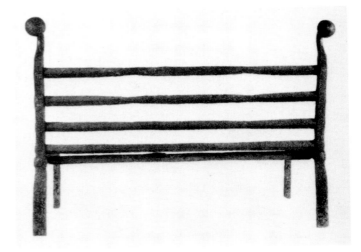

A.

B.

C.

A. Grate, early 18th c., probably American, 27 3/4" wide, 10" long.

This grate could have been used for burning chunks of wood or soft coal.

B. Miniature grate, cast iron, early 19th c., English, 9 7/8" high, 8 3/8" wide, 2" deep, Victoria and Albert Museum.

Coal burning grates were placed in fireplaces and in many cases were original to their house. This miniature was a sample, or built for a large doll house.

C. Jamb hooks, wrought iron, late 18th c., American.

Few pairs of iron jamb hooks have survived. The known examples range from this pair with turned finials to one with chamfered finials and one with brass chamfered base and flame finial.

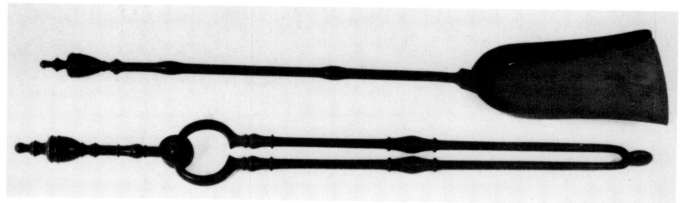

A.

B.

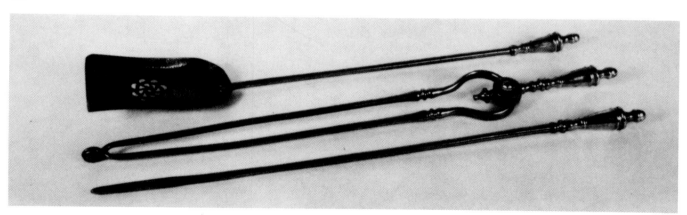

A. Fire tools, iron, American, late 18th century.

It is quite unusual to find all-iron fire tools dating from the 18th century. This pair has quite sophisticated urn finials.

B. Fire tools, iron and brass, late 18th century, American.

C. Fire tongs, iron and brass, American, the urn top, late 18th c., the turned top, early 19th c.

Many iron fire tools have brass ornamental finials which often correspond to finials of andirons. The designs reflect the fashionable motifs of their periods from turned to ball finials.

C.

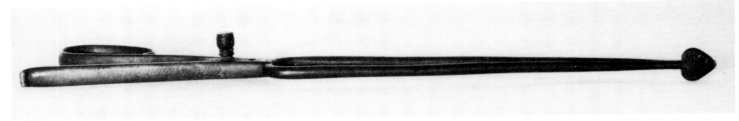

A.

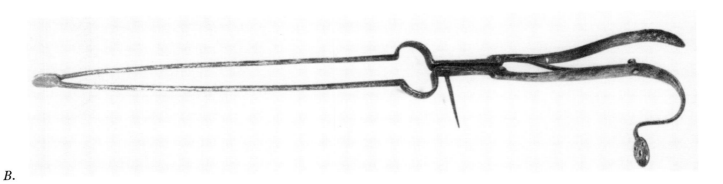

B.

A. Ember or pipe tongs, iron, dated 1764, American.
These pipe tongs are inscribed for their original owner Caleb Cresson, a prominent Philadelphian. This amount of detail is unusual in a utilitarian piece.

B. Ember or pipe tongs, iron, 18th c., Essex Institute, Salem, Massachusetts.

This type of tong was used to take an ember from a fire to light a pipe. They are a complicated form to make, and fine examples in both America and England sometimes are dated and inscribed.

C.

C. Lazy tongs, wrought iron, late 18th or early 19th c., American or Engliah, Wallace Nutting Collection, Wadsworth Atheneum.

This form of ember tongs retracts when the handles are opened and extends to grasp embers when the handles are closed. Some lazy tongs have more joints than these. Steel examples are known.

CHAPTER 7
Fire marks

Fire marks originated in London after the Great Fire of 1666 as fire brigades were formed by insurance companies to fight blazes on insured houses. When a fire brigade was called to a fire, it looked for the fire mark on a house to indicate that it was insured by their company. If there was no mark, or that of another company, the fire brigade would simply watch the fire, or return to their quarters. Later, fire brigades were merged to a single organization that fought all fires.

In America, the first organized fire brigade was organized by Benjamin Franklin and others in 1736. By 1752 six brigades were in Philadelphia working together for the mutual assistance of the membership. In this year, the Philadelphia Contributionship for the Insurance of Houses from Loss by Fire was formed. Over the years other companies in other cities adopted fire marks of their own designs. These American marks were primarily a means of advertising the insurance companies, since firefighting in America was a cooperative endeavor. By the late nineteenth century, when cities were setting up their own professional fire fighting departments, fire marks lost their usefulness and were discontinued.

B.

Except as noted, these fire marks are by courtesy of the Historical Collection of the Insurance Company of North America.

A. Fire mark, Philadelphia Contributionship, issued 1752, lead hands on a white pine board, 12 7/8" high, 12 1/4" wide.

In 1752, the Philadelphia Contributionship insurance company was founded by a group including Benjamin Franklin. The Contributionship ordered 100 of these fire marks from John Stow, who recast the cracked Liberty Bell a year later. Two of these earliest American fire marks are known to have survived.

B. Fire mark, The Mutual Insurance Company, Philadelphia, issued 1784, lead on pine board, 15" high, 12" wide.

The Philadelphia Contributionship Insurance Company would not insure houses that were surrounded by trees for fear that lightning would be attracted to increase the fisk for fire. Therefore, The Mutual Assurance Company for Insuring Houses from Loss by Fire was founded in 1784 to write insurance for houses with trees nearby. The company's fire mark was this tree — giving the company the popular name "The Green Tree".

A.

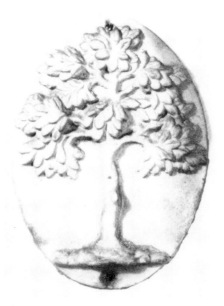

A.

B.

C.

A. Fire mark, Mutual Assurance Company, Philadelphia, issued 1805, first all iron mark, 13 1/4" high, 9 1/2" wide.

B. Fire mark, Mutual Assurance Company, Philadelphia, issued 1806, cast iron, 12 3/4" high, 8 3/4" wide.

C. Fire mark, Mutual Assurance Company, Philadelphia, issued 1810, cast iron, 12 1/4" high, 8 1/4" wide.

D. Fire mark, Mutual Assurance Company, Philadelphia, issued about 1827, cast iron, 8 1/4" high, 8 3/4" wide.

D.

E. Fire mark, Baltimore Equitable Society, issued about 1795, cast iron on pine board, 10 1/8" high, 13 7/8" wide.

This was the second mark of this company. The iron hands were originally gilded.

E.

A.

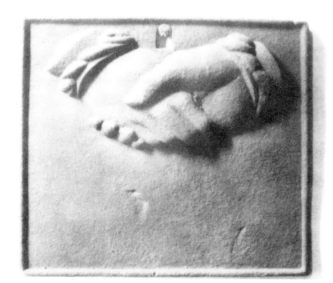

B.

C.

A. Fire mark, Baltimore Equitable Society, issued about 1820, cast iron on pine board, 10 1/4" high, 12 3/4" wide.

B. Fire mark, Baltimore Equitable Society, issued about 1847, cast iron, 10" high, 10 1/2" wide.

C. Fire mark, Baltimore Equitable Society, issued about 1845, cast iron, 9 3/4" high, 10 1/4" wide.

D. Fire mark, Insurance Company of North America, Philadelphia, issued 1830, cast iron, 11 1/2" high, 8 1/2" wide.

The first fire mark issued by this company was a lead six-pointed wavy star in a wood board. This is the fourth design with the eagle that has become a symbol for the company.

D.

A.

B.

C.

A. Fire mark, Fire Association of Philadelphia, now the Reliance Insurance Company, issued 1835, cast iron, 10 1/3" high, 7 3/4" wide.

This design has been used consistently by the Reliance Company since its founding in 1817. Slight variations help determine the date of the fire mark.

B. Fire mark, Fire Association of Philadelphia, now the Reliance Insurance Company, issued 1867, cast iron, 11 1/2" high, 7 1/4" wide.

C. Fire mark, Mutual Insurance Company, Charleston, South Carolina, issued about 1798, cast iron, 8" high, 10 1/2" wide.

This was the first iron fire mark in America.

D. Fire mark, an English insurance company, 19th c., Cast iron, courtesy the Museum of London.

D.

A.

B.

A. Fire mark, Chambersburg Fire Insurance Company, Chambersburg, Pennsylvania, cast iron, 1833-1872, 9 3/4" high, 9 1/4" wide.

B. Fire mark, Firemen's Insurance Company of Baltimore, Maryland, c. 1835, cast, courtesy Index of American Design, National Gallery of Art.

The Firemen's Insurance Company of Baltimore, Maryland was founded in 1825 and closed in 1904 when it was burned out by the Baltimore conflagration. This fire mark is the second design issued — with no border and six wheel spokes. An example of the first design has not been found.

C.

D.

C. Fire mark, Niagara District Mutual Fire Insurance Company, Niagara Falls, New York, c. 1836, cast iron, 5 1/2" high, 7" wide.

D. Fire mark, Firemen's Insurance Company of the District of Columbia, George town, District of Columbia, issued about 1838, cast iron, 12 1/4" high, 13 1/4" wide.

A.

A. Fire mark, Lexington Fire, Life and Marine Insurance Company, Lexington, Kentucky, issued about 1836, cast iron, 8 3/4" high, 11 3/4" wide.

B. Fire mark, Associated Firemen's Insurance Company, Pittsburgh, Pennsylvania, issued 1851, cast iron, 8 1/2" high, 8" wide.

B.

C.

D.

E.

C. Fire mark, City Insurance Company, Cincinnati, Ohio, issued about 1846, cast iron, 9 1/2" high, 13" wide.

D. Fire mark, Milwaukee Mechanics' Mutual Insurance Company, Milwaukee, Wisconsin, issued 1853, cast iron, 5 3/4" high, 8" wide.

E. Fire mark, Citizens' Fire, Marine and Life Insurance Company, Wheeling, West Virginia, issued about 1856, cast iron, 5 1/2" high, 12 3/4" wide.

A.

B.

A. *Fire mark, Home Insurance Company, New Haven, Connecticut, 1859-1871, cast iron, 6" high, 8" wide.*

B. *Fire mark, Clay Fire and Marine Insurance Company, Newport, Kentucky, issued about 1856, cast iron, 4 1/2" high, 8 1/2" wide.*

C.

D.

C. *Fire mark, American Insurance Company, Chicago, Illinois, issued 1865, tin, 3 1/4" high, 6 3/4" wide.*

This is the second firemark design for this company.

D. *Fire mark, Peabody Fire and Marine Insurance Company, Wheeling, West Virginia, issued about 1869, cast iron, 5 3/4" high, 13 3/4" wide.*

E. *Fire mark, State Mutual Fire and Marine Insurance Company, Hannibal, Missouri, issued about 1865, zinc, 6" high, 8" wide.*

E.

A.

A. Fire mark, Union Fire Insurance Company, Nashville, Tennessee, issued about 1870, cast iron, 10" high, 7" wide.

B. Fire mark, Lumbermen's Insurance Company, Philadelphia, Pennsylvania, issued about 1873, cast iron, 11 1/2" high, 11 1/2" wide.

C. Fire mark, Protection Fire Insurance Company, Charleston, West Virginia, 1892-1894, cast iron, 7" high, 9 1/4" wide.

B.

C.

CHAPTER 8
Furniture

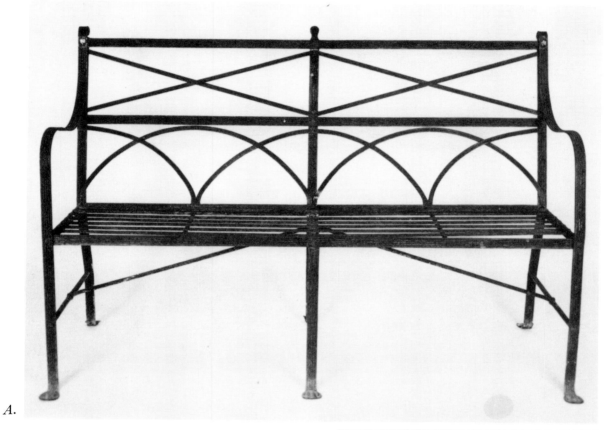

A.

A. Bench, cast iron, c. 1790-1820, English, 3' 4" high, 5' 4" wide, seat height 19".

Cast iron outdoor furniture is of great interest and was made by known makers. Late eighteenth century wrought iron garden benches and chairs were designed in the height of the Classical style. Some knowledgable people have attributed them to the English Colebrookdale Furnace. The metal often is decorated with lines that could have been made by a roller.

B. Child's Windsor chair, wrought iron, mid-18th c., English.

This exquisitely-made child's Windsor chair is a rarity of great charm.

B.

A. Table, cast and wrought iron, late 18th c., American or English, 15 3/4" high, 14 5/8" diameter. The Henry Francis du Pont Winterthur Museum.

This table is a rare and early example of iron furniture.

B. Bench, wrought iron, 1780-1810, English, 39" high, 4' 7" wide, seat height 18".

This bench was probably made at the Colebrookdale Furnace in England. It has had its feet rusted off and replaced. It was designed to stand in front of a tree, curving around the trunk.

A.

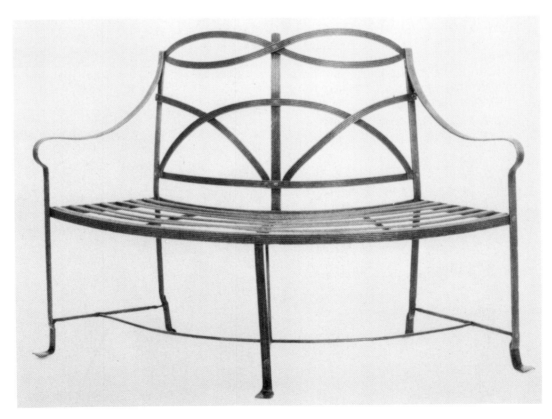

B.

A.

B.

A. Chair, wrought iron, 1780-1810, English.
Iron chairs are extremely rare; far fewer have
survived than iron benches. This chair was
probably made at the Colebrookdale Furnace.
B. Chair, cast iron, early 19th century, American.
This style reflects the interest in Classical design
popular at the beginning of the nineteenth century. Garden furniture was popularized as peo-

ple spent more time at leisure in a booming
world economy.
C. Bench, wrought iron, late 18th century, English.
This design reflects a preference for ornate detail
popular at the end of the eighteenth century. The
outline is similar to fine upholstered sofas of the
period.

C.

A.

A-B. Garden arm chair, cast iron, 1804, made by Robert Wood, 34" high, 22 1/4" wide, Courtesy of Israel Sack, Inc., N.Y.C.

This cast iron chair is one of a set which appears in the *Blue Book of Philadelphia Furniture* by William McPherson Hornor. It was made and marked by Robert Wood, Ridge Road, Philadelphia.

C. Chair, cast iron, early 19th c., Robert Wood, Philadelphia, Herbert Schiffer Antiques.

Another view of the signature on a different chair from the same set. Cast iron furniture gets painted year after year and ultimately has all its details obscured by coats of paint. The fastest way to remove the paint is to send it to the people who strip finishes off furniture. The iron emerges ready for a coat of rust-repellent paint. Many pieces of early cast iron have the founders' name on them. You may be sitting on a piece of American industrial history and never know.

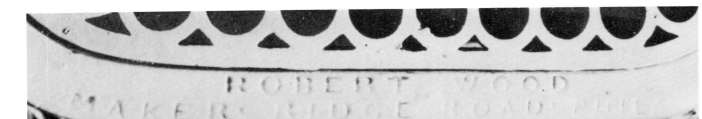

B.

C.

A.

A. Two chairs and table, cast iron, 1859-1861, New Orleans, Museum of Rural Life, Louisianna State University.

These two rococo revival side chairs are marked "W M S Co./N. Orleans, La." (Wood and Miltenberger, c. 1859-1861) The wood of this partnership is Robert Wood of Philadelphia, who did not come to Louisiana, but provided Miltenberger with patterns and some iron work. From 1859 to 1861, Miltenberger had a foundry in New Or-

leans. The cast iron table shown with them is Victorian Renaissance period and unmarked, circa 1855-1880, and was made either in New Orleans or the East.

B. Bench, cast iron, c. 1858-1865, Philadelphia, 36 3/4" high, 73 1/2" long, Museum of Rural Life, Louisiana State University.

The patterns for this type of furniture were made by Wood and Perot of Philadelphia. Some patterns were shipped south to founders. This rococo revival bench is marked "Wood and Perot makers".

B.

*A. Garden bench, cast iron, c. 1885, made by
E. T. Barnum, Wire and Iron Works, Detriot,
Michigan, Greenfield Village and the Henry Ford
Museum, Dearborn, Michigan.*

The same type of garden bench that was made
before the Civil War in Philadelphia and the
South was made in the mid-West after the war.
The grapes in the back and well developed leaves
on the legs make this a very pleasing Victorian
design.

*B. Umbrella stand, cast iron, late 19th c.,
American, National Gallery of Art, Index of
American Design.*

This Victorian rococo cane and umbrella stand is
typical of the door knockers, foot scrapers and
latches made from the 1850's.

*C. Plant stand, iron wire, late 19th c., Ameri-
can or English.*

This small plant stand represents a group with
many variations. Others have two, three,
four or more shelves and often loopes for hanging baskets.

A.

B.

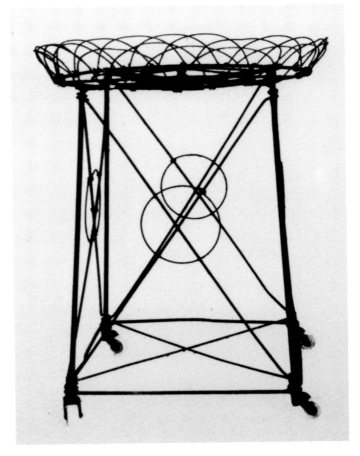

C.

A.

B.

C.

A. Bird cage, wire and rolled and tinned iron, late 19th c., American, Herbert Schiffer Antiques.

Wire and tin Victorian bird cages were made in many charming forms. This one suggests a Swiss chalet. Note the tiny deer's head over each door.

B. Bird cage, iron wire and rolled and tinned iron, late 19th c., American, Herbert Schiffer Antiques.

Some of these cages must have been produced in enormous quantity. The pierced roof pattern suggests the same manufacturer as the previous examples.

C. Bird cage, iron wire, rolled and tinned iron, and wood, late l9th century, American.

A.

B.

C.

A-B-C. Bird cages, iron wire, rolled and tinned iron, and wood, late 19th century.

*A. Bird cage, iron wire and wood,
late 19th century.*

A. Squirrel cage, iron, rolled and tinned iron, and glass, 19th c., American.

Squirrel cages were extremely popular in the nineteenth century. This one imitates a Victorian mansion.

B. Squirrel cage, rolled and tinned iron, early 19th c., American.

Here is a simpler, but equally functional, squirrel cage. Note that it has a loop for hanging or carrying.

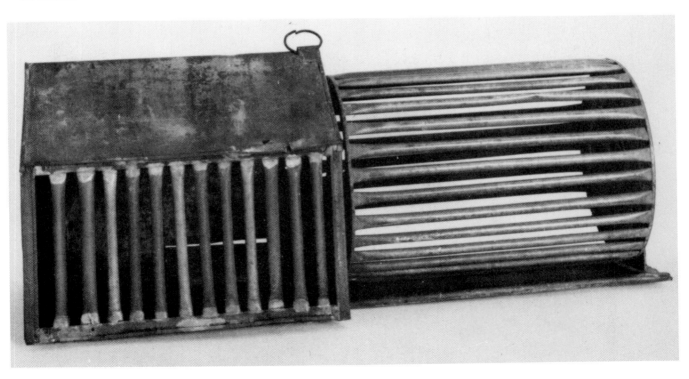

CHAPTER 9
Garden Ornaments

A.

After the Civil War, many foundries went out of business because there was no longer need for large supplies of armaments. Many animals were cast as garden ornaments to supply the developing, peacetime culture.

Of these animals, the rabbit is life size. The Boston Bull dog and the German Shepard are small door stops. These animals are often cast in two parts, screwed together and painted.

B.

C.

A-B-C. Animals, cast iron, late 19th century, National Gallery of Art and private collection.

A.

B.

A. Eagle, cast iron, probably 19th c., American, National Gallery of Art, Index of American Design.

This iron eagle was probably made as a wall ornament.

B. Eagle, cast iron, early 19th c., American, Old Sturbridge Village.

Here is an example of a roof eagle that was used to prevent ice and snow from sliding off a roof onto people below. There is an indecipherable raised name on the eagle's stomach.

C. Roof eagle, cast iron, 19th c., American, James C. Sorber.

Roof eagles were used on barns and houses to prevent ice or snow from sliding down the roof. Barns with over 100 and houses with several dozen are known. There were large numbers made and many are still in use.

D. Eagle, cast iron, 8 1/8" high, 15 1/4" wide.

This cast iron eagle's purpose is elusive. Hundreds of people have looked at this but have not concluded the purpose of its design.

C.

D.

A.

A. *Iron figure of a lion, painted late 19th century, American.*

B. *Iron figure of a deer, painted, late 19th century, American.*

C. *Screen, iron, late 17th c., English, Frome Parish Church, 6' 5" high, Victoria and Albert Museum.*
The quality of this work and design indicate familiarity with French design books, or this may have been constructed by a refugee Huguenot.

B.

A.

C.

B.

A. Corner and section of railing, wrought iron, 18th c., American.

This is an exquisitely designed and beautifully executed railing.

B. Ballustrade, wrought iron and lead, late 18th c., English, 2' 9 1/2" long, 3' 4" wide, Victoria and Albert Museum.

The delicate design of bell flowers has a strong Adam influence. The loops are held together with lead joints, a usual method of joining wrought iron parts.

C. Element of railing, wrought iron, mid-18th c., Victoria and Albert Museum.

This extremely refined ornamental railing is made in the French manner, inspired by design books with strong Huguenot influence.

In Laurel Hill Cemetery in Philadelphia today, may be seen outstanding examples of architecture and iron work of the nineteenth century. Extensive records have been kept and excellent research has recently been done on the cemetery.

Like plants struggling for light in a jungle, typical Philadelphians have always struggled for recognition, position, and importance in life. A study of the tombs at Laurel Hill cemetery, where the struggle continues after death, was very interesting both from the standpoint of fine iron work and sociology.

People have paid and continue to pay ten times the price of an obscure grave for a place on a "good" corner or in the center of an avenue. For the people who seek greatness and social importance by association, competitive locations are near the wealthy and socially elite. Here lies General Hugh Mercer — victor of the Revolutionary battle of Princeton. Politicians cluster near Charles Thompson, secretary of the Continental Congress. Simon Gratz, who helped finance the Revolution, lies near Peter Weidner, the traction multimillionaire. Captain Biddle and Admiral John A. Dahlgren crowd the editor of *Godey's Ladies Book*, Sarah Josephine Hale. Abner Doubleday, father of baseball, should be an attraction to sports fans.

The cemetery was the first to be laid out by an architect of note, John Notman. He also laid out Hollywood cemetery, Richmond, Virginia and Spring Grove near Cincinatti, Ohio.

The first interment was in 1836. The most prominent people engaged the finest architects for their tombs, including Thomas U. Walter, John Strickland (architect of the Atheneum of Philadelphia). Naturally, the cast iron here was the finest money could buy and most of it was made locally. As tastes changed, so did the iron work — from Greek revival to Gothic revival and on to Ecclectic, Art Nouveau, and Neoclassic. Alexander Calder's work is visible here.

A.

A. Fence, wrought iron, mid-19th c., Philadelphia, Laurel Hill Cemetery.

An interesting cemetery lot fence showing a Greek key type of design on top; but a later Gothic revival or early Victorian element below. This is on "Lewis Point" overlooking the Schuylkill River and above the burial site of Charles Thomson, the first Secretary of Congress.

B.

B. Fence, wrought iron, mid-19th c., Laurel Hill Cemetery, Philadelphia.

This fence is Classical in design, suggesting a date as early as 1790, but actually it was probably made after 1830. This is the Wurts family plot.

A.

A. *Cemetary fence and retaining wall, cast iron, early 19th c., Mobile, Alabama, Library of Congress.*

In many wet places it has been a tradition to raise graves. These beautifully designed panels incorporate the Classical motifs of vases and scrolled leaves.

B. *Fence, wrought iron, mid-19th c., Laurel Hill Cemetery, Philadelphia.*

The Joseph S. Lewis monument was designed by John Notman and stone work was executed by Struthers. The Lewis monument has carving on the south side showing the Philadelphia Fairmount waterworks cut by John Hill. Lewis was the Chairman of the Watering Committee on the Philadelphia Council when the water of the Schuylkill was introduced by the present means.

B.

A.

A. Fence detail, wrought iron, 1810-1840, American, National Gallery of Art, Index of American Design.

The anthemion design also was used on furniture and brass mounts of the period. The pattern depicts palm leaves in a radiating cluster, a motif first used in Greek art.

B. Balcony and fence, cast iron, mid-19th c., Mobile, Alabama, Library of Congress.

Here is a fine example of Victorian cast iron so popular and practical in the South where termites and other wood destroying insects abound.

B.

A. Stairs and railing, cast iron, early 19th c., Alabama, Library of Congress.

Good quality early Victorian iron work of Empire design enhances this classic building facade.

B. Lithograph of the Wood and Perot Iron Works of Philadelphia, Library Company of Philadelphia.

This charming print shows one of the Wood iron works. Here one can see sections of cast iron fence being loaded on wagons. It is interesting to note that railings, verandas, balconies, stairs, and counters, are being advertised. Cast iron animals can be seen on the pavement.

A.

B.

A. Elements of fence, cast iron, mid-19th c., American, National Gallery of Art, Index of American Design.

Grape and grape leaves were a popular motif from the late eighteenth century through the late nineteenth century. This motif appears on Wedgwood pottery, Chinese porcelain, silver, and iron work of the period.

B. Fence section, cast iron, 19th c., American, National Gallery of Art, Index of American Design.

A lamb under a weeping tree was a typical sentimental design of the nineteenth century.

C. Fence section and posts, cast iron, mid-19th c., American, National Gallery of Art, Index of American Design.

Instead of urn finials, this example has weak baskets with foliage and pointed finials. This design was used well into the mid-Victorian period.

A.

B.   *C.*

A.

A. Fence, cast iron, mid-19th c., Laurel Hill Cemetery, Philadelphia.

This fence encloses a group of sculptures named "Old Mortality". The building is designed by John Notman. The group represents Sir Walter Scott with "Old Mortality," who is re-cutting on their tombstones the names of the Covenanters who died for their faith in Scotland.

Sculptor James Thorn also did the well known group "Tam O'Shanter."

B. Fence, cast iron, mid-19th c., Laurel Hill Cemetery, Philadelphia.

The fence shows a group of Victorian details on top, but the rest is earlier, quite Empire in design. Were these old sections used again, or was this cast at a later date than its style? We can ask, but we will never know the answer.

B.

A.

A. Gate, wrought iron, early 18th c., English,
Victoria and Albert Museum.

This carefully built and designed gate is a fine example
with French Huguenot influence.

A.

A. Gate and fanlights, wrought iron, early 19th c., Mobile, Alabama, Library of Congress.

These iron grills and fanlights over the outdoor gateways were designed in the high Classical style of the late eighteenth century even though they were made a little later. Some of the pieces connecting the wrought iron elements are missing.

B. Gate, wrought iron, mid-19th c., Laurel Hill Cemetery, Philadelphia.

B.

A.

B.

C.

*A. Gate and fence, wrought iron, mid-19th c.,
Laurel Hill Cemetery, Philadelphia.*

This simple and elegant gate and fence is in the
Empire style. Nearby is the burial lot of Mercy
Carlisle, a Friend, aged 67, who selected her own
lot two weeks before her death and was the
first interment on October 19, 1836.

*B. Fence and gate, cast iron and stone, mid-
19th c., Laurel Hill Cemetery, Philadelphia.*

This has a bold, simple design — quite impossible
to date. This is William Duane's lot.   He success-
fully drew up the will of Stephen Girard and was
appointed Secretary of the Treasury by President
Jackson.

*C. Gate and fence, wrought iron, mid-19th c.,
Laurel Hill Cemetery, Philadelphia.*

Here is a Victorian Gothic revival design, even
though the urns are earlier in feeling. This fence
and gate are adjacent to the grave   of General
Hugh Mercer. General Mercer fought with General
Washington in the Indian Wars, served under
Braddock and took part in the battles of Trenton
and Princeton.

A.

A. Gates, cast iron, mid-19th c., Laurel Hill Cemetery, Philadelphia.

This gate is an example of restrained early Victorian style.

B. Gate, cast iron, 19th c., American, National Gallery of Art, Index of American Design.

Cemeteries of the nineteenth century used very imaginatively designed cast iron gates. Two common symbols of grief and sacrifice often found in cemetaries are the weeping willow and the lamb, combined in this example.

B.

A. Gate, cast iron, mid-19th c., American, National Gallery of Art, Index of American Design.

This cemetery gate is full of Victorian symbolism: the weeping angel, the extinguished torch, the wreaths, the grapes and the roses on top.

B. Gate, and post, cast iron, 1830-1840, American, National Gallery of Art, Index of American Design.

The leaf details and scrolls are typical of the end of the Empire period and the beginning of the Victorian period.

A.

B.

A.

B.

C.

A. Post, gate and fence, cast iron, mid-19th c., National Gallery of Art, Index of American Design.

Victorian rococo scrolled motifs are seen here in the 1840's. The urn motifs were popular as early as the 1780's.

B. Gate, wrought iron, late 19th c., American.

Here is the Victorian Gothic style at its most romantic. This Brownstone mausoleum is a fine example of the Gothic revival style of architecture.

C.   Counterweight for a gate, cast iron, American, 19th century, 10" long, 4" high.

A.

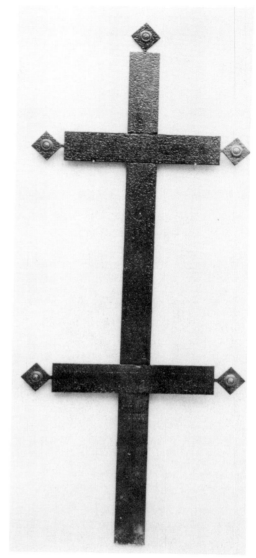

B.

A. Four grave crosses, wrought iron, early 19th c., Louisiana, Museum of Rural Life, Louisiana State University.

B. Graveyard cross, iron and brass, c. 1850-1853, Louisiana, 62" high, 25" wide, Louisiana Museum of Rural Life, Baton Rouge.

In the French and Spanish tradition, grave markers were made of iron. This one is from Louisiana.

C. Tomb front, cast iron, 19th c., Laurel Hill Cemetery, Philadelphia.

The use of cast iron in architecture was spreading by the late nineteenth century. Entire office buildings were made of cast iron. This arch and pilaster supports typify the Neo-classical style of the period.

C.

A.

A. Hitching post, wrought iron, late 18th or early 19th c., American, National Gallery of Art, Index of American Design.

Wrought iron hitching posts and rings or spikes to be driven into buildings preceed hitching posts of cast iron.

B-C. Hitching posts, cast iron, mid-18th c., J. W. Fiske, New York, National Gallery of Art, Index of American Design.

The taller horse head hitching posts is missing its tying ring, while the shorter one has the ring intact.

B.

C.

D.

D. Hitching post, cast iron, 19th c., American, National Gallery of Art, Index of American Design.

Jockeys, both Caucasian and Negro, were popular hitching posts. Owners in the racing world painted them with their own Jockey Club approved racing colors. Other owners made up pleasing combinations for their decorations.

A.

A. Sundial, wrought iron, early 19th century, American.

B.   Garden urn, cast iron, 19th c., American, National Gallery of Art, Index of American Design.

Every Victorian garden displayed by anyone with reasonable social aspirations was adorned by quantities of cast iron. The earliest of these were rather Classical and elegant in shape and later Gothic revival and Rococo.

B.

A.

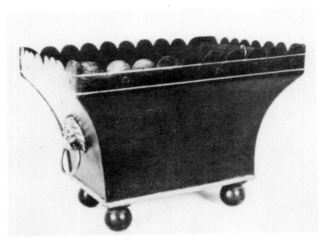

B.

A. Fruit baskets with liners, iron wire, 19th c., English or French, 6" high, 11 1/2" wide, 8 3/4" long.

Many decorative objects were made with iron wire which was tinned and painted. This pair of fruit baskets have liners of a later date.

B. Jardinier, iron, 19th c., probably English.

Jardiniers in metal were very popular in the last years of the eighteenth and the first years of the nineteenth centuries.

C. Garden urn, cast iron, 1852, signed by Wallace Lithgow and Company, Louisville, Kentucky, 38 3/4" high, Museum of Rural Life, Louisiana State University.

C.

CHAPTER 10
Kitchen Utensils

A.

A. *Cask, oak and wrought iron, 19th c., American, National Gallery of Art, Index of American Design.*

Wrought iron hoops were often used to hold wooden casks, tubs, tanks, and pails together.

B. *Miniature collander, tin, 19th c., American, 5 1/2" diameter, 2" high, Walter Himmelreich.*

C. *Collander, tin, 19th c., American, Herbert Schiffer Antiques.*

B.

C.

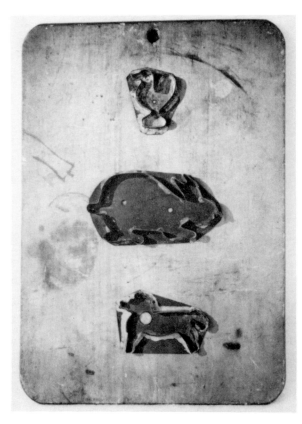

A.

B.

A-C. Cookie cutter, rolled and tinned iron, 19th c., American.

There are so many different shapes of cookie cutters that an entire book this size could not contain them all. This is a selection of a few interesting ones.

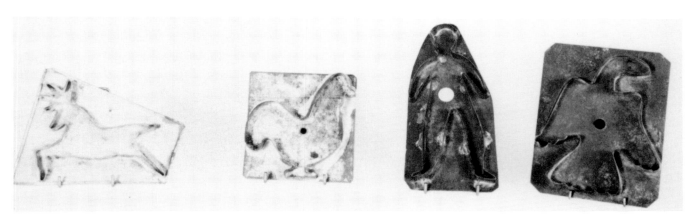

C.

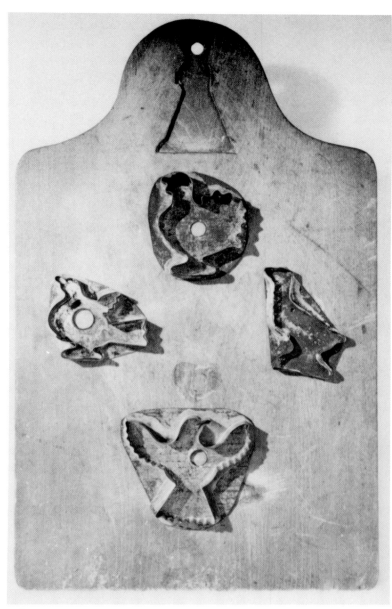

A.

B.

A. *Four cookie cutters, tin, American, 19th century.*

B. *Cookie cutter, tin, American, 19th century, Index of American Design, National Gallery of Art.*

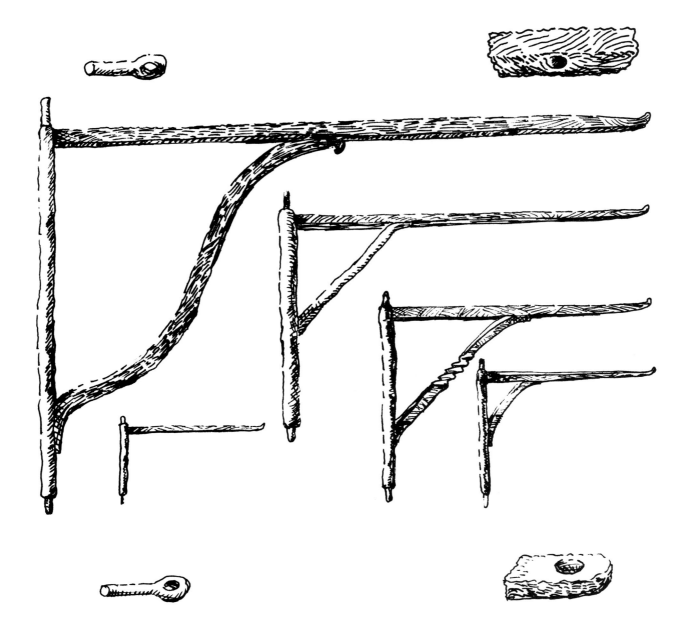

Cranes were suspended from wrought iron supports or from stone pintles held through holes in the fireplace beam. Cranes were used in both large cooking fireplaces and heating fireplaces. The heating fireplaces were smaller and probably supported only a kettle or bowl for warm water. American cranes are simple and functional with little added ornament.

A.

C.

B.

A. Cabbage cutter, wrought iron and wood, 19th c., northern European or Pennsylvania Dutch, Anonymous,

This cabbage cutter has the blade decorated and initialed in a highly personal and unusual style.

B. Cabbage cutter, brass and iron, 19th c., American, Walter Himmelreich.

This form is traditionally known as a cabbage cutter, but also may have been used for tobacco. It is highly amusing and decorative.

C. Meat cleaver, wrought iron and wood, early 19th c., American, 14 1/8" long, Pennsylvania Farm Museum at Landis Valley.

This primitive example was made from a sythe blade thus demonstrating the frugality of our ancestors. An additional iron piece is riveted under the flange to withstand the hammering necessary to cut through bone.

D. Cutter, cast iron, probably 19th c., American, Old Sturbridge Village.

This cutter is of functional design that was made over a period from the early eighteenth century until the early nineteenth century.

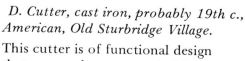
D.

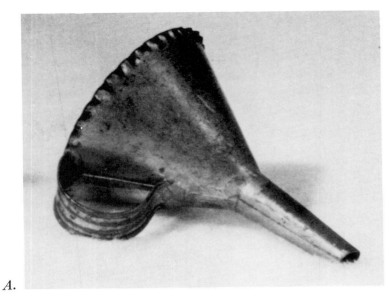

A.

B.

A. Funnel, rolled and tinned iron, early 19th c., American.

The ruffled top and ribbed handle give this utilitarian funnel extra style.

B. Goffering iron, iron, brass and steel, 1775-1810, American or English, The Henry Francis du Pont Winterthur Museum.

This special form of pressing iron was devised in Italy in the early 1500's to press ruffles and small pleats which became fashionable at that time. The French term for fluting or crimping is gauffering, and the English version became goffering. They are listed in laundering catalogs up to 1900. The barrels were heated by inserting hot irons, and ruffles were made by pressing the cloth over the heated barrel with both thumbs. Only one ruffle could be made at a time.

This double goffering iron has two barrels on one stand making it possible to work with one iron while the other was heating. The legs of the stand are made of brass.

C. Goffering iron, wrought iron, 1720-1780, English or American, stand 7 3/16" high, 6 5/8" wide, The Henry Francis du Pont Winterthur Museum.

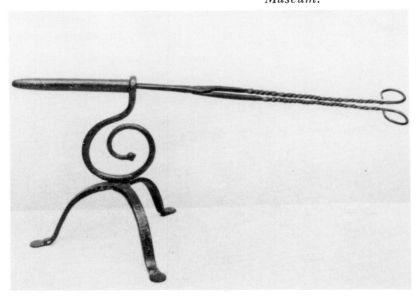

C.

A.

A. Griddle, wrought iron, 18th c., American.

Griddles of this type have been used since the Renaissance in every country. Hung from either a trammel or a crane, they provided a flat hot cooking surface over the fire.

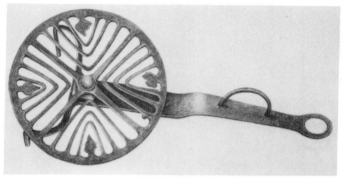

B.

C.

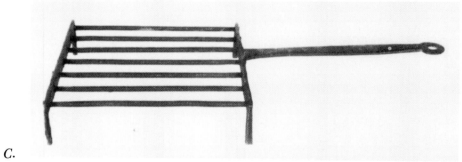

D.

B-E. Griddles, wrought iron, American or European.

Round griddles are found in both American and European iron. Because of the elaboration of the handle, their is a possibility that this example is European. The next few examples are American.

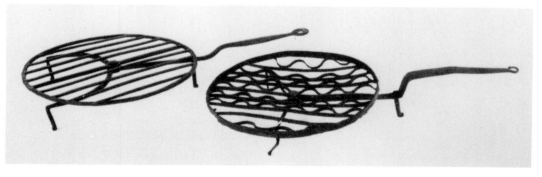

E.

A.

B.

C.

A. Tea kettle and tilter, cast iron, marked SC, English or American, W. Himmelreich.

One of the earliest shapes of iron tea kettles is shown here suspended from a kettle tilter. The legs are an early feature, derived from the first cooking pots that were held above embers. However, the handle is late eighteenth or early nineteenth century in date. The raised initials SC and leaves is probably the mark of the founder.

B. Kettle, cast iron, probably mid-18th c., American, Old Sturbridge Village.

This kettle was designed either to be hung from a crane or placed over embers. It has its own attached tilting mechanism.

C. Tea kettle, cast iron, c. 1800, American, 8" high, 11" diameter, National Gallery of Art, Index of American Design.

This kettle has been owned continuously by the Hubbard Family of Berlin, Connecticut. It dates from the end of the eighteenth or beginning of the nineteenth century. The handle's shape can be compared with brass and copper kettles of this date.

A. Kettle tilter, wrought iron and wood, late 18th or early 19th c., American or English.

The most unusual feature of this tilter is the wooden handle which might burn if the cook were careless, but because it conducted heat poorly, the cook had far less chance of getting her hand burned.

B. Kettle tilter, wrought iron, mid-18th c., probably English, 14" high, W. Himmelreich.

The carefully constructed joints and overall care of workmanship suggest an English origin for this tilter.

C. Kettle tilter, wrought iron, mid-18th c., American or English, National Gallery of Art, Index of American Design.

The interesting design and simplicity indicate a possible American origin.

A.

B.

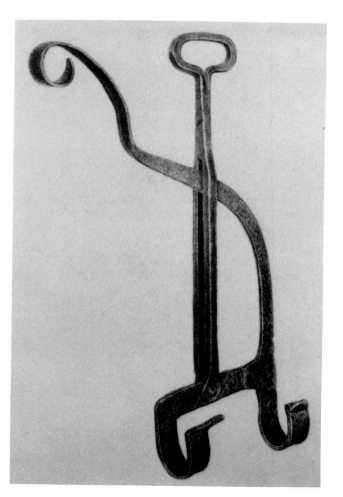

C.

A.

B.

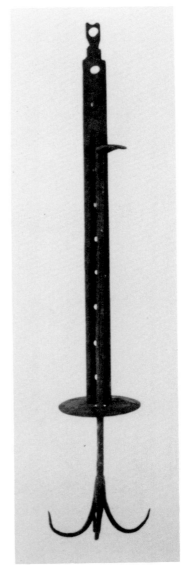

A. Group of measures, rolled and tinned iron, early 19th c., American.

These tin measures are lighter and would have been cheaper than pewter measures.

B. Grain measure, wrought iron and wood, late 18th or early 19th c.

Grain measures of wood with iron handles and bindings were cheaper and are lighter than ones made of brass, bronze or cast iron.

C. Meat hook, wrought iron, probably 18th c., probably European, Herbert Schiffer Antiques.

Meat hooks were made continuously from the Middle Ages until the mid-nineteenth century and are extremely difficult to date. This one hangs from a brass arm of a later period.

C.

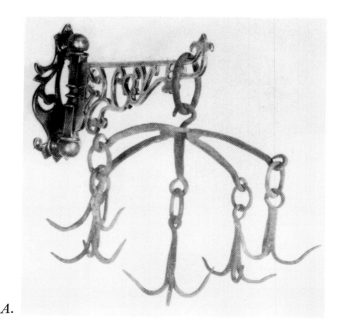

A.

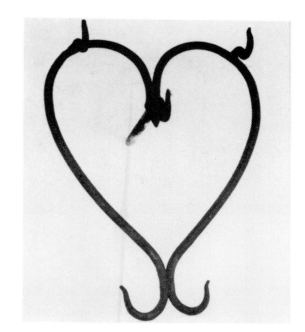

D.

B.

C.

A. Meat hook, wrought iron, 18th c., possibly European, 7" high, 10 1/4" diameter.

Meat hooks are found throughout Europe and America. The Basque and Southern France examples have the most ornate work. This one does not have any strong regional characteristics.

B. Meat hook, sheet and wrought iron, probably early 19th c., Philip Bradley Antiques.

C. Meat hook, wrought iron, 18th c., possibly European, 7" high, 10 1/4" diameter.

A slightly different version is shown here, a bit more elaborate, possibly Continental or even Basque.

D. Meat hook, wrought iron, mid-18th c., Pennsylvania.

This hook screws into a wall. It came from an old Pennsylvania inn.

A.   *B.*

A. Cake mold, rolled and tinned iron, 19th c., W. Himmelreich.

Old heart shaped cake molds are quite rare.

B. Cake mold, rolled and tinned iron, 19th c., American, W. Himmelreich.

A horse shoe shaped bread or cake mold is quite unusual.

C. Mold or pan, rolled and tinned iron, 19th c., American, W. Himmelreich.

This is a half pie pan or cake mold.

D. Cooking mold, cast iron, 19th c., American, Old Sturbridge Village.

This type of cooking mold is known as a turk's head. They are customarily made of rolled and tinned iron or pottery, so this cast iron one is a rarity.

C.

D.

B.

A.

C.

A. Mop holder, wrought iron, 1820-1830, possibly New York State, 8 1/2" across, Old Sturbridge Village.

This homely mop holder required ingenuity to design and skill to make. A wooden handle attaches to the shaft and rag strips fit into the vice. This is the type of specialized item people went to the local blacksmith for preceeding the days of hardware manufacture and distribution by peddlers, or hardware stores.

B. Mortar, cast iron, late 18th c., Wallace Nutting collection, Wadsworth Atheneum.

Iron mortars are quite rare as most were made of bronze or brass.

C. Reflector oven and bottle jack, rolled and tinned iron and wrought iron, brass cover on bottle jack, early 19th c., American, Old Sturbridge Village.

This is a rare, complete reflector oven. The flame was where the viewer is. At the top is the brass bottle jack, a spring mechanism that winds and runs like a crude clock turning the meat. The cone below the jack is a weight which serves as a governor. Small hooks held small pieces of meat or birds, while other hooks could be placed in the loops below. A door at the back of the oven allows the cook to baste or check the meat. At the base of the oven is a well to collect drippings and into which seasonings were added for basting.

Because this is made of rolled and tinned iron, it is light enough that it can be moved as the handles on the sides indicate.

A.

B.

A. Reflector oven, rolled and tinned iron, late 18th or early 19th c., American or English.

A small reflector oven was useful next to an open fire. The meat hung on the hooks. The top is hinged to facilitate basting from the pan below. A surprising number of these have survived.

B. Oven door, cast iron, after 1792, Berks County, Pennsylvania, 13 5/8" high, 21 1/2" wide.

Doors of this type were set into the stone at the front of ovens. Before this style was derived, sheet iron was placed against the opening without hinges. This example was made at Joanna Furnace, Berks County, Pennsylvania, which was started in 1792 by Thomas Bull and John Smith. At the time lead patterns nailed to wooden backs were used to make the molds.

C. Oven door, cast iron, c. 1800, Portland, Maine.

This door has been cast with Classical details and a small air regulating door at the center. There was a Portland stove foundry at a later date.

C.

A.

B. Three pails, rolled and tinned iron, 19th c., American, W. Himmelreich.

Thousands of useful items were made of rolled tin. Note the decorative lines stamped or rolled into the tinned iron.

B. Covered pail, rolled and tinned iron, 19th c., American, W. Himmelreich.

Many products were sold in tinned containers which could be used again. These containers often had the names of the product and manufacturer stamped on the sides.

C.Pan, wrought iron, late 18th c., American.

This pan may have been a type of fat lamp, yet this form has been traditionally used to catch the drippings from a piece of meat on a spit.

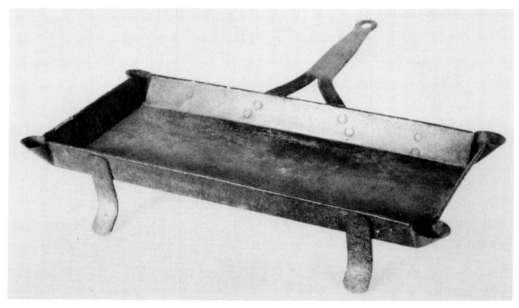

C.

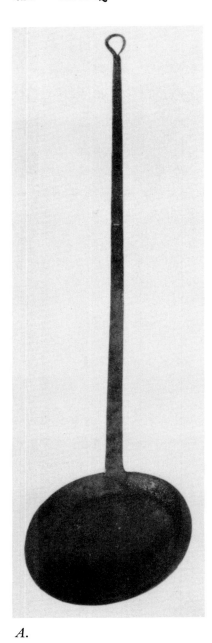

A. Frying Pan, wrought iron, late 18th or early 19th c., American.

Long handled frying pans were useful near a hot fire.

B. Baking pan, wrought iron, early 19th c., American, 11 5/8" diameter, Pennsylvania Farm Museum at Landis Valley.

This baking pan was hammered from a single sheet of iron over a form. These came in many sizes.

C. Pie crimper, first half of the 19th c., American, 5 3/4" long, Pennsylvania Farm Museum at Landis Valley.

A pie crimper was used to trim excess dough from around the edge of the pie while it also sealed the top and bottom crust. This fine example was probably made by a whitesmith in the nineteenth century.

Pie crimpers were generally not made in wrought iron, as they took mastery of the trade, precision, and time to make.

D. Pie crimpers, wrought iron, late 18th or early 19th c.

The center crimper has a beautifully decorated shaft of an interesting shape.

C.

A.

B.

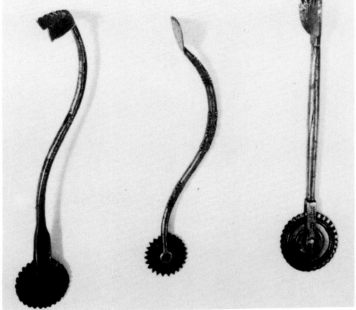

D.

A.

A. Kitchen tool, steel, early 19th c., American.

This multiple purpose baking tool for crimping and scraping dough is interesting in having a cross pierced in its center. Could it have been used in a Convent?

B.

B. Pitcher, rolled and tinned iron, 19th c., American, W. Himmelreich.

On this pitcher the solder that holds tin objects together is seen as light lines. Solder runs smoothly over newly tinned surfaces, but when oxidized tin is repaired and resoldered, as on antique tin, solder flows unevenly with high edges like water on cellophane.

C.

C. Porringer, cast iron, early 19th c., American, Old Sturbridge Village.

American iron porringers are rarities.

A.

B.

A-B. Covered pot, rolled and tinned iron, 19th c., American, W. Himmelreich.

A large number of tin covered pots of this sort were made. This one has an attractive heart cut out on its spout and the original finial was made from a desk interior drawer pull, the type that was in continuous use from the 1730's on.

C-E. Three coffee pots, rolled and tinned iron, 19th c., American, W. Himmelreich.

C.

E.

D.

A. Cooking pot with lid, cast iron, American, 9" high, 11" diameter, Philip Bradley Antiques.

B. Pot, cast iron, signed Ellis Griffeth, American, Old Sturbridge Village.

Pots did not change greatly from the Middle Ages to the mid-nineteenth century. It is a great help when one finds a dated or signed example such as this. The advent of the cooking stove brought a change in the shapes of equipment.

Pots and kettles with legs were meant to go in the fireplace above hot embers.

C. Cooking pot, cast iron, early 19th c., Savory and Son, Philadelphia, James C. Sorber.

This cooking pot has changed little from those used in the Middle Ages; and yet because of the raised letters cast on its side we know this to be a nineteenth century pot.

A.

B.

C.

A.

A. Pot, cast iron, probably mid-19th c., American, 5" high, 10" diameter, Philip Bradley Antiques.

A pot like this could stand on a stove or fit into a hole on top of a stove up to the flanges.

B. Pot, cast iron, American, Wallace Nutting collection, Wadsworth Atheneum.

This pot could either hang steadily from two hooks on a crane or sit flat on a stove or trivet.

C. Skillet, wrought iron, late 18th c., Pennsylvania, National Gallery of Art, Index of American Design.

This is an early form in iron derived from bronze medieval skillets. The bowl was beaten from a sheet and the legs and handle riveted on.

B.

C.

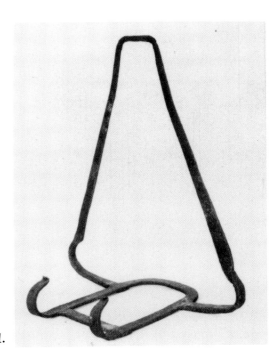

A.

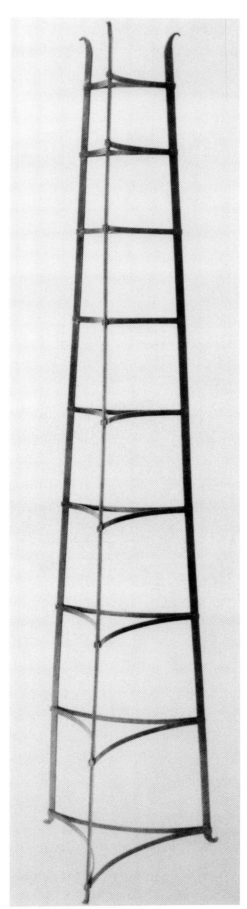

A. Pot hanger, wrought iron, 18th c., American, Herbert Schiffer Antiques.

This type of apparatus hung on an S-hook to hold a pot.

B. Pot stand, wrought iron, early 19th c., English.

Pot stands come in all sizes from approximately three feet to six feet high. Some mid-nineteenth century ones have the capacity of the pot marked in raised letters on each level.

Old wrought iron stands are held together with rivets that are peened over. The modern copies are electrically welded.

B.

A.

B.

A. Pressing iron, wrought and cast iron, early 19th c., American.

A door at the back of this pressing iron can be raised to insert a hot wedge of cast iron. The pressing plate was thus heated, and when it cooled, another hot wedge could reheat it.

B. Pressing iron, cast iron, mid-19th c., American or European, National Gallery of Art, Index of American Design.

The definitive book about pressing irons is *The Evolution of the Sad-Iron* by A. H. Glissman which is informative and well illustrated.

C. Trivet for pressing iron, wrought iron, 18th c., American, Walter Himmelreich.

Trivets for pressing irons can be found made of wrought iron and cast iron. There is infinite variety in their designs. The wrought iron ones are generally earlier than those of cast iron.

D. Trivet for pressing iron, wrought iron, 18th c., American, National Gallery of Art, Index of American Design.

E. Trivet for pressing iron, wrought iron, mid-18th c., American, Walter Himmelreich.

C.

D.

E.

A.

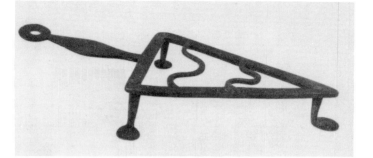

B.

A. Trivet for a pressing iron, wrought iron, late 18th or early 19th c., American, National Gallery of Art, Index of American Design.

B. Trivet for a pressing iron, wrought iron, late 18th c., American, 12" long, 4 1/2" wide, Walter Himmelreich.

C. Trivet for a pressing iron, wrought iron, 18th c., American, National Gallery of Art, Index of American Design.

Besides having a pleasant form, the leaves are punched to show veins, and a heart is punched at the center.

D. Trivet for a pressing iron, wrought iron and wood, late 18th c., American, National Gallery of Art, Index of American Design.

E. Trivet for a pressing iron, wrought iron, late 18th c., American, National Gallery of Art, Index of American Design.

The use of two stylized hearts on the trivet and a repeat on the handle is a very clever design.

F. Three trivets, two wrought iron, one cast iron, 1810-1860, American, left, 1 1/4" high, 10 7/8" long; middle, 1 1/4" high, 5 5/8" long; right, 2 1/8" high, 11 9/16" long, maker, J. Sellers, dated 1837, Henry Francis du Pont Winterthur Museum.

The cast iron trivet can be dated c. 1860, while the two wrought iron ones date from the first quarter of the nineteenth century. The Pennsylvania tulip design is distinctive here.

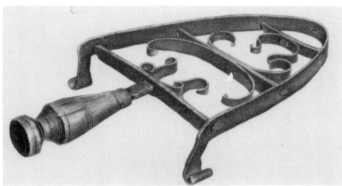

C.

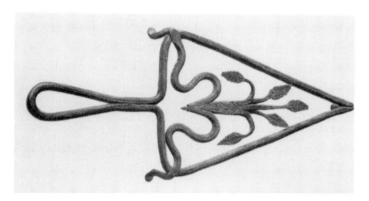

D.

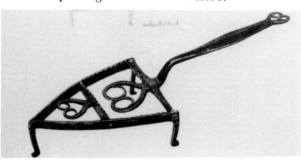

E.

F.

A.

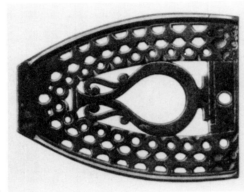

B.

C.

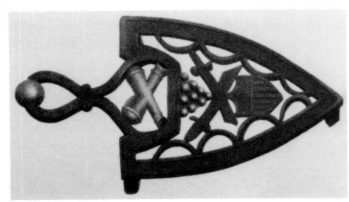

D.

A. Trivet for a pressing iron, cast iron, marked Enterprise Mfg. C. Philadelphia, late 19th c., National Gallery of Art, Index of American Design.

The manufacturer's name forms both a decorative and a functional part of this iron stand. The raised edge would secure the hot pressing iron.

B. Trivet for pressing iron, cast iron, mid-19th c., American, National Gallery of Art, Index of American Design.

The Classical urn motif that was popular in the early nineteenth century is incorporated into this later design. The raised sides are noteworthy.

C. Trivet for a pressing iron, cast iron, late 19th c., American, National Gallery of Art, Index of American Design.

The anthemion was a popular motif of the 1810 period and is incorporated into this later trivet with raised inscription "Purity, Love, and Truth."

D. Trivet for a pressing iron, cast iron, mid-19th c., American, National Gallery of Art, Index of American Design.

The crossed cannons, cannon balls, and shield of the United States make this a very patriotic trivet.

E. Trivet for a pressing iron, cast iron,,end of the 19th c., American, National Gallery of Art, Index of American Design.

Strouse Gas Iron C., Phila. Pa. USA, IWANTU COMFORT IRON is a marvelous inscription. The tube extending from the back of the iron is for gas which burned to heat the iron.

E.

A. Skewer holder, wrought iron, 18th century, American, Metropolitan Museum of Art, gift of Alice Porter, 1927.

B. Skewer holder, wrought iron, 18th c., American, Herbert Schiffer Antiques.

In the early days of American iron collecting, there were many skewer holders available. They have always been sought after. Now the skewers are as hard to find as the holders.

C. Skewer holder and skewers, wrought iron, 18th c., American.

D. Skewer holder, wrought iron, early 19th c., American or English, 16" high, 6" wide.

This extremely simple skewer holder could have been the type issued to the British army from the time of the Napoleonic wars to the Crimean.

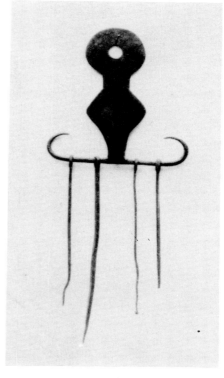

A.

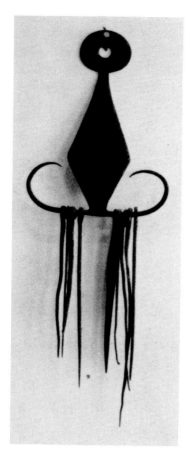

B.

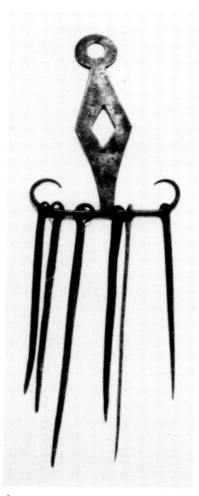

C.

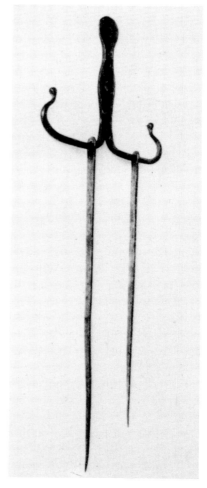

D.

Many table articles were made of painted tinned iron. This type of object was sold by peddlers.

A. Spice sifter, rolled and tinned iron and wrought iron, 19th c., American, National Gallery of Art, Index of American Design.

B. Spice set, rolled and tinned and painted iron, mid-19th c., American, W. Himmelreich.

A.

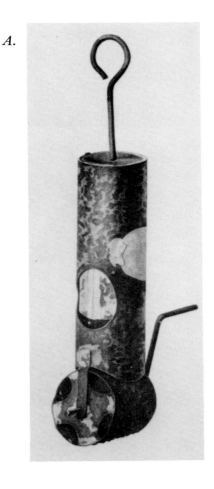

B.

In the eighteenth century, sugar was poured as a saturated solution over a heated bisque-fired ceramic cone. It then crystalized and dried. To be used, it had to be cut into bricks with instruments like these.

C. Sugar cutter, wrought iron, brass and wood, 18th c., probably English, Herbert Schiffer Antiques.

D. Sugar cutter, late 18th to early 19th c., signed "B. Smith", 10" long, Pennsylvania Farm Museum at Landis Valley.

This sugar cutter has wonderful decorative engraving at the joint.

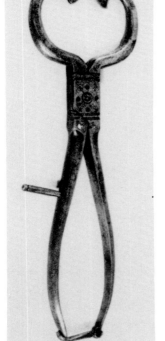

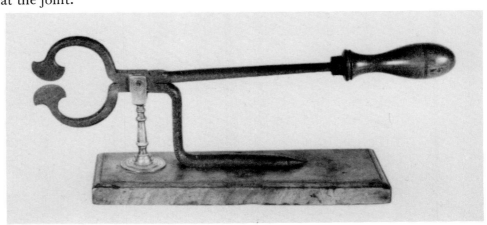

C.   D.

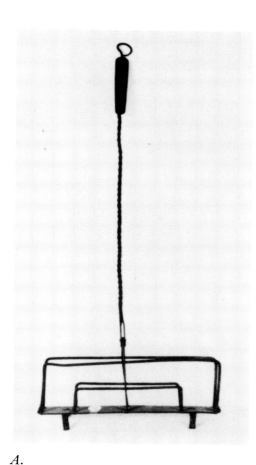

A.

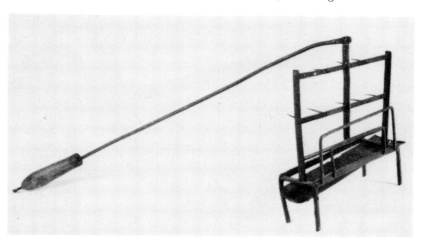

B.

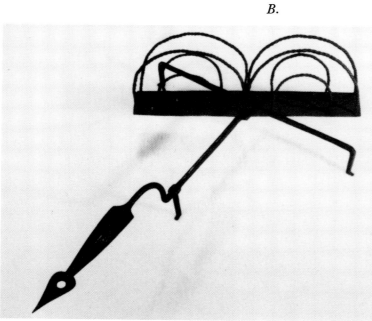

C.

A. Toaster, wrought iron and wood, late 18th c., probably American, possibly English, Herbert Schiffer Antiques.

Slices of bread were held vertically in these toasters to be placed in front of a fire. These range in design from simple to elegant.

B. Toaster with dripping pan, wrought iron, and wood, 18th c., English or American, Wallace Nutting collection, Wadsworth Atheneum.

This toaster is also designed to roast small birds like quail or small pieces of meat. Note the pan to catch fat for basting.

C. Toaster, wrought iron, 18th c., American, W. Himmelreich.

This toaster swivels for easy turning.

A.

B.

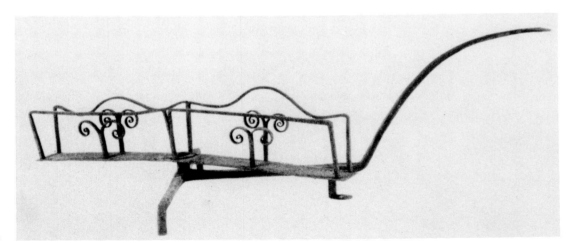

C.

A. Toaster, wrought iron, 18th c., European, 19" long, 13" wide, 6 1/2" high, W. Himmelreich.

This very elaborate toaster may be European, Basque, French or German.

B. Toaster, wrought iron, 18th c., probably European, W. Himmelriech.

C. Toaster, wrought iron, 18th c., American, 18 1/4" wide, 19 1/4" long.

A.

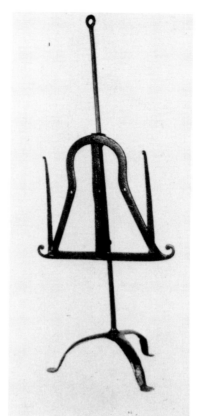

B.

A. Standing toaster, steel, 18th c., English.

Exquisitely wrought and well designed, this steel toaster is a beautiful object from the finial to the graceful legs and feet. It was used for small game, pieces of meat, or toast as were the usual toasters. The toasting area is kept at the desired height by a spring.

B. Standing toaster, wrought iron, 18th c., English.

The two uprights swing across to clasp meat or toast. The holes in the frame could hold spikes, hooks, or other moveable clips.

C. Toaster on trivet, wrought iron, c. 1770, 15 1/2" high, 15 1/2" wide, 18" long.

This toaster is mounted on a trivet. There are holes in the handle to adjust the rack from nearly vertical to horizontal.

D. Fender toaster, wrought iron, mid-18th c., American or English.

This exquisitely designed toaster was made to be attached to a fender. It is one of the most attractive pieces of design in iron. Even the wing nut is scrolled!

C.

D.

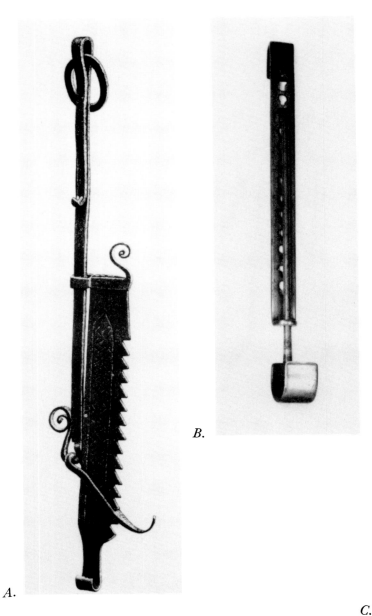

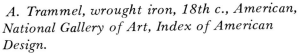

A.

B.

C.

D.

A. *Trammel, wrought iron, 18th c., American, National Gallery of Art, Index of American Design.*

Trammels were made in sizes and strengths ranging from extremely heavy ones to hold large pots to tiny, delicate ones to hold a lighting device such as a betty lamp. There are many variations in strength, decoration, and quality. Some of the French and German trammels are elaborately scrolled and decorated. This example has some stamped decoration.

B. *Trammel, wrought iron, 18th c., probably American.*

Another very simple example. The trammel enabled a pot to be suspended at a height according to the size of the fire and the cooking heat needed.

C. *Trammel, dated 1751, signed three times KM, American, Pennsylvania, Pennsylvania Farm Museum of Landis Valley.*

This trammel was made to hang from a lug pole, an oak or hickory sapling which spanned the width of the fireplace. The trammel is of fine workmanship with stamped decoration and the original owner's name, Christian Hochstetter.

D. *Trammel, wrought iron, 18th c., American, Wallace Nutting collection, Wadsworth Atheneum.*

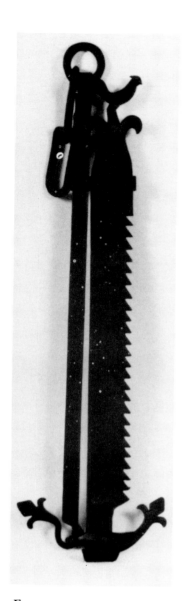

F.

E.

E. Trammel, wrought iron, 18th c., American.

F. *Trammel, wrought iron, end of the 18th c., signed Whal, American, James C. Sorber.*

This trammel is a variation of a European shape. The maker was probably taught by a German blacksmith, but the quality of this work is not as fine as a European blacksmith. Few trammels of this type were used in America.

G. *Triangle, wrought iron, American.*

This triangle was probably struck to call people to dinner, warn of a fire, or some other disaster.

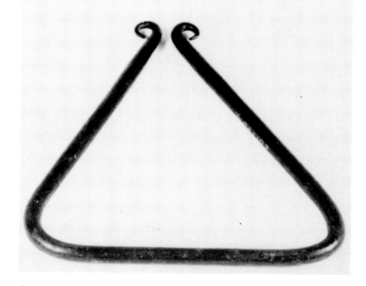

G.

A.

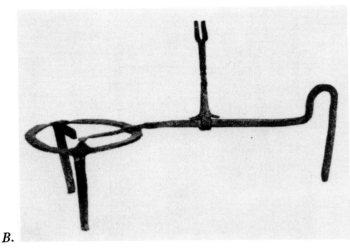

B.

A. Trivet, wrought iron, early 18th c., English or American, 16" high, 20 1/2" wide, 10 1/8" diameter.

Trivets were absolutely essential when cooking over embers in a fireplace. The earlier ones were made of iron or iron and brass to be both heavy and heat resistant. Later examples were made of brass and stood elegantly in front of the fireplace to keep a teapot or other small pot warm. This trivet has a vertical element forked at the end to steady the handle of a pan.

B. Trivet, wrought iron, early 18th c., English or American.

The vertical element to hold a pot handle is adjustable along the horizontal bar.

C.

C. Trivet, wrought iron and wood, late 18th c., English or American.

This is a rather unusual trivet because it can be used to hold a pot or suspend meat for cooking. The forks to hold the meat can be raised or lowered. It was built with refinement.

D. Trivet, wrought iron, mid-18th c., American.

Triangular iron trivets are rare. This one has some niceties of design.

D.

A.

A. Trivet, wrought iron, 18th c., American, Wallace Nutting collection, Wadsworth Atheneum.

Most of the early wrought iron trivets were round and many had no handles.

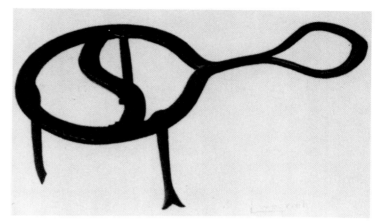

B.

B. Trivet, wrought iron, late 18th c., American, National Gallery of Art, Index of American Design.

A logical successor to the simple round trivet was one with a handle, thus making it possible to move the trivet without burning one's hand or smearing ashes.

C. Trivet, wrought iron, late 18th c., American, W. Himmelreich.

D. Two trivets, iron and brass, c. 1800, English, larger: 11" high, 7 1/2" wide, 15" long, Herbert Schiffer Antiques.

A standard size and a miniature iron and brass trivet make an interesting comparison.

E. Trivet, steel, late 18th c., English.

This is a very sophisticated and beautifully designed trivet, which could also be used to hold a round bottomed pan or bowl.

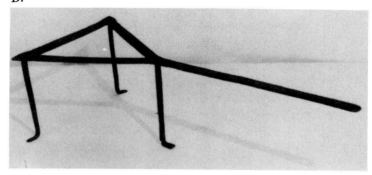

C.

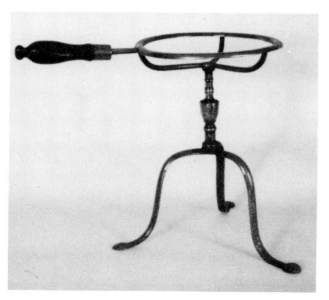

E.

D.

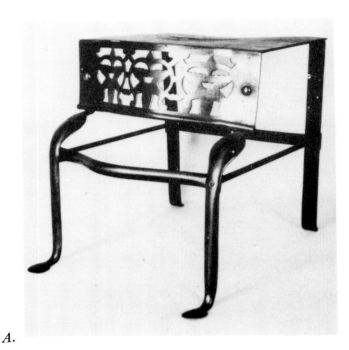

A.

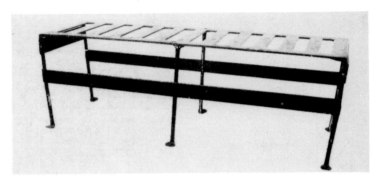

B.

A. Trivet, Steel, probably early 19th c., English.
This elaborate steel trivet is a form called a footman. It is attractively pierced on one side. This form is often made of brass or has a brass top.

B. Trivet, steel, probably early 19th c., American.
An elongated trivet is shown here, intended to hold several kettles and pans at a time.

C-E. Three trivets, cast iron, probably American, mid- to late 19th c., National Gallery of Art, Index of American Design.
This group of highly ornamented trivets typify the use of cast iron for everyday items during the industrialized nineteenth century.

C.

D.

E.

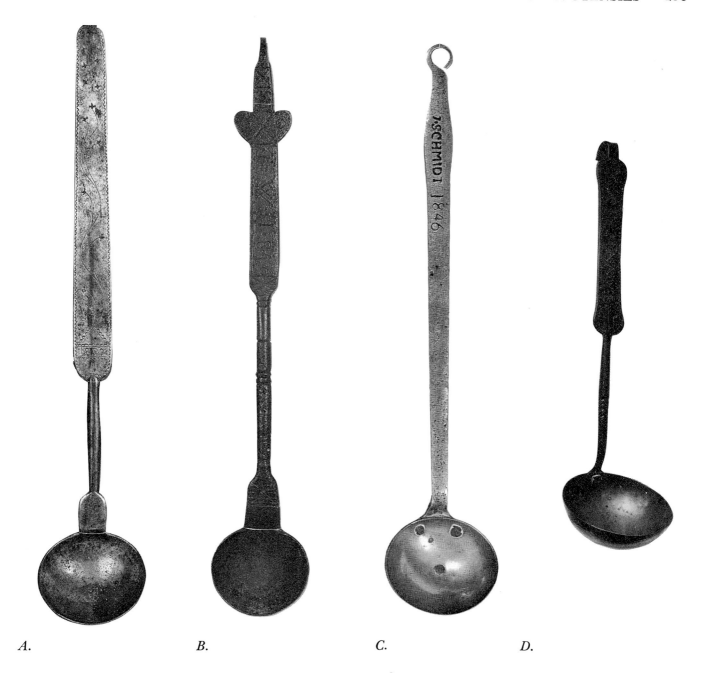

A.   B.   C.   D.

A. Ladle, wrought iron, dated 1822, American. Walter Himmelreich.

The "wiggle" work border and floral design are adaptations of the Classical motifs found on silver and furniture of the period. This is a very fine example.

B. Ladle, wrought iron, dated 1840, Pennsylvania, Walter Himmelreich.

This is another fine ladle. The design is complimented by the unusual shape of the handle.

C. Ladle, wrought iron and brass, dated 1846, Pennsylvania, Walter Himmelreich.

J. SCHMIDT stamped this ladle. He was undoubtedly the maker because few others would own a specialized stamp for iron.

D. Ladle, iron and brass, American, dated 1821.

This ladle has a decorated handle inscribed by punching the metal while hot. The bowl is brass.

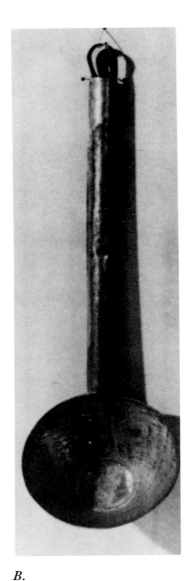

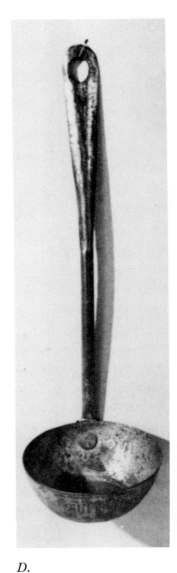

A.   *B.*   *C.*   *D.*

*A. Ladle, wrought iron, early 19th c., 14 3/4"
long, Pennsylvania Farm Museum of Landis
Valley.*

A few ladles, such as this one, show lavish care,
good design, and were probably intended as gifts.

*B. Dipper, rolled and tinned iron, 19th c.,
American, Walter Himmelreich.*

*C. Dipper, rolled and tinned iron, 19th c.,
American, Walter Himmelreich.*

*D. Ladle, rolled and tinned iron, 19th c., Ameri-
can, W. Himmelreich.*

A.

A. Peel, wrought iron, late 18th or early 19th c., American, W. Himmelreich.

To remove bread and pastries from the oven a cook needs a tool with a flattened end and a long handle. Blacksmiths considered this form a challenge.

B. Peel, wrought iron, American, Wallace Nutting collection, Wadsworth Atheneum.

C-D. Group of peel handles, wrought iron, 18th and early 19th c., American, Wallace Nutting collection, Wadsworth Atheneum.

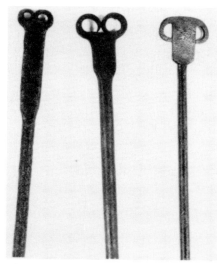

C.

D.

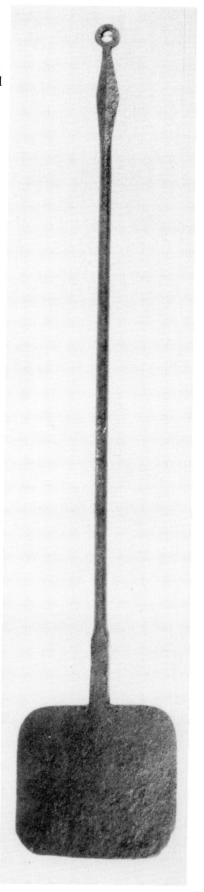

B.

A.

A. *Skimmers, 19th c., American, Walter Himmel-reich.*

B. *Skimmer, wrought iron, late 18th c., English or American, Wallace Nutting collection, Wadsworth Atheneum.*

C. *Skimmer, wrought iron, early 19th c., Wal-Himmelreich.*

The pierced design in this skimmer is unusual.

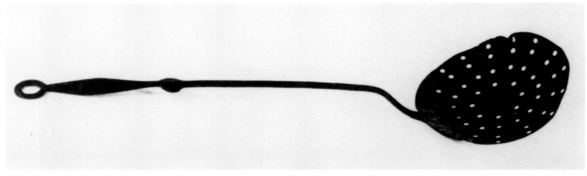

B.

C.

A.

B.

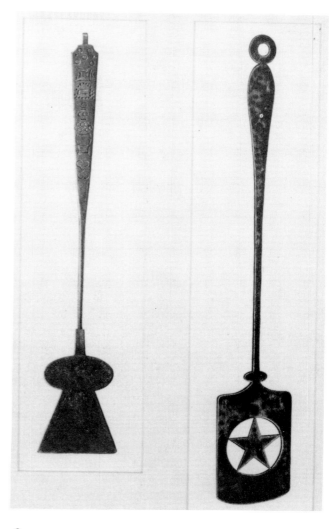

C.

A. Spatula, wrought iron and brass, dated 1797, Pennsylvania, 18 1/2" long, 2 9/16" wide, Henry Francis du Pont Winterthur Museum.

This very decorative spatula with initials is very rare. The flat end is brass.

B. Spatula, wrought iron, mid-18th to early 19th c., American, Herbert Schiffer Antiques.

A simple spatula like this would have been in most American kitchens.

C. Two Spatulas, wrought iron or milled steel, early 19th c., American, National Gallery of Art, Index of American Design.

The handle of the left spatula is stamped 1816. These have pleasing and unusual outlines.

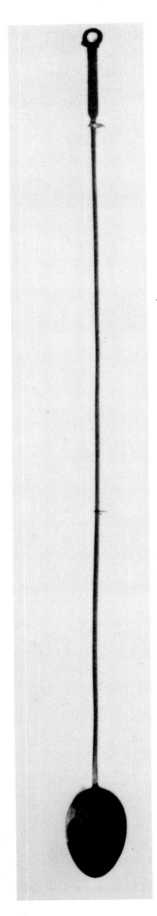

A-B. Spoons, wrought iron, 18th c.

The long handle was useful for cooking over an open fire.

C. Tableware in case, steel, early 18th c., English, Museum of London.

This set of tableware includes a cork screw, nutmeg grater, detachable handles, spoon, fork, and knife all fitting compactly into the shagreen covered box. A set like this would be useful today at fashionable Hunt lunches or hiking in rugged mountains.

D. Tableware, bone and steel, early 19th c., American or English, Walter Himmelreich.

Most sets like this were made with English or Continental blades.

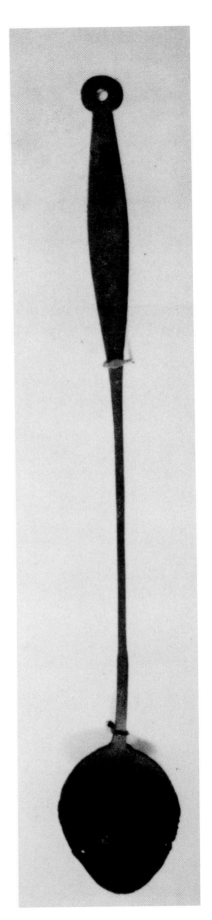

A.

B.

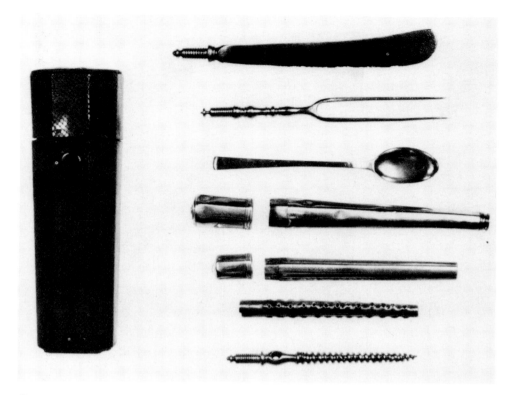

C.

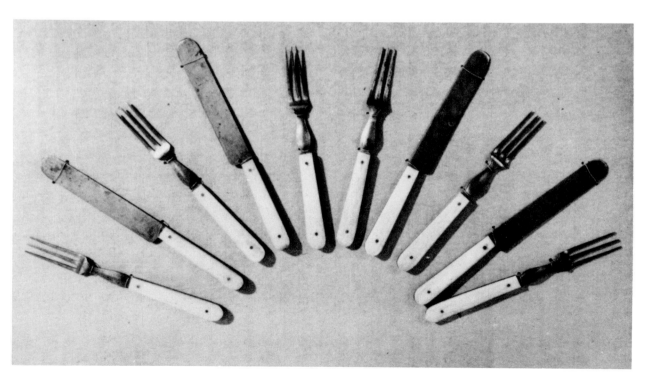

D.

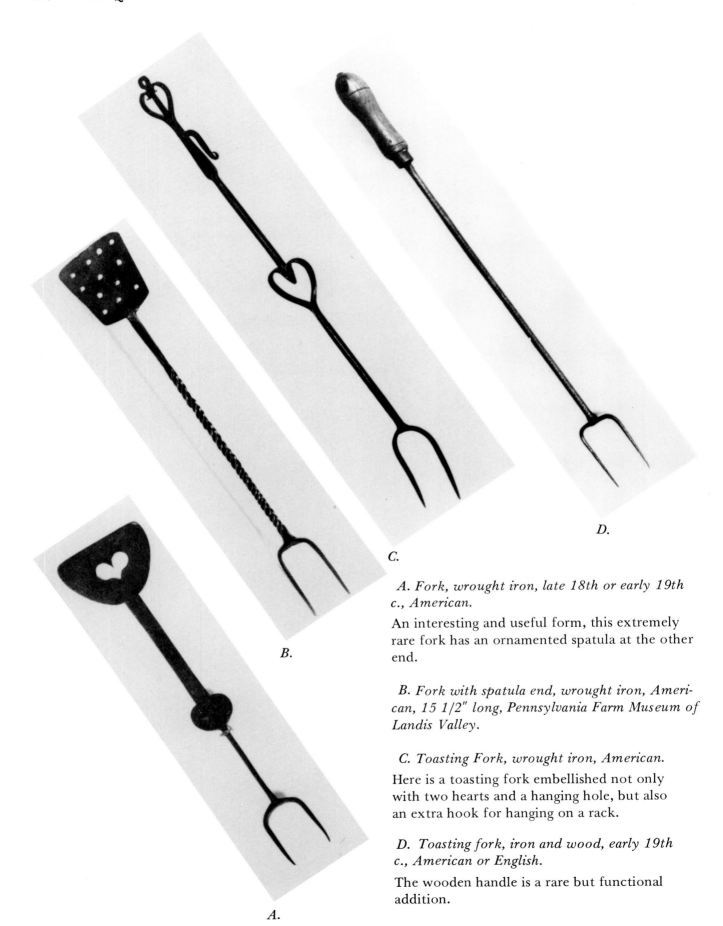

A.

B.

C.

D.

A. Fork, wrought iron, late 18th or early 19th c., American.

An interesting and useful form, this extremely rare fork has an ornamented spatula at the other end.

B. Fork with spatula end, wrought iron, American, 15 1/2" long, Pennsylvania Farm Museum of Landis Valley.

C. Toasting Fork, wrought iron, American.

Here is a toasting fork embellished not only with two hearts and a hanging hole, but also an extra hook for hanging on a rack.

D. Toasting fork, iron and wood, early 19th c., American or English.

The wooden handle is a rare but functional addition.

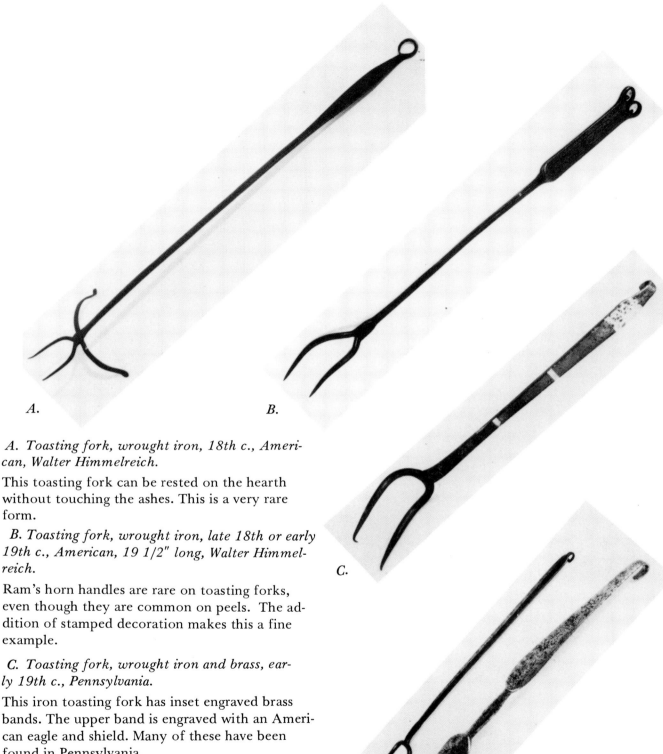

A.

B.

C.

D.

A. Toasting fork, wrought iron, 18th c., American, Walter Himmelreich.

This toasting fork can be rested on the hearth without touching the ashes. This is a very rare form.

B. Toasting fork, wrought iron, late 18th or early 19th c., American, 19 1/2" long, Walter Himmelreich.

Ram's horn handles are rare on toasting forks, even though they are common on peels. The addition of stamped decoration makes this a fine example.

C. Toasting fork, wrought iron and brass, early 19th c., Pennsylvania.

This iron toasting fork has inset engraved brass bands. The upper band is engraved with an American eagle and shield. Many of these have been found in Pennsylvania.

D. Two toasting forks, wrought iron, early 19th c., 13" long and 16 1/2" long, W. Himmelreich.

The top fork displays expert workmanship with stars on the handle, while the lower one is a more unusual type.

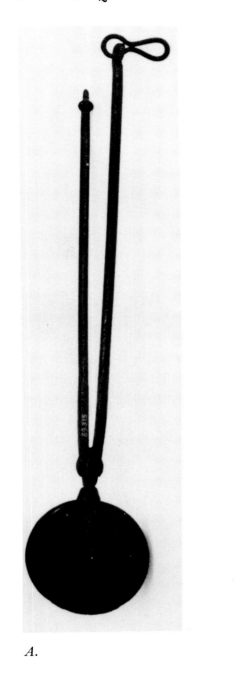

A.

B.

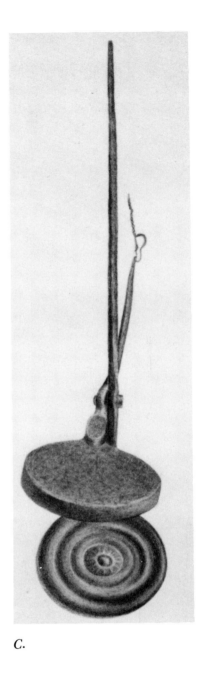

C.

Waffle irons were used for ordinary eating while smaller wafer irons were used to make Communion wafers. Some of the finer examples have the name and picture of the church to which they were made as part of the decoration. Pennsylvania German designs were frequently used. The handles are made of wrought iron, while the cooking parts are cast iron.

A. Wafer iron, cast and wrought iron, c.1820-1850, English, 27 3/4" long, 5 1/2" diameter, Henry Francis du Pont Winterthur Museum.

B. Waffle iron, cast and wrought iron, 18th or 19th c., American, W. Himmelreich.

C. Wafer iron, cast and wrought iron, late 18th or early 19th c., American, National Gallery of Art, Index of American Design.

CHAPTER 11
Lighting

A.

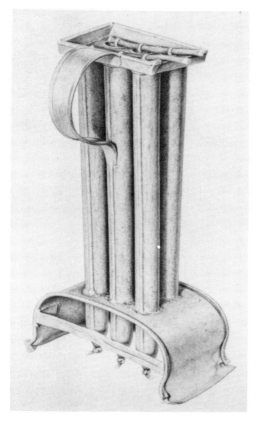

C.

B.

A-B. Candle molds, rolled and tinned iron, late 18th to early 19th c., American, 6" tall, 5" wide, W. Himmelreich.

The earliest candle molds were usually made of pewter in wooden frames, but most are made of rolled and tinned iron. Of the three shown here, the round one is the rarest.

C. Candle mold, rolled and tinned iron, late 18th or early 19th c., American, National Gallery of Art, Index of American Design.

This candle mold is drawn that one can see the sticks holding the strings placed in the center of the molds, ready to pour the wax. The noted strings will be the wick ends. After the wax has hardened, the knot at the bottom is cut, leaving an exposed wick and the entire mold is put in a bath of hot water. Shortly there after the candles can be removed.

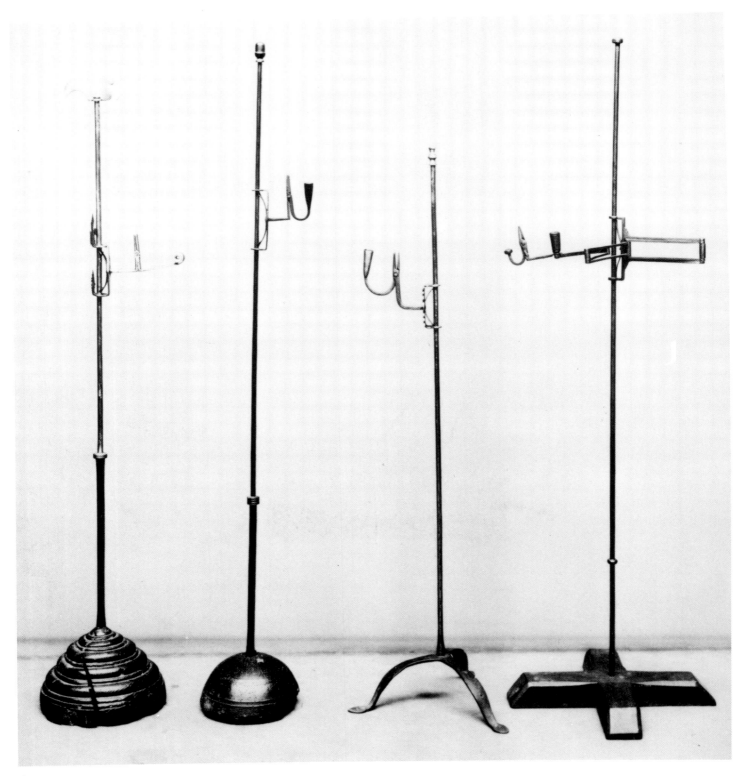

A.

A-B. Seven candlestands, wrought iron and wood, late 17th and early 18th c., English, Suffolk, tallest 4' 8" high, Victoria and Albert Museum.

The late Joseph Kindig Jr., a revered authority on antique lighting devices, felt that standing candlestands made in England often had rush lights as a utilitarian feature as well as candle cups, while those made in America almost never did. The wooden bases are very typical of English iron candlestands.

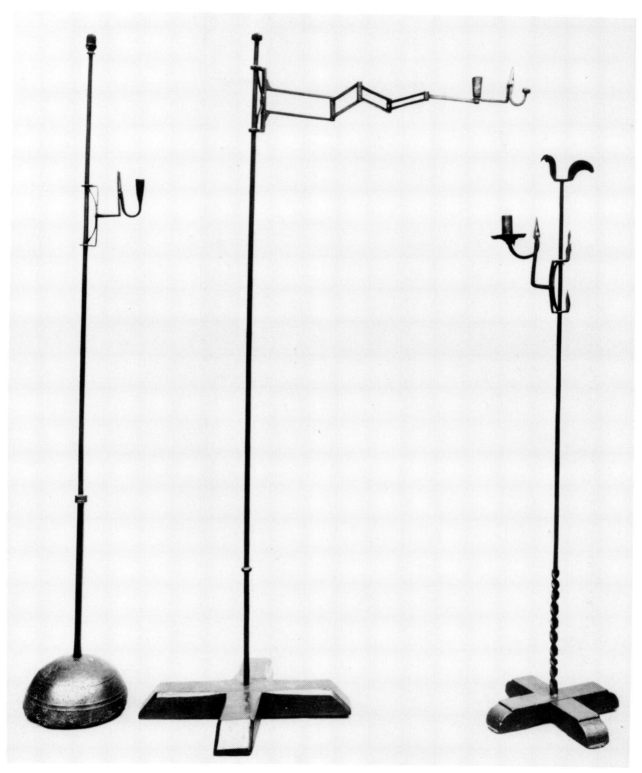

B.

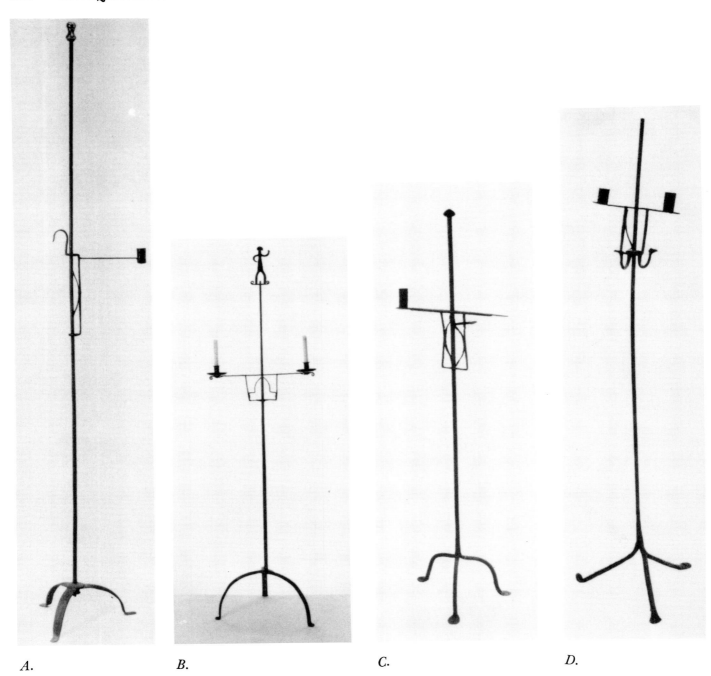

A.

B.

C.

D.

A. Candlestand, wrought iron, early 18th c., English or American.

The small proportions of the base, and lack of a deep pan make this an awkward example of an early candlestand.

B. Candlestand, wrought iron, 1720-1780, American, 67" high, 19 3/8" wide, 17" wide (at base), Henry Francis du Pont Winterthur Museum.

This is one of the most charming American iron candlestands. Of all iron decorative objects, no form has been faked as much as tall iron candlestands.

C. Standing candlestand, early 18th c., American, 45 1/2" high.

D. Candlestand, wrought iron, early 18th c., American, 44 3/4" high.

The feet of this candlestand are poorly designed and a finial is lacking. Some fake candlestands are accurate artistically and almost impossible to distinguish from original, old candlestands.

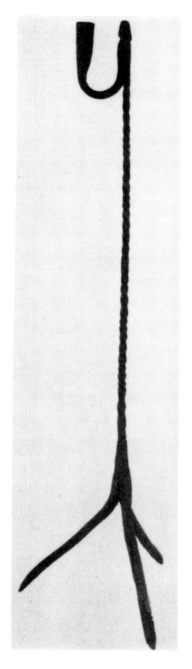

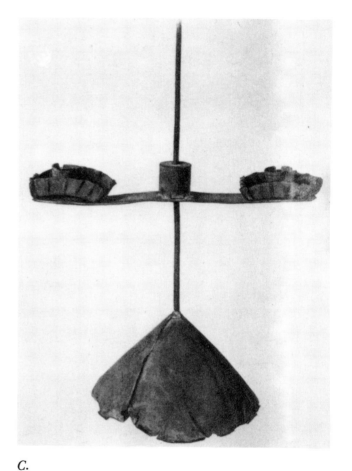

A.   *B.*   *C.*

*A. Standing candlestand, wrought iron, early
17th c., European, Wallace Nutting collection,
Wadsworth Atheneum.*

This candlestand is also a rush light holder. It
is not a graceful example.

B. Candleholder, rolled and tinned iron, American, W. Himmelreich.

This is a tin table model of the candlestand. The
conical base is weighted with sand an the arm
can be adjusted up and down.

C. Candlestand, rolled and tinned iron, American, National Gallery of Art, Index of American Design.

This version of the table candlestand has an adjustable two-light stem. Perhaps this one is earlier than the preceeding, but it is not as well
proportioned as the taller one.

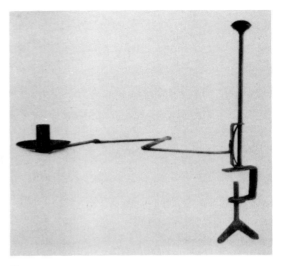

A.

B.

C.

D.

A. Candlestand, wrought iron, American, W. Himmelreich.

This table or hanging model of a candlestand can also be used as a fat lamp. The feet are boldly designed.

B. Candlestick, wrought iron, Continental, 14 3/4" high, Timothy Trace.

Here is another table model candlestand with adjustable candle arm. The lower pan could be used as a fat lamp, although it probably was intended to catch drippings from the candle.

C. Clamp candleholder, wrought iron, possibly American, 18" high.

Extension arm candleholders are quite rare. This one can be fastened to a table or arm of a chair, and can be raised or lowered on the stem.

D. Lamp, wrought iron, 17th c. or earlier, Continental or English, 12 1/4" high, 4 5/8" wide.

A very unusual lighting device that could have burned pine knots, candle stubs or oil.

E. Candlestick, sheet iron, early 19th century American.

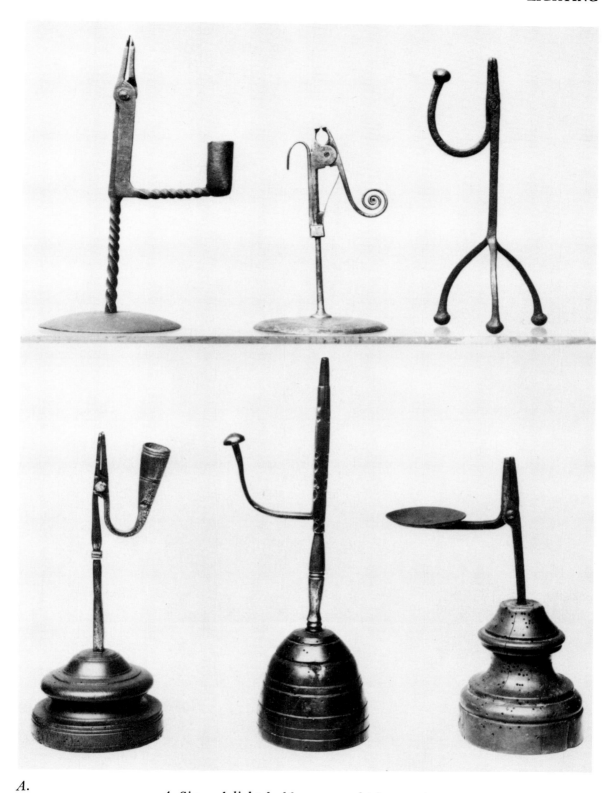

A.

A. Six rush light holders, wrought iron and wood, 18th c., English, tallest 11 5/8", Victoria and Albert Museum.

Here are six rush light holders with the upper and lower left ones being adapted to use with candles. All have a counter weight arm to keep the rush light grippers tight.

A.

B.

C.

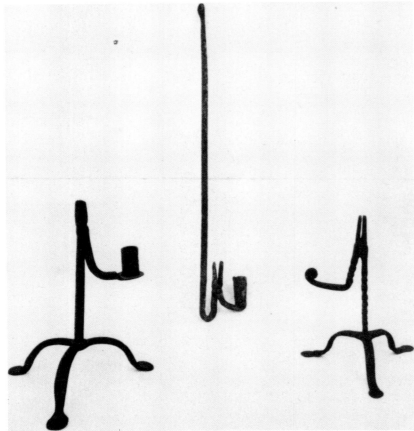

D.

A. Rush light and candleholder, wrought iron and wood, American, National Gallery of Art, Index of American Design.

A combination of candleholder and rush light holder was a fairly common seventeenth and early eighteenth century lighting device in Europe and America.

B. Rush light and candleholder, wrought iron, probably 18th c., American, National Gallery of Art, Index of American Design.

The base is unusual in this example, probably to give added stability.

C. Rush light and candleholder, wrought iron, possibly American, 18th c., National Gallery of Art, Index of American Design.

D. Rush light and candleholders, wrought iron, English or American, Herbert Schiffer Antiques.

The hanging device could slide along a rod hanging parallel to the ceiling to allow a large area to be lighted when needed.

A.

B.

C.

A. Hanging candlestick, wrought iron, 18th c., probably American.

Hanging candlesticks were used in cellars or hung from a mantle to provide light in awkward spaces. This candlestick also can stand.

B. Candlestick, rolled and tinned iron and wood, 18th c., American, National Gallery of Art, Index of American Design.

An unusual and primitive tin push-up candlestick with a tinned and wooden base is shown here.

C. Candlestick, wrought iron and wood, late 17th or early 18th c., English, National Gallery of Art, Index of American Design.

This is the earliest type of push-up candlestick with a spiral twisted iron stem that supported the candle on a moveable flat plug within the spiral.

D. Candlestick, rolled iron, late 18th c., American, 8″ high, Pennsylvania Farm Museum of Landis Valley.

This early style of iron push-up candlestick is designed to be hung from the back of a chair or mantle.

D.

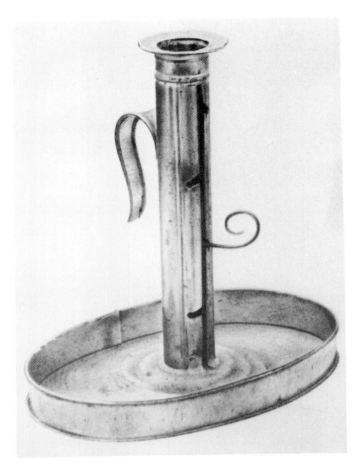

A.

B.

C.

A. Candlestick, rolled and tinned iron, early 19th c., American, National Gallery of Art, Index of American Design.

The oval pan of the push-up candlestick is an unusual variation, as are the open handle which can be used to hang, and the twisted stem of the platform.

B. Chamberstick, rolled and tinned iron, early 19th c., American, National Gallery of Art, Index of American Design.

Candlesticks with deep saucer bases are called chambersticks, since they were traditionally used to light the way to bed. The deep saucer would catch wax, while the device is being carried. The handle has an extra loop to hold a snuffer.

C. Chamberstick, rolled and tinned iron, c.1800, American or English.

The snuffer is attached by a chain to the handle. This was a very popular model.

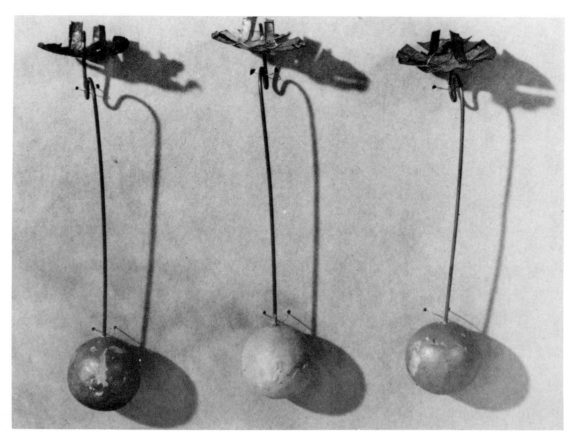

A.

B.

C.

A. Christmas tree candleholders, tin, wire and wood, American or German, late 19th c., W. Himmelreich.

Our friends in the insurance industry would not approve of these lighted in close proximity to dry resinous evergreens. They must have looked as nice as they were dangerous. The weights kept the candle upright.

B. Candleholder, rolled and tinned iron, 19th c., probably American.

This candleholder is designed with a handle and wind screen, making it possible to move it around like a flashlight with less danger of the candle blowing out. The screen was silvered with tin providing a reflector to intensify the light.

C. Candlesticks, rolled iron, early 19th c., American, 7" high, 3 7/8" long.

Push-up candlesticks with bases like these are called hog scrapers. They really will scrape a scaled hog and the base is designed very much like the utensil used. Many of these have a maker's name stamped on the thumb piece.

A.

B.

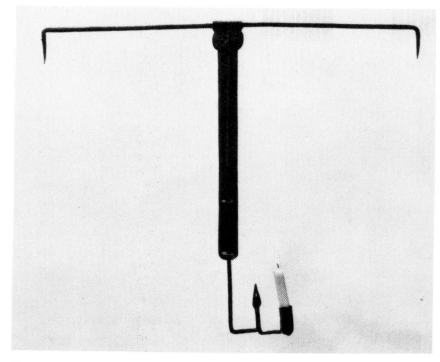

C.

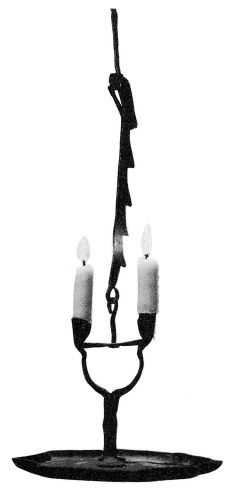

D.

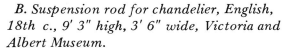

A. Section of suspending rod for chandelier, wrought iron and gilt, 17th c., English, 6' 5" long, 2' 7" wide, Victoria and Albert Museum.

This design shows dragons' heads which derive from the days of the Viking invasions of 800 to 1100 A.D.

B. Suspension rod for chandelier, English, 18th c., 9' 3" high, 3' 6" wide, Victoria and Albert Museum.

These ornate rods were used in churches to suspend chandeliers.

C. Candleholder, wrought iron, 18th c., probably English, Herbert Schiffer Antiques.

A rare "loom" light or moveable hanging candlestick with rush holder. This was adjustable in height and could be moved down a trammel. The sharp ends of the top element were driven into ceiling beams.

D. Hanging candleholder, wrought iron, 18th c., English or American, Herbert Schiffer Antiques.

A rachet controlls the height of this hanging device with two candle holders.

E. Adjustable candleholder, wrought iron, 18th c., American, Herbert Schiffer Antiques.

The hanging candleholder has a rachet-like trammel to adjust its height.

E.

A.

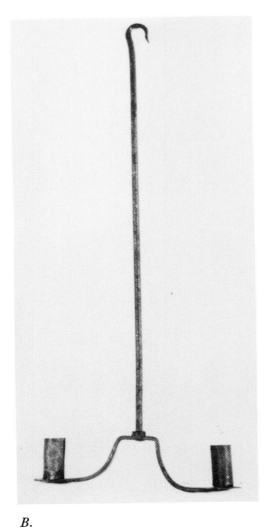

B.

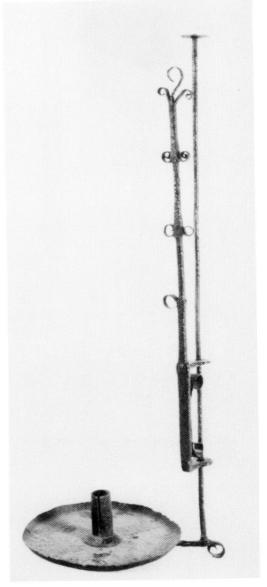

C.

A. Hanging candleholder, wrought iron, 18th c., possibly English.

This very simple hanging candleholder can be jambed upwards into the ceiling or sideways into a wall. It was possibly for use in a coal mine or cellar.

B. Hanging candleholder, wrought iron, 18th c., American or English.

A two-candle chandelier was a versatile home device.

C. Hanging candleholder, wrought iron, American, 23" high.

A hanging lighting device of adjustable height, possibly French or Basque.

A.

B.

A. Double rush light holder, wrought iron, 18th c., American.

A double rush light holder that is devised to hang from a rod, with adjustable height in the use of the rachet. Instead of candle cups being used for weights to keep the rush lights closed on the rushes, chamfered balls are used.

B. Chandelier, wrought iron, 18th c., English.

This very early type of hanging iron chandelier could have been made any time from the fifteenth century to the early nineteenth century. We are inclined to think this is early eighteenth century at the latest because of the use of the prickets rather than candle cups.

A.

A. Chandelier, Old Sturbridge Village.
This type of wonderful iron and wooden chandelier has been found in America, French Canada, England and Scandinavia. Without wood, analysis, it is very difficult to place their origins. Most have had ecclesiastical use from the mid-eighteenth to early nineteenth centuries.

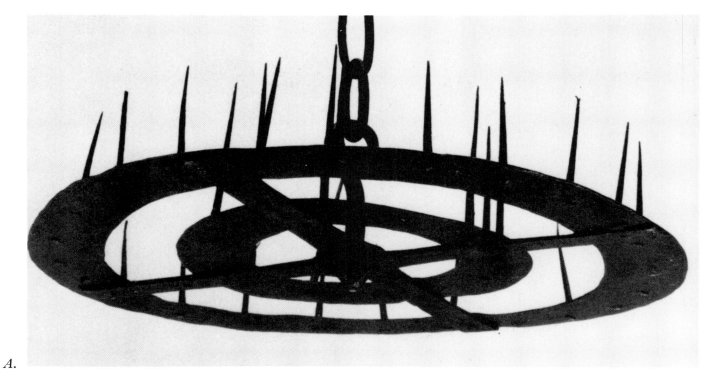

A.

A. *Chandelier, wrought iron, late 18th c., probably American, Old Sturbridge Village.*

This chandelier with prickets was made to hold candles in two rows.

B. *Chandelier, pressed and wrought iron, late 18th c., American or European, Old Sturbridge Village.*

Another chandelier with tinned leaves as a decorative device. Note the flaring cups.

B.

A.

A. Chandelier, iron and wood, 18th c., American.
Tin leaves may have been available since they were
bought from tinsmiths to add to your chandelier
to give more light by reflection. Sometimes the
wooden part was painted or gilded.

*B. Chandelier, wrought iron and wood, early
18th c., American, Old Sturbridge Village.*
This graceful and primitive chandelier can be
adjusted in height by the rachet, which is an in-
tegral part of the chandelier.

B.

A.

A. *Chandelier, rolled and tinned iron, Old Sturbridge Village.*

This chandelier was a type quite typical in American inns and churches from the mid-eighteenth to the early nineteenth century. Originally this was bright and shiny with its new tinned surface. This type has been reproduced extensively.

B. *Chandelier, rolled and tinned iron, American, Old Sturbridge Village.*

B.

A.

A. Chandelier, rolled and tinned iron, late 18th c., possibly American, 18" high, 18 1/2" wide.

B. Chandelier, rolled and tinned iron, American, Old Sturbridge Village.

C. Chandelier, rolled and tinned iron, early 19th c., probably American, Old Sturbridge Village.

D. Chandelier, rolled and tinned iron, American, Old Sturbridge Village.

This is a simple, but very graceful, chandelier.

B.

C.

D.

A.

A. Chandelier, rolled and tinned iron, American, Old Sturbridge Village.

Here is a most unusual type. Note the chain is made with loops that have been tinned.

B. Chandelier, rolled and tinned iron, 19th c., possibly American or European, National Gallery of Art, Index of American Design.

Another chandelier with some possibility of European origin due to the stamped design.

B.

A. Chandelier, rolled and tinned iron, 19th c., American, Old Sturbridge Village.

B. Chandelier, rolled and tinned iron, probably early 19th c., American, Old Sturbridge Village.

This chandelier has a simple and practical design.

A.

B.

The fat lamp did not change much from pre-Roman civilizations until the nineteenth century. Crusie lamps are hanging grease-burning lamps with open saucers. little or no wick support, and sometimes a second, lower pan to catch dripping fuel.

Crusie lamps have been found from Viking lands to Arab territories dating from Roman times to the early nineteenth century.

The first real improvement in lighting was by Ami Argand in 1793. Franklin also improved lighting when he put two wicks tightly spaced in street lamps in the mid-eighteenth century.

A. Grease lamp, wrought iron, probably 18th c., 7 3/4" high, Pennsylvania Farm Museum at Landis Valley.

The shallow saucer contained grease in which one or more wicks were soaked and burned.

B. Crusie lamp and stand, wrought iron and wood, early 18th c., American, W. Himmelreich.

This stand is a very rare piece of furniture — probably many existed originally. Crusie lamps were used for generations in the periods before the nineteenth century.

C. Crusie lamp, sheet iron, probably Continental, National Gallery of Art, Index of American Design.

A.

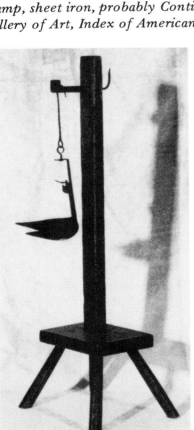

B.

C.

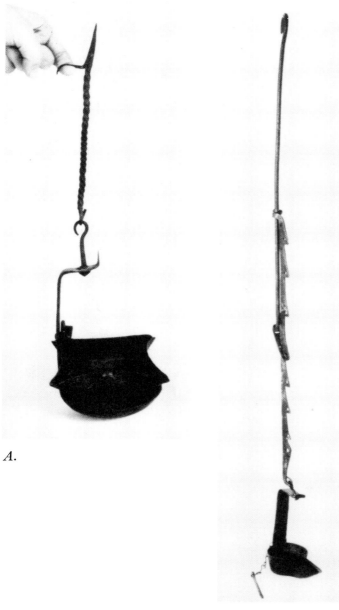

A.

B.

C.

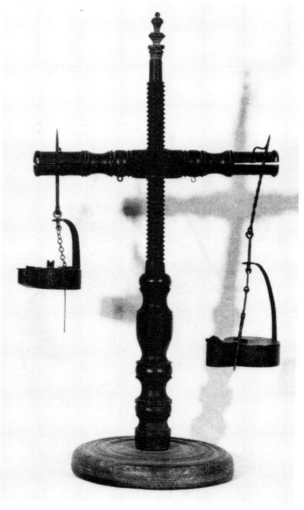

D.

*A. Four-channel fat lamp, sheet iron, 16 1/2"
high, 4 1/2" wide.*

This is an unusual variation.

*B. Crusie lamp on trammel, wrought iron, 18th
or 19th c., English or American.*

Crusie lamps were often used on trammels. These
trammels can be delicate and refined, like the
one shown here and are quite different from
those found at fireplaces.

*C. Betty lamp, sheet iron, early 19th c., possibly
American, 5 1/4" high, Pennsylvania Farm Museum
at Landis Valley.*

*D. Betty lamps on stand, wrought iron and
wood, dated 1815, one by Peter Derr, American,
W. Himmelreich.*

One of these lamps is marked "Peter Derr, 1815"
a noted maker from Lancaster, Pennsylvania.

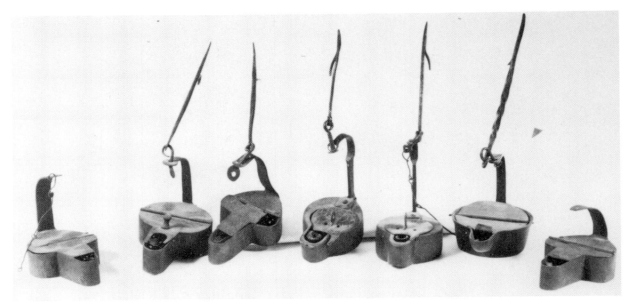

A.

B.

C.

Betty lamps are derived from crusies but with hinged lids and definite wick supports.

A. Betty lamps, sheet iron, Wallace Nutting collection, Wadsworth Atheneum.

B. Adjustable height betty lamp, wrought, rolled and tinned iron, early 19th c., American, National Gallery of Art, Index of American Design.

This betty lamp can be adjusted on the iron rod above the sand filled base.

C. Betty lamp and stand, rolled and tinned iron, 19th c., American, National Gallery of Art, Index of American Design.

A. Oil lamp on stand, rolled and tinned iron, 19th c., American, W. Himmelreich

B. Lighting devices, rolled and tinned iron, 19th c., American, Old Sturbridge Village.

This collection of tinned lighting devices includes a fat lamp with a drip collector, a betty lamp, an oil lamp sconce, a nineteenth century tinned version of a Roman lamp, and a whale oil lamp on a candlestick type base.

A.

B.

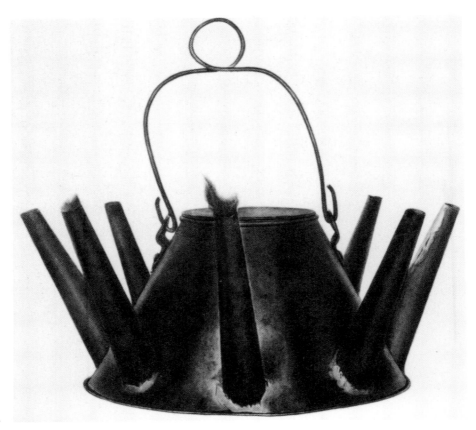

A.

A. *Oil lamp, sheet iron, 19th c., probably American, National Gallery of Art, Index of American Design.*

This lamp would give a lot of light, but also a vile odor.

B. *Miner's torch, rolled and tinned iron, mid-19th c., American, National Gallery of Art, Index of American Design.*

This oil lamp could be carried or hung. It is cer-tainly utilitarian with no pretense of elegance or decoration.

C. *Whale oil lamp, rolled and tinned iron, 19th c., American, National Gallery of Art, Index of American Design.*

This lamp can hang, stand or be carried; it is particularly useful on a table or hung on a wall. The double wick gave more then double light as Benjamin Franklin discovered.

B.

C.

A.

A.Whale oil lamp, tinned and rolled iron, 19th c., American, National Gallery of Art, Index of American Design.

This lamp gave a great deal of light due to its wide wick.

B. Lard lamp, rolled and tinned iron, mid-19th c., American, National Gallery of Art, Index of American Design.

This unusual lamp, was probably designed for the cheaper fuels that competed with sperm oil.

C. Pole lantern, rolled and tinned iron and wood, 19th c., American, National Gallery of Art, Index of American Design.

Lanterns of this type were carried in processions and at night, since they hung in gambrels they always stayed upright.

B.

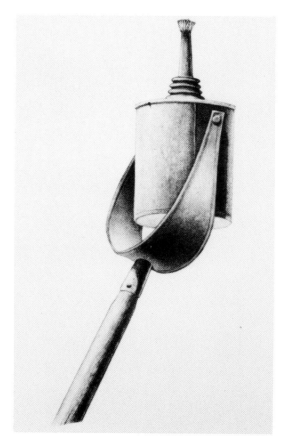

C.

A.

A. Lamp, rolled and tinned iron and steel, late 18th or early 19th c., American, English or French, Museum of the City of London.

Both the shade height and candle height are adjustable. This type of lamp usually was made in France, but labeled examples of American and English ones have been found.

B. Lamp, rolled and tinned iron, c.1800-1840, French or American, Herbert Schiffer Antiques.

B.

A. Trade card, early 18th c., English, Museum of London.

B.

B.

C.

A. Trade card, early 18th c., English, Museum of London.

It is interesting to note that besides repairing and tinning copper and brass, Daniel Ross, also sold and made lanterns. Here we see the break down of the early guild system — under which he could not have been a merchant, a tinsmith, a manufacturer of lanterns, and a repairer of copper and brass.

It is also worthy of note, that he rented lamps by week, or quarter, a practice also of Ami Argand in London at the end of the eighteenth century.

B. Pocket lantern, rolled and tinned iron and glass, 18th c., English, Herbert Schiffer Antiques.

When closed, this lantern looks like a book and can be carried in a pocket. Open, it is a useful, small lantern.

C. Two lanterns, rolled and tinned iron, 18th c., English or European.

The round lantern was designed to use thinly peeled sheets of animal horn within the frame. Horn was less expensive than glass in the eighteenth century and could be bent to a curve, yet less light could pass through the horn than through glass. The flat sided lantern is pierced in a style typical of the period.

A.

B.

C.

D.

E.

A. Four light lantern, rolled and tinned iron and glass, 18th c., English or American, 19 1/2" high, Timothy Trace.

This lantern was very efficient as air entered below the glass and heat escaped by a well developed chimney. The four glass sides give a great deal of light since they are far from the candle. Glass that is closer to a candle will discolor from smoke. The punched decoration is very nice.

B. Revere lantern, rolled and tinned iron, 18th and 19th c., National Gallery of Art, Index of American Design.

Lanterns of this type have been called "Paul Revere" lanterns after the silversmith and patriot who supposedly placed lanterns of this type in a church tower to signal the invasion of British troops. It was disillusioning to find them in a book of early lighting of Central Hungary.

They burn well, but give little light. The piercing is done by striking flat tinned iron with a "cold chisel" or center punch.

C. Belt lantern, rolled and tinned iron and glass, English or American, 19th c.,

This useful lantern enabled a person to use both hands.

D. Lantern, rolled and tinned iron, late 18th or early 19th c., European, Old Sturbridge Village.

This type of handsome lantern has been found in Denmark, Sweden, and England. They probably were used extensively throughout northern Europe.

E. Lantern, rolled and tinned iron, late 18th c., American or possibly English.

This stylish lantern is similar to the type Benjamin Franklin designed as street lamps with flat outward slanted sides. The rosettes are a little touch of elegance.

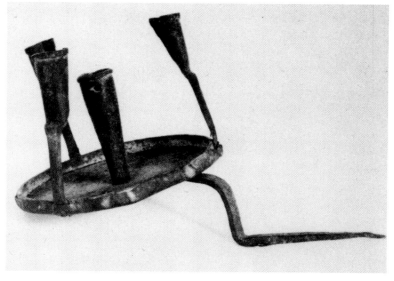

A.

B.

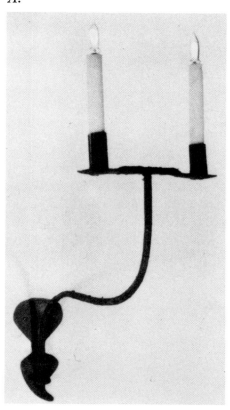

C.

*A. Wood holder, wrought iron, early 18th c.,
English or European, Victoria and Albert Museum.*

This type of bracket and holder was attached to
the side of a building and used to burn pieces of
wood for light from the Middle Ages to the
beginning of the eighteenth century.

*B. Candle sconce, wrought iron, early 18th
c., possibly American, 11" high, 11" long.*

The removal holes in the sides of the candle cups
indicate this as a very early sconce. The construction of the pan and the number of candle holders
are very unusual. The fact that the sconce is driven
into the wall is also unusual.

*C. Candle sconce, wrought iron, mid-18th c.,
probably American, 17 3/8" high, 7 7/8" wide,
Henry Francis du Pont Winterthur Museum.*

Most iron sconces had just one candle, two are
very rare. Surviving iron sconces are surprisingly
rare. This one screws or is nailed to the wall.

A.

B.

*A-B.Three sconces, rolled and tinned iron, late
18th or early 19th c.*

The crimping and ridging are two of the common-
est decorative and strengthening devices of the
tinsmith. These were made shiny originally by
dipping thin rolled cleaned sheets of iron into
molten tin. When thicker coatings were required,
further dippings were possible.

A.

C.

B.

D.

A. Sconce, cast iron, 19th c., probably American, 14 1/4" wide.

This sconce had a glass shade to protect the candle from winds and drafts. Few of these have survived.

B. Candle sconce, tinned and rolled iron, mid-18th c., American.

The punched decoration and braced sides make this is a rare and attractive sconce.

C. Sconce, rolled and tinned iron, American, late 18th c., 14" high, 8 3/4" wide, Timothy Trace.

The even ruffles surrounding the oval back served to reflect the light.

D. Double candle sconce, rolled and tinned iron, 18th c., American.

A wide double candle sconce is an unusual item.

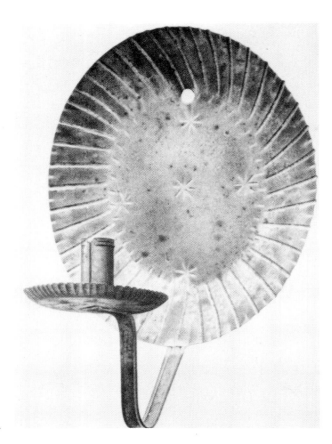

A.

B.

C.

A. Candle sconce, rolled and tinned iron, late 18th c., American.

The punched back plate with a short ruffled edge and the large drip pan make this an unusual sconce.

B. Candle sconce, rolled and tinned iron, mid-to late 18th c., American, National Gallery of Art, Index of American Design.

The juxtaposition of the round reflector placed on top of the elongated back is a rare combination.

C. Sconce, rolled and tinned iron and glass, mid-18th c., American, Old Sturbridge Village.

Clean tin reflectors, protected from oxidation here by a sheet of glass, gave more light than a smooth back plate. Some sconces had little pieces of glass mirrors glued to the backs. These are excellent. This type has been reproduced so steadily that old ones are very difficult to find.

A.

*A. Snuffer, wrought iron, 18th c.,
American or English, Wallace Nutting
collection, Wadsworth Atheneum.*

The shape of the point, the detail
of the nut and the curlicue at the ends
of the handles are all extra nicities.

*B. Tray and two snuffers, rolled,
tinned and painted iron and wrought
iron, 18th c., American, National
Gallery of Art, Index of American
Design.*

Iron snuffers follow silver and brass
ones very closely in design. The iron
snuffers were purely functional, but
in a period when high quality, workmanship and design were second
nature, many are found beautifully
made. Early trays are thicker than
later ones and often have stamped
decoration.

B.

The advanced state of Roman civilization is expressed in many fields by useful inventions, not the least of which is a record of street lighting at Antioch, Syria in the fourth century. With the fall of the Roman Empire gradually in successive centuries, inventions of this type were forgotten and the Middle Ages were spent primarily in darkness at night.

In the modern era, "Beckman has traced the periods when the custom of lighting streets was first introduced in various cities, and towns, upon the continent."[33] His work provides the information for the following list:

1417	London
1524	Paris
1553	LaHague
1669	Amsterdam
1675	Hamburg
1679	Berlin
1681	Copenhagen
1687	Vienna
1696	Hanover
1702	Liepzig
1705	Dresden
1721	Cassel
1728	Halle
1735	Gottingen
1765	Brunswick
1778	Zurich

In 1416, London's mayor Sir Henry Barton ordered lanterns to be hung out in winter, but this order was apparently only casually enforced. Cressets were iron basket-like containers that supported burning pine knots or wood splints and were used for stationery lighting in this period.

In 1512 the steeple of Bow Church in Cheapside, London, was reconstructed with "arches, or bows, to support five lanterns, one at each corner, and one upon the top, for the purpose of bearing lights hightly in the winter."[34] In Paris in 1558, police set up gallots (large vases filled with burnable material) on street corners at night. By 1662, Paris and other French towns contracted an Italian named Laudate to erect booths where lanterns were rented to carriage passengers and pedestrians with hourglasses to determine the length of rental.[35]

A man named Hemig patented a reflector for oil burning street lights in 1694 and was contracted to light London's streets for 10 years. He agreed to place a light in front of every tenth door and keep it lit from 6:00 to 12:00 p.m. in the winter. In 1716 he lost this contract and no one was named to replace him, so London's streets were dark once more. About 1720 the London Court of Council ordered housekeepers to "hang out one or more lights, with sufficient cotton wicks, to continue burning from 6:00 p.m. to 1:00 a.m. under penalty of one shilling."[36] This system was apparently not effective, for in 1729 a company was contracted by the city to furnish street lights to those housekeepers who preferred to pay for them rather than provide their own. Then in 1736 the City Corporation ordered London's streets lit with glass lamps throughout the year, and nearly 5,000 street lights were erected. "The act for completing this department, according to the present regulations, was passed in 1744. The lamps are lighted . . . every day in the year, at sunset; . . . The lamps are all of clear glass, in which are burnt good oil, with cotton wicks: they are trimmed every morning, and are cleaned as often as occasion requires . . . The lamp-lighters are employed in the forenoon, in trimming and cleaning the lamps; in the evening in lighting them; and they are obliged to take their turns, to go about at midnight to replenish such as are burning out."[37]

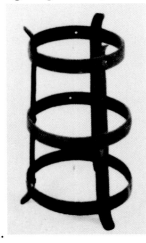 

A. Cresset, wrought iron, 18th or early 19th century, American, James C. Soeber.

B. Lantern, wrought iron with blown glass globe, 18th century, English.

A.   B.

The problems with street lighting in London were repeated in each other city at that period. In Philadelphia, for example, citizens groups formed by 1749 to address the problems.

> those who have put up, or intend to put up LAMPS at their doors in this city, are desired to meet at the Widow PRATT'S, on Thursday, the 21st instant . . . in order to concert measures for having them regularly lighted by persons to be agreed with for the purpose.[38]

Their action apparently prompted the government to take action in this matter, for "the Streets of this City began to be illuminated with Lamps in Pursuance of a late Act of Assembly."[39] When this act was renewed five years later, Benjamin Franklin made a significant contribution to the science of street lighting by proposing a change in the design of lanterns. Franklin wrote that the lamps imported from London were

> . . . inconvient in these respects: they admitted no air below; the smoke, therefore, did not readily go out above, but circulated in the globe, lodg'd on its inside, and soon obstructed the light they were intended to afford; giving, besides, the daily trouble of wiping them clean; and an accidental stroke on one of them would demolish it, and render it totally useless. I therefore suggested the composing them of four flat panes, with a long funnel above to draw up the smoke and crevices admitting air below, to facilitate the ascent of the smoke; by this means they were kept clean, and did not grow dark in a few hours, as the London lamps do . . . and an accidental stroke would generally break but a single pane, easily repaired. [39]

In Philadelphia, correct street lighting reproductions were constructed in the 1960's at the Independence National Historical Park after exhaustive research. The study of period lighting there was guided by contemporary prints, newspaper advertments, court records, and writings. Thomas Birch's *Views of Philadelphia,* published in 1801, was particularly useful.

All pictorial evidence for eighteenth century street lighting in this study shows Franklin's type of lantern used exclusively. None of the English globe lamps were illustrated.

A.

A. *Tinted engraving of a lamplighter, from an unidentified book of the late 18th century, English.*

A.

B.

Benjamin Franklin, always interested in the improvement of lighting devices, made an important discovery which increased the efficiency of wick tube lamps, a type common in the latter half of the eighteenth century. (*Heating and Lighting*, p. 64-65) Through experimentation, Franklin found that two wick tubes "ranged up side by side and a certain distance apart gave a greater amount of light than would be furnished by two single-tube lamps." (Ibid., p. 65.) This discovery was of immense practical value, was taken up at once and enjoyed great popularity as a feature of interior lighting devices for nearly a century. Certainly, its superior design would have commended it to the gentlemen entrusted with providing the city with proper illumination.[40]

The streets of London began to be lit by gas in 1807 when gas fixtures were installed on Pall Mall Street. Electricity was slow to become popular for street lighting after it was first tried in Cleveland in 1877 with electric arc lamps.

C.

A. Street lights appear here in Philadelphia as they were seen by Thomas Birch who engraved the scene in 1799.

B. View of street lamps and watch box lamps with lamplighter in the vicinity of Robert Morris's unfinished house on Chestnut street in Philadelphia, from an engraving by Thomas Birch in 1800.

C. This authentically restored street lamp is seen in Philadelphia today outside the Thaddeus Kosciuszko National Memorial. National Park Service, Independence National Historical Park.

A.

A-B. *Restored street lighting in Philadelphia
at Independence National Historical Park,
National Park Service photo.*

B.

B.

A.

C.

A. Taper jack, wrought iron, 18th c., English, Herbert Schiffer Antiques.

This iron taper or snake jack is far rarer than a brass or silver one. A long taper was twisted around the column and secured at the upper end in the spring-tightened clamp.

B. Flint lighter, wrought iron, steel, and wood, 18th c., English or American.

This pistol type lighter is rare. The trigger releases a hammer holding a piece of flint. The flint strikes the metal plate creating a spark, which starts a fire in the tinder held in a box below.

C. Flint lighter, steel and wood, 18th c., English.

Here the flint strikes the steel plate causing a spark to shoot into the hole where flammable material such as "punk" was kept.

B.

A.

A. Tinder box and candleholder, rolled iron, late 18th or early 19th c., American or English.

The candle cup and pan lift up to reveal a cavity in which flint, steel, and tinder were kept.

B. Tinder box, candleholder and striker, rolled and tinned iron, wood and wrought iron, late 18th c., American or English, National Gallery of Art, Index of American Design.

The wooden handle on this tinder box is a nice addition. The metal striker was used against a flint to start a fire.

[33] "Lamplighter", illustrated page from an unknown book published after 1778 in England.

[34] Ibid.

[35] F.W. Robins, *The Story of the Lamp*, (Bath: Kingsmead Reprints 1970), p. 140.

[36] Ibid., p. 141.

[37] "Lamplighter", illustrated page from an unknown book published after 1778 in England.

[38] *Pennsylvania Gazette*, December 19, 1749.

[39] *Pennsylvania Gazette*, October 3, 1751.

[40] Robert J. Colborn, *Lamps in Eighteenth Century Philadelphia*, Independence National Historical Park, 1961, p. 10.

CHAPTER 12
Miscellaneous

A.

B.

After the Civil War, many American iron foundries had excess metal. The proprietors tried to find alternate uses for their product instead of releasing the workmen. Therefore, many door stops and other non-essential cast iron dates from this period.

A. Figures, cast iron, 19th c., American, rabbit 4 1/2" long.

B. Animals, wrought iron, 18th c., or earlier, Phil Cowan.

Primitive iron animals represented a Pennsylvania German legendary method of keeping evil spirits away from the barn. The Scandinavians also claim to have used this method of magic.

A.

A. Two decoys, cast iron, c.1880-1890, Charles-town, Maryland, Black Water Antiques.

The first of these decoys represents a "red head" duck, the second, a canvasback. They were used on the wings of sneak boxes by market gunners about 1885. The ducks were made from a pattern carved by decoy maker John D. Graham, of Charlestown, Maryland, and cast in foundries in adjoining settlements along the Susquehanna Flats.

B. Door stops, cast iron, 19th c., American.

Foundry men must have gotten bored and made these whimsies for their own amusement.

B.

C.Snake, wrought iron, 19th c., American, 8 1/2" wide

Judicious placement of an object like this could make you the life of the party or perhaps asked to leave.

C.

D. Boot jack, cast iron, late 19th c., American, 9½ by 4 inches, Philip Bradley Antiques.

E. Boot jack, cast iron, mid-19th c., American, National Gallery of Art, Index of American Design.

Another type of Victorian boot jack is this most unattractive large insect.

D.

E.

A.

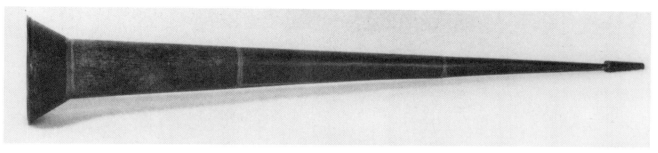

B.

A. Coaching horns, rolled and tinned iron, late 18th c., English or American, Anonymous.

The graceful design makes these lovely things. They were used to announce the arrival of the coach from a distance so the next team of horses could be harnessed and ready.

B. Coaching horn, rolled and tinned iron, late 18th c., English or American, W. Himmelreich.

C. Commission pennant, sheet iron, 1840-1900, American, 74 inches long, Courtesy the Henry Francis duPont Winterthur Museum.

This charming rarity is listed as a commission pennant. Commission pennants are flown at the mainmast of government ships which are commissioned, but not under the command of officers entitled to personal flags.

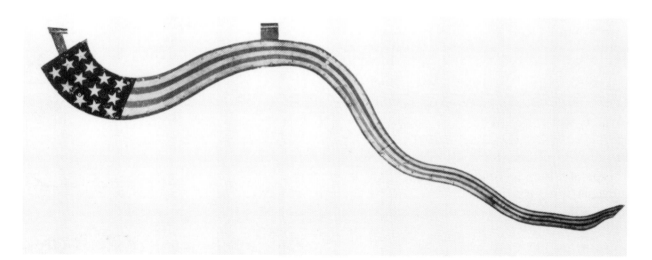

D. Flask, rolled and tinned iron, early 19th c., English or American, W. Himmelreich.

The rings on the end could have been attached to a strap over one's shoulder. This would have been lighter and less breakable than glass or ceramic flasks.

D.

A.

B.

C.

A. Hat box, rolled and tinned iron, early 19th century, English or American, W. Himmelreich.
The name "cocked" hat may be derived from "cockade", the ribbon badge often worn on tri-cornered hats. The tri-cornered British and American Naval officers' hats were difficult to pack and carry, so boxes such as this would have been useful. Epaulettes were also carried in their own specially designed tin boxes.

B. Looking glass, cast iron and glass, mid-19th century, American.
Many cast iron objects were painted originally such as porch railings and columns with grape decoration in purple and green tones. This "Jenny Lind" looking glass was not discolored by weather and has brilliant remaining paint.

C. Looking glass, cast iron, late 19th century, American, Index of American Design, National Gallery of Art.

The looking glass frame has decoration of the Victorian Renaissance revival style.

A.

A. Group of miniature pieces, cast iron, mid-19th c., American.

These were toys or gifts with the possible exception of the anvil.

B. Pipe, wrought iron, 18th c., English,

Iron pipes are very rare. Clay was cheap, but was fragile. The length and refinement of this iron pipe suggests that the smoke would cool before reaching the mouth.

B.

C. Shop sign, iron, 19th century, American, Index of American Design, National Gallery of Art.

This butcher's shop sign shows the tools of his trade.

C.

A.

A. Weathervane and shop sign, rolled iron, late 19th c., Pennsylvania, Pennsylvania Farm Museum of Landis Valley.

This example is both a shop sign and a weathervane. It is a puzzle, a rebus, that tells us that Mr. W. Gerfin was both a blacksmith and a horseshoer. These trades were originally separate, but in the nineteenth century when machines began to produce iron items, the blacksmith added horseshoeing to his trade. This is a rare and delightful metal creation.

B. Shop sign, wrought and cast iron, c.1800, English, Museum of the City of London.

This splendid locksmith's sign is one of few remaining. They were once common trade signs.

B.

A.

A. *Tinsmith's sign, tin, 1858, Winston-Salem, North Carolina, 7' 3" high, 64" diameter, Historic Winston-Salem.*

In the 1850's, Julius Mickey conducted a merchantile business in the building and opened a tinsmith's shop in the upper portion. He wanted a sign that would attract attention and chose this coffee pot to inform the public of his roofing, tin and stove business. It has been estimated that the pot could contain 740½ gallons of coffee. Tradition has it that a Yankee soldier hid in the pot at one time during the Civil War. The pot can be seen today at Old Salem.

B. *Tinsmith's sign, tin, 19th century, American.*

This handsome tea pot trade sign represents the tradesman's abilities admirably.

C. *Brazier, sheet iron, American, early l9th century. Index of American Design, National Gallery of Art.*

D. *Foot warmer, pierced sheet iron and wood, American, late l8th century, Index of American Design, National Gallery of Art.*

B.

C.

D.

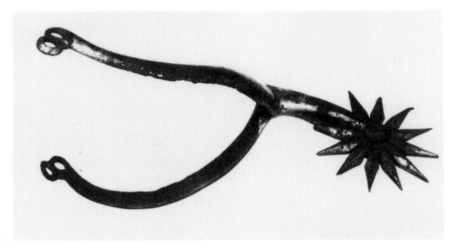

A.

B.

C.

A. Spur, steel, 16th c., English, Museum of London.

Steel spurs have remained essentially unchanged from the Middle Ages to the present.

B. Spur, 19th c., American, National Gallery of Art, Index of American Design.

This spur from the American southwest is similar to those worn by the Spanish Conquistadores in the eighteenth century, and English and European knights in the fourteenth and fifteenth centuries.

C. Watch holder, mid-19th c., American, 12" high, 6 3/4" wide, 4" long.

Men's large pocket watches were placed in the slot at night so that the face could be seen. Most surviving watch holders are made of carved wood.

CHAPTER 13
Stoves

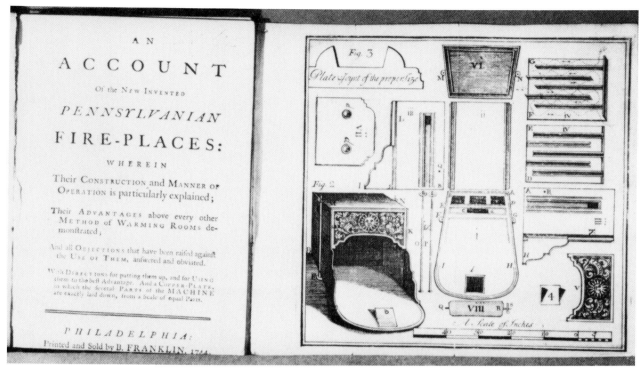

Pennsylvania State Library.

Benjamin Franklin described his newly invented stove to the American Philosophical Society in 1742. Two years later this brochure was published by him to explain the stove to everyone.

On February 1, 1745, the *Boston News Letter* advertised the "New Fashion Fireplaces or Stoves from Philadelphia," and announced as "just published, and account of the New-invented Pennsylvania Fireplace." This was Franklin's contribution to heating. It was an adaptation from the fireplace built in England for Prince Rupert — one with a descending flue, and from the French fireplace of Nicolas Gauger, from which he borrowed the caliducts and the soufflet or blower in the hearth. The open fire burned on an iron hearth, and the smoke rose in front of a hollow metal back, passed over the top and down the other side where it entered the flue by a curved channel at the level of the hearth.

Franklin never profited from his invention. He wrote, in later years, "That, as we enjoy great advantages from the inventions of others, we should be glad of an opportunity to serve others by any invention of ours; and this we should do freely and generously." [41]
The stoves were made at furnaces such as Warwick Furnace in Pennsylvania until the Revolution interrupted production there, and after the Revolution the stoves were made at several furnaces including Batsto in New Jersey.

It is interesting to note the length of time for which these Franklin stoves were manufactured. It is amusing that stoves like these are being manufactured today and with our fuel problems may once again be a primary source of heat.

[41]Josephine H. Pierce, "Franklin-type Stoves," *Antiques*, LIII, 351-53.

A.

B.

C.

D.

A. Franklin stove, cast iron, signed Hopewell Furnace, Pennsylvania, c.1790, National Park Service, Hopewell Village.

The draped garland cast decoration suggests a late eighteenth century date for this stove.

B. Stove, cast iron, mid-19th c., Pennsylvania, Hopewell Village, National Park Service, Hopewell Village.

The back of a Franklin stove shows the large metal surface and smoke chamber which radiated heat into a room. These features made the stove more efficient than previous wood-burning fires.

C. Front plate of Franklin stove, cast iron, marked Bird, Hopewell Furnace, Pennsylvania, dated 1772, National Park Service, Hopewell Village.

This is the arching front plate of a Franklin stove cast by Mark Bird at Hopewell Furnace in 1772. The design was carved in wood in the same rococo style popular at the time for furniture made in Philadelphia.

D. Stove, cast iron, c.1790-1800, Catoctin Furnace, Frederick County, Maryland, 31 1/2" high, 39 1/2" wide, Museum of Early Southern Decorative Arts.

Catoctin Furnace was operating in 1774 and was rebuilt in 1787 and 1831. It was in operation under the name of James Johnson and Company as late as 1880.

A.

A. *Franklin stove and grate, cast iron, late 18th c., American.*

Here is a carefully designed and decorated grate in a Franklin stove. American grates are extremely rare. The Franklin stove has a pattern in the design of its hood suggesting a date after 1780 and before 1810.

B. *Franklin stove, cast iron, c.1780-1810, United States, 26" high, 31 3/4" wide, 36 3/8" deep, Henry Francis du Pont Winterthur Museum.*

The motto "Be Liberty Thine" across the top of this stove suggests a date after the Revolution.

C. *Stove, cast iron, 1840-1880, Pennsylvania Hopewell Furnace, Pennsylvania, National Park Service, Hopewell Village.*

B.

C.

A.   *B.*

A. Stove, cast iron, c.1790-1820, English, probably Carron Company, Victoria and Albert Museum.

This urn shaped stove is exquisitely designed and cast. Besides being decorative, this stove was quite efficient since there is a great deal of surface area to radiate heat.

B. Dumb stove, cast iron, 19th c., American, 47 1/2" high, 19" diameter, Henry Francis du Pont Winterthur Museum.

Calling this a dumb stove is not disrespectful to the Father of our Country, but is a style of stove with no opening in the room where it was used. The hot air from a flue turned this into a radiator. The Winterthur Museum also has a Martha Washington dumb stove.

A.

A. Pattern for a stove plate, carved wood, 18th c., New Jersey, Batsto Furnace, National Park Service, Hopewell Village.

This elegant Chippendale carving is the wooden pattern for the side of a stove. The patterns were pressed into casting sand. This pattern was used about 1770. Doctor Mercer has written that the earliest stoves were not decorated.

B. Stove plate, cast iron, dated 1769, Pennsylvania, Lancaster County, Henry Francis du Pont Winterthur Museum.

This stove plate is number one of "the series of great American Industrialists" that Baron Stiegle was planning to manufacture. Unfortunately six years after casting this he went bankrupt; before he proclaimed to the world the name of the second greatest American industrialist. His choice would have been interesting. Elizabeth Furnace was named after his wife whose money backed the furnace. He also owned Charming Forge. For whom that was named we may never know. Masonic emblems may be seen in the lower section of this plate.

B.

A.

B.

A-B.Stove, cast iron, dated 1772, Pennsylvania, Hopewell Furnace, National Park Service, Hopewell Village.

This is the earliest stove pattern made at Hopewell Furnace. The decorative leaves are of such quality that the pattern was undoubtedly carved by one of the fine Philadelphia carvers. Since many Hopewell-made stoves were cast for other firms with their own patterns, Hopewell's name is found on very few stoves.

C. Five plate stove or jamb stove, dated 1773, Marlboro Furnace, Frederick County, Virginia, 21 3/4" high, 18" wide, 23 3/4" deep, Museum of Early Southern Decorative Arts.

These stoves were also called "non-ventilating stoves," as they took no draft from the room they heated, but were fired from the fireplace of an adjoining room.

Five plate stoves were usually placed through a wall so that the wood and ashes were in the kitchen.

The primitive quality of the plates of this stove stand in stark contrast to the Fairfax fireback, and reflect the art and abilities of a Valley of Virginia carver versus those of a professional urban carver of Philadelphia.

The side plates are inscribed from Isaiah 11:6, 7, and translate, "I look for a better time, when all strife shall cease (and when) cows and bears shall feed together (and) the wolves shall dwell with the lambs." The dated end plate translates "Every one shall live without fear under his own vine and fig tree," and is taken from Micah 4:4.

The stone base has been restored.

C.

A.

B.

A-B. Six plate stove, Catoctin Furnace, Frederick County, Maryland, dated 1786, 32" high, 29 1/2" long, 12" wide, Old Salem Inc.

Note the typical Classical design of the "lady in mourning" and the funeral urn.

C. Stove, cast iron, 19th c., American, Old Sturbridge Village.

The baskets of flowers in the decoration indicate the design to be in the Classical period between 1780 and 1810.

C.

A.

B.

A. Stove, cast iron, c.1800, Delaware, Daniel Royer, Springfield Furnace, State of Delaware, Division of Historical and Cultural Affairs.

This stove was found in the New Castle County, Delaware, Court House.

B. Tailor's stove, cast iron, c.1810-1840, American, National Gallery of Art, Index of American Design.

The additional flat space enabled more pressing irons to be heated for the tailors who used the stoves and room for a kettle for steaming. The designs on the sides are similar to motifs found on Empire furniture.

C. Two stoves, cast iron, early 19th c., Pennsylvania, Hopewell Furnace, National Park Service, Hopewell Village.

At Hopewell Village one can see a spectacular demonstration of early nineteenth century casting. There is also a visitor's center with a museum. Hopewell produced a great variety of cooking and heating stoves. At one period as many as 60 types and sizes were being cast. In 1841, a peak year, about 5,000 stoves were sold.

C.

A.

B.

C.

A. Ten plate stove, cast iron, mid-19th c., Pennsylvania, Hopewell Furnace.

Hopewell Furnace sold thousands of stoves, although most were made for other companies.

B. Ten plate stove, cast iron, 1834-1850, Ohio, Zoar Furnace, Greenfield Village and the Henry Ford Museum, Dearborn, Michigan.

Zoar was a specialized community, somewhat like the Shakers. The members manufactured many products . Their architecture is quite interesting as it appears to be much earlier in style than actual dates.

C. Stove, cast iron, dated 1830, American, Old Sturbridge Village.

This barrel sided stove is decorated with raised sailing ships. The top is designed for one large kettle or a flat stove plate. This was apparently primarily a room-heating stove.

The Shakers are known for functionalism, simplicity, and cleanliness of design. This is one of the many types of stoves they made free of all unnecessary trimmings, embellishments, and ornamentation. Their stoves worked well and are handsome because of design becoming an object of stark beauty. The simple modern designs are "discovering" what the Shakers accomplished.

A. Stove, cast iron, 1790, American, Shaker, by Anthony Pierce, Dighton, Massachusetts, Old Colony, Taunton, Massachusetts.

B. Sisters' room in building number one, dwelling house, Mt. Lebanon Shakers South Family, near New Lebanon, New York. Photo taken about 1929, Library of Congress.

B.

A.

A. Ironing stove in laundry room, sisters' workshop, Mt. Lebanon Shakers Church Family, New Lebanon, New York, photo taken 1931, Library of Congress.

B. Ironing stove in Sisters' Chair-making shop. Mt. Lebanon Shakers South Family, near New Lebanon, New York, photo taken 1930, Library of Congress.

A.

B.

A.

B. Bolt, wrought iron, American, 3" wide
This type of bolt with ram's horns was found on everything from Conestoga wagons to stoves in the eighteenth and nineteenth centuries.

B.

A. Stove, cast iron, mid-19th c., American, Old Sturbridge Village.

From an engineering standpoint, the heat transfer and efficiency of this stove was better than most because of more surface to radiate heat. There is a space for a kettle or a humidifier even though this was primarily a heating stove.

C. Vessels, cast iron.

Low humidity came with extensive heating by stoves. As an effort to combat this problem, cast iron urns were often placed on stoves and filled with water. In the foreground two of these are shown.

C.

CHAPTER 14
Tools

A.

A. *Plate, Delftware, dated 1769, Holland, James C. Sorber.*

In this carpenter's shop an adz can be seen being used to smooth a plank, a drawknife being used at the bench, and a full range of tools hanging on the wall.

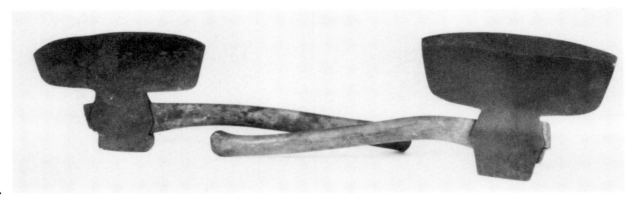

A.

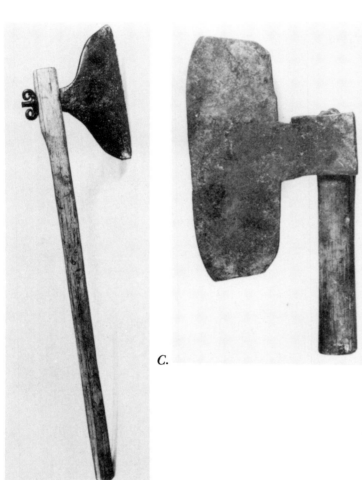

B.

C.

D.

A. Broad axes, wrought iron and wood, 19th c., American, Wallace Nutting collection, Wadsworth Atheneum.

A wonderful book written by Henry J. Kauffman on American axes is highly recommended for its quantity of styles, descriptions, instruction and manufacturers' details.

B. Broad axe, wrought iron and wood, 18th c., American, 9" long, Pennsylvania Farm Museum of Landis Valley.

A large and very interesting wing nut secures the broad axe to its handle.

C. Carpenter's hewing hatchet, wrought iron and wood, probably 19th c., American, blade 9 1/2" long, Pennsylvania Farm Museum of Landis Valley.

The carpenter's hewing hatchet is a small version of a broad axe used for finish dressing and trimming timbers. The blade is stamped twice "D. Pugh."

D. Pruning and grafting tool, 19th c., 11 3/4" long, Pennsylvania Farm Museum of Landis Valley.

Three tree worker's tools are combined in one here. The saw edge, chopping edge, and bill hook would all be useful at the end of a long pole upon which this was mounted for work in trees.

A.

C.

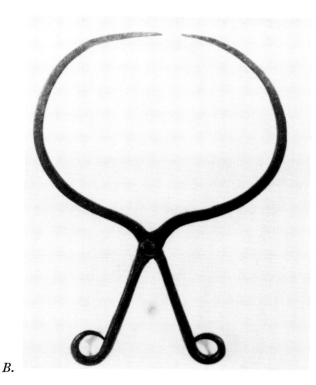

B.

A. Splitting wedge, wrought iron, 18th or 19th c., American, 16″ long, Pennsylvania Farm Museum of Landis Valley.

Today it is hard to comprehend embellishing a humble tool such as a splitting wedge, yet this example is profusely decorated on both sides with a stamped tree-like design.

B. Calipers, 19th c., American, 9 1/4″ long, Pennsylvania Farm Museum of Landis Valley.

Calipers were an important measuring device in many trades including blacksmithing, wood turning and tinsmithing. This example calibrates from 5/8″ to 4 1/8″.

C. Stamp, wrought iron and wood, 19th c., probably American, National Gallery of Art, Index of American Design.

An unusual stamp is shown here, possibly used to identify objects such as sawmill logs.

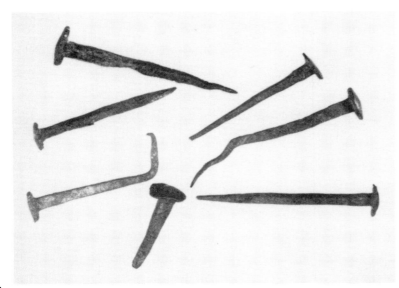

A.

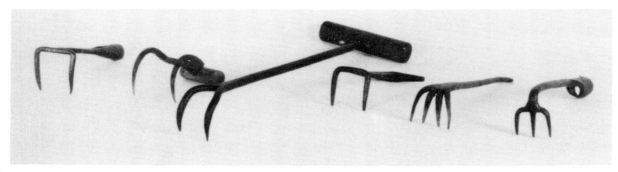

B.

*A. Nails, 18th and early 19th c., 3 1/4" to
2 1/4" long, Pennsylvania Farm Museum of
Landis Valley.*

Nails were made by the blacksmith in many
shapes and sizes for particular purposes. The
longitudinal grain of wrought iron enabled these
nails to be bent or clinched over. Such nails
were used to fasten hardware to doors, shutters,
drawers. chest lids, and other general purposes.

*B. Tools, wrought iron, 19th c., American,
James C. Sorber.*

These tools were used for taking nails and other
objects out of barrels. Some of them had wooden
handles which are not shown here.

*C. Carpenter's brace, 18th to early 19th c.,
American, 11 1/4" long, Pennsylvania Farm
Museum of Landis Valley.*

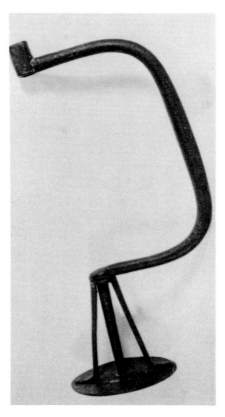

C.

A. *Druggist's tools, wrought iron,*
18th century, tongs 8" long, James
C. Sorber.

These small shovels and tongs resemble fire tools, but probably
were used by druggists to measure small amounts of medicine.
The flaring shape of the shovels
indicates an early date.

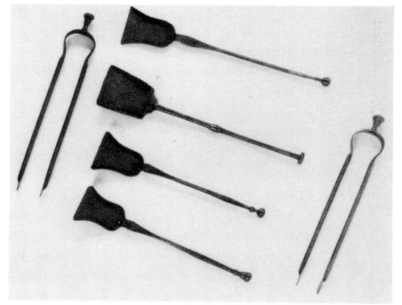

A.

B.

B. *Plow, late 18th to early 19th c., 7' 9 1/2"*
long, Pennsylvania Farm Museum of Landis
Valley.

Characteristics of ancient plow design are present
here. The wrought iron coulter and wooden
mold board are separate elements. In the modern
plow, these are combined into one unit which
efficiently cuts and turns the earth.

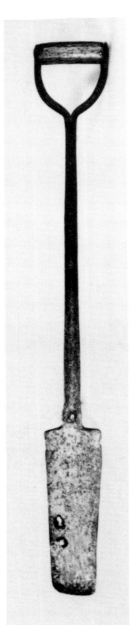

A.

B.

A. Spade, 18th or early 19th c., American, 11 1/4" high, 8 1/4" wide, Pennsylvania Farm Museum of Landis Valley.

This tradition form of spade is ageless. Drawings from the sixteenth century depict similar iron spades in use at that period.

B. Spade, wrought iron, possibly late 18th c., possibly Dutch.

This specialized spade may have been used to keep narrow ditches open or in a foundry to cut passages for iron to flow into molds for pig bars.

C. Model of manure fork, wrought iron, mid-19th c., American, 9" long, Pennsylvania Farm Museum of Landis Valley.

This model may have served as a salesmen's sample or been intended for a patent model. The full scale implement was horse drawn and used to clean manure from stables.

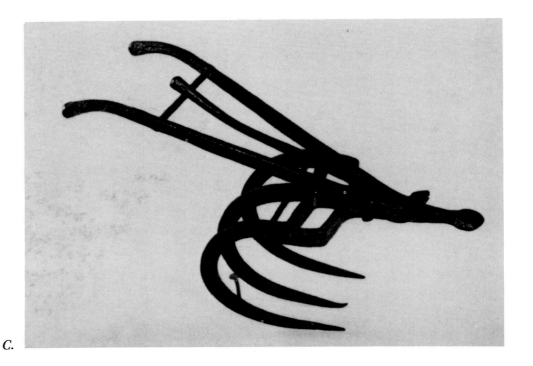

C.

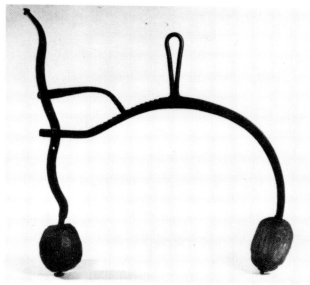

A.

B.

A. Cow restraint, wrought iron and wood, early 19th c., 25" long, Pennsylvania Farm Museum of Landis Valley.

This device was placed over the cow's body immediately forward of the hind legs and pulled tight. The tightening forced the wooden bells into the animal's sides, thus immobilizing the hind legs to prevent the cow from kicking during milking.

B. Horse, wrought iron, 18th c., American.

This iron "horse" may have been part of the equipment in a wheelright's shop. These were made from the early eighteenth to the mid-nineteenth century with no change in style.

C.

C. Bear trap, wrought iron, last half of the 19th c., American, 32" long, Pennsylvania Farm Museum of Landis Valley.

Metal animal traps were a popular item of manufacture for blacksmiths until they became factory made. They are really fairly difficult to make because the springs must be tempered.

D. Chains, wrought iron, 18th and 19th c., American, James C. Sorber.

Chains have traditionally been one of the products of a blacksmith. Here we show some that took great skill. The chain on the left with a lock is believed to have been made as a slave collar and is very fine work. The next three held cotter pins from Conestoga wagons. The extreme right one is a very complicated and difficult chain to make and bends very tightly.

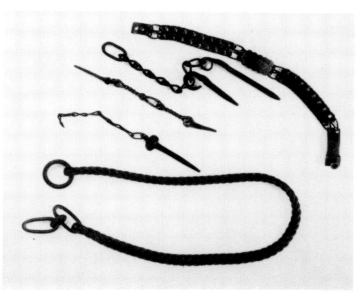

D.

A.

A. Fire engine model, iron, l854, The Mutual Assurance Company.

Model of a Philadelphia-style double-deck hand pump fire engine built in l854, attributed to Robert and Henry Eichholtz, gunsmiths of Lancaster, Pennsylvania, the sons of the portrait painter, Jacob Eichholtz. Nineteenth-century fire engines were nearly always gaily painted and ornamented, but the octagonal condenser case and skill-fully engraved brass trim make this a particularly handsome model.

B. Fire axes, iron and wood, 19th c., American, Insurance Company of North America.

Fire axes have a sharp point at the opposite end from the blade.

C. Group of fireman's tools, cast and wrought iron, brass, 19th c., American, 9" to 22" long, Insurance Company of North America.

1. open box wrench and spanner
2. brass wrench with pinch bar (to lift hydrant caps)
3. wrench
4. hydrant wrench
5. double box wrench
6. box wrench.

B.

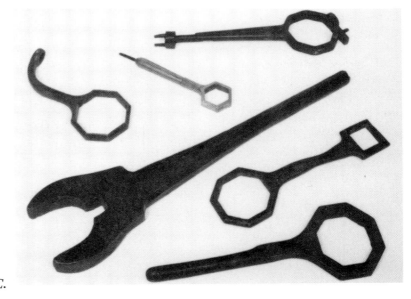

C.

A.

A. Hook and ladder wagon, wrought iron, wood and brass, Philadelphia, 1799, 7' 2" wide, 22' 5" long, 4' 10" high, Insurance Company of North America.

Fire axes and oil lamps (shown separately in other sections) are shown here in place. This wagon was built for a Philadelphia fire company in 1799 and sold to a Delaware fire company in 1825 where it was used until 1850. It is a hand pulled wagon. The lantern is marked "Lakeview I. H&R."

B. Fire engine jack, wood and iron, 19th c., American, Insurance Company of North America.

This jack belonged to an engine of the Union Fire Company. The iron foot plate has two spikes to anchor in the ground. The spike part of the handle is missing. This is very similar to jacks made for Conestoga wagons.

C. Flambeau, rolled and tinned iron, 19th c. American, 19 1/2" high, 4" diameter, Insurance Company of North America.

The container was packed with tallow and topped by bunched wicks. The flambeau was lighted and hand carried to guide fire fighting equipment to nocturnal fires.

B.

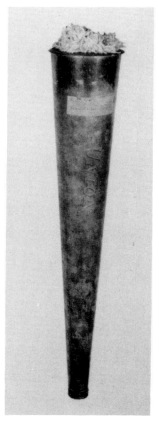

C.

A. Eel spear, wrought iron and wood, 19th c., probably American, Pennsylvania Farm Museum of Landis Valley.

Eel spears were in use frequently until the early twentieth century when eels were no longer considered a delicacy.

B-C. Harpoon, wrought iron, c. 1833, signed J.D., made by James Dumphee, New Bedford, Massachusetts, collection of Frank Sommer, courtesy of the Henry Francis du Pont Winterthur Museum Libraries.

A Negro blacksmith, James Dumphee, made this and many other harpoons for the whaling trade. It took a great knowledge of tempering to make these, for if the harpoon was too hard it would snap, yet the cutting surface had to hold a fine edge.

C.

A.

B.

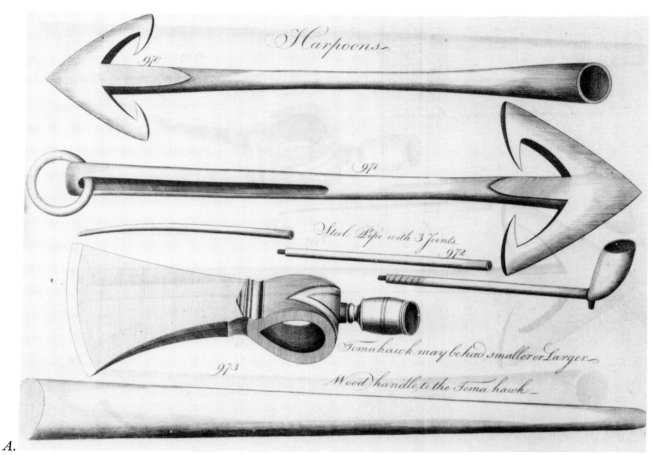

A.

B.

A. Page from an iron merchant's catalog, 18th century, Courtesy, Essex Institute, Salem, Massachusetts.

The harpoons, steel pipe, and tomahawk were each available with variations in the late 18th century when catalogs such as this were engraved.

B. Corporate seal press, cast iron, Merrick and Agnew, Philadelphia, 1830, The Mutual Assurance Company.

The directors of The Mutual Assurance Company purchased this press in 1830 to mark important documents with their corporate seal. The firm of Merrick and Agnew made this press as well as fire engines in the mid-19th century.

A.

B.

A. Blacksmith's cutters, wrought iron, 19th c., American.

The dog's head and the chamfered ball end make these cutters a very unusual tool.

B. Creasing swedge, early 19th c., signed "J. and E. North, Berlin, Conn.", 14 1/2" long, Pennsylvania Farm Museum of Landis Valley.

Creasing swedges are essential to the tinsmith for creasing or making a furrow in tinplate. Jedediah and Edmund North were brothers and blacksmiths who specialized in tool making. The swedge fits into a hole at the top of an anvil.

C. Tongs, wrought iron, 19th c., Wallace Nutting collection, Wadsworth Atheneum.

Many types of tongs are used in a blacksmith's shop. The tongs with long flat ends enable a blacksmith to grip a flat surface too hot to touch.

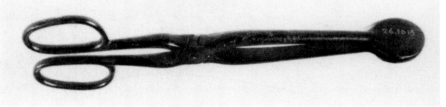

C.

D. This tool is used by a blacksmith to hold a horse's hoof up while he is attaching an iron shoe.

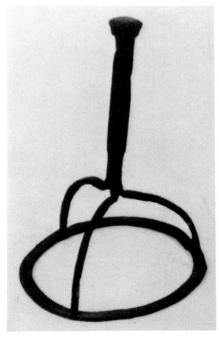

D.

A.

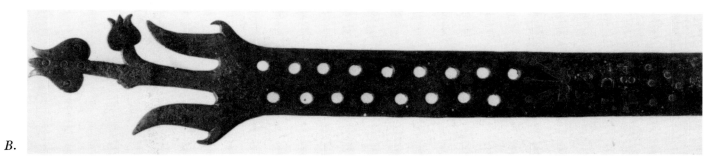

B.

A-B. Mill iron, dated 1784, 5' 10" long, Pennsylvania Farm Museum of Landis Valley.

This tool was used to measure the separation of mill stones. It is beautifully decorated with punch work.

C-D. Mill iron, wrought iron, dated 1799, American.

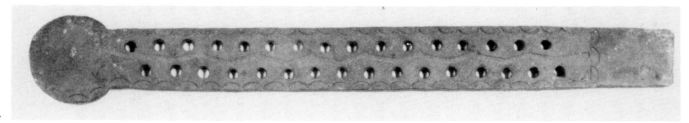

C.

D.

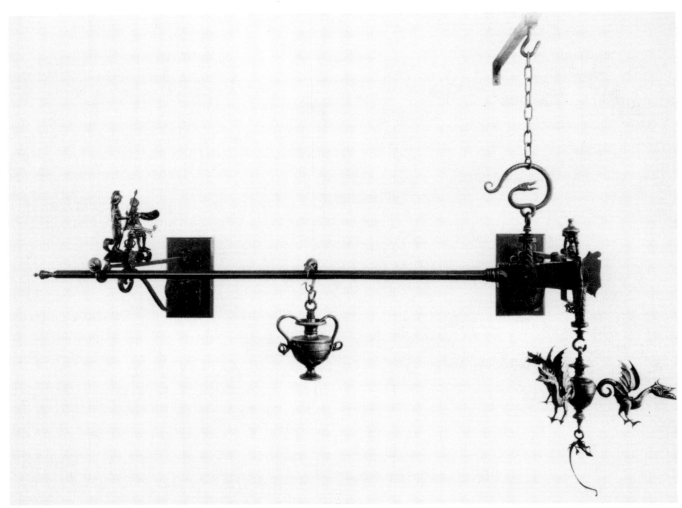

A.

B.

A-B. Scales, steel, late 16th or early 17th c., English or Continental, Museum of London.

These may be the finest steel scales ever made and are called the "Gresham Scales" after the founder of the "Royal Exchange" in England. Possibly these are of northern Italian or southern German manufacture. The quality of the work is similar to the armor and clocks made in those areas. It is possible that they were made by one of the immigrant craftsmen attracted to England at this period.

A.

B.

C.

A. *Trade card, early 18th century, English, Museum of London.*

Small scales shown in the middle of the cartouch were money scales. These were absolute necessities to all mechanics in the days of nearly pure gold and silver coins. The weight of coins often was altered by unscrupulous people by a practice called *clipping,* for which one quite appropriate punishment was to clip the tops of the culprit's ears.

B. *Scales, wrought iron, 18th c., probably European, 22" long.*

This is one of the most common types of scales, made from the Middle Ages to the mid-nineteenth century.

C. *Scales, wrought iron, dated 1770, signed H. Jackson, Old Sturbridge Village.*

Many scales are elaborately decorated and show interesting dates and maker's marks.

A. Trade card for Thomas Hazelton, 1826
Carnegie Library.

*B. Weights, cast iron, dated 1767, English or
American, 5" high, 4 1/2" wide, 8" long, Herbert
Schiffer Antiques.*

Weights like this have been used by Mennonite
people to "anchor" their buggy horses. Engravings
also show similar weights used on commercial
scales.

B.

A.

A. *Flax hatchels, iron and wood, dated 1804 and 1806, American, 12 1/4" long, 13" long.*

In the processing of flax fibers for eventual spinning into linen thread, hatchels were used to straighten and grade the fibers. These were needed by American colonists and one of the reasons iron furnaces and slitting mills were started was to provide the iron teeth for hatchels.

B. *Wool winder, wrought iron, 18th c., American, Henry Francis du Pont Winterthur Museum.*

Wool winders were made principally of wood, and sometimes of whale bone. This is the only iron example we have seen. It is exquisitely made, obviously by an extremely confident blacksmith.

C. *Loom fitting, wrought iron, late 18th or early 19th c., Allentown, Pennsylvania, James C. Sorber.*

These were found by the owner in an early house in Allentown, Pennsylvania. The two fanciful punch decorated straps held the large wooden roller. The catch stopped a ratchet on the roller to keep tension.

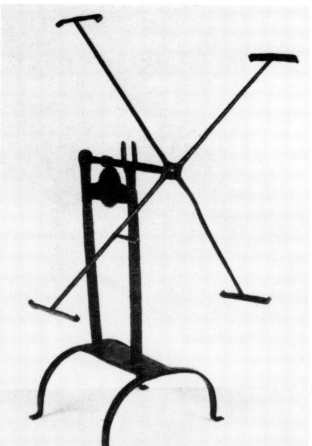

C.

B.

A.

Five quilting patterns, rolled and tinned iron, 19th c., American, W. Himmelreich.

Few quilting patterns have survived, yet they were quite abundant in the nineteenth century. The designs are simple geometric configurations that became known by regional names in varied quilted combinations.

B.

C.

D.

E.

A. Quilting clamp, wrought iron, late 18th c., American, James C. Sorber.

This quilting frame clamp has diamond shaped chamfering and a stylishly shaped wing nut.

B. Sewing bird, wrought iron, 19th c., American, Wallace Nutting Collection, Hartford Atheneum.

This primitive pin cushion and clamp has a frame to hold the pin cushion. The heart shaped wing nut adds to its charm.

A.

B.

A.

A. Sewing bird, stamped, rolled and tinned iron and cast iron, 19th c., American, National Gallery of Art, Index of American Design.

B. Sewing bird, wrought iron, late 18th c., American, W. Himmelreich.

This wonderful sewing bird is shown upside down. The round plate formed the base of a pin cushion. The heart and little birds on the tightening screw are exceptionally pleasing.

B.

A. Seam cutter, wrought iron, 18th c., Pennsylvania, 3 3/4" long, Pennsylvania Farm Museum of Landis Valley.

The chamfered head on this seam cutter is reminiscent of the tops of andirons and jamb hooks in the eighteenth century. The workmanship is exquisite.

B-C. Shears, steel and wrought iron, late 19th c., American, National Gallery of Art, Index of American Design.

Scissors are usually made of steel.

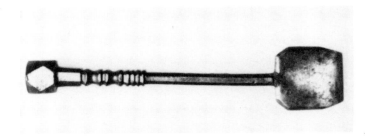

A.

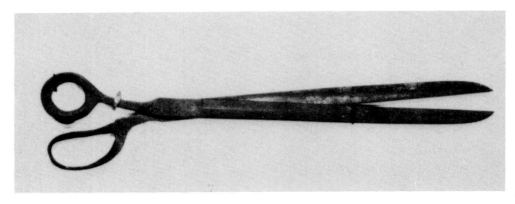

B.

C.

CHAPTER 15
Toys

Penny banks were made of cast iron by the thousands. There were still banks, like "Independence Hall", and mechanical banks that had moveable parts, sometimes doing remarkable things like "Jonah and the Whale". Many were social commentaries such as "The Dark Town Group" which had anti-negro intent. "The Mason and Hod- Carrier" is anti-Irish. "Teddy" is Theodore Roosevelt and had political conotations at the time it was made. Many of these banks retain their original paint. Some of the rarer ones are valuable, even through made at the end of the nineteenth century and early twentieth century. This work is not a study of penny banks, but here we are just showing a few banks at random to indicate the variety that exists.

A. Mechanical bank, cast iron, c. 1900, American, Teddy and the Bear by J. E. Stevens Company, Cromwell, Connecticut, patented February 19, 1907, National Gallery of Art, Index of American Design.

This bank celebrates an incident on one of Theodore Roosevelt's hunting adventures in Mississippi where he said he only wanted to shoot big bears. A coin is placed in the gun, when a button is pressed, the coin shoots into a hole in the tree and the bear's head appears on top.

B. Penny bank, cast iron, "Dark Town Battery" by J. and E. Stevens, Cromwell, Connecticut, patented January 17, 1888, National Gallery of Art, Index of American Design.

C. Mechancial penny bank, "The Mason and the Hod-Carrier" by Shepard Hardware Company, Buffalo, New York, patented February 8, 1887, National Gallery of Art, Index of American Design.

The brick layer snaps the coin from the hod in the laborer's hands.

D. Mechanical bank, cast iron, "Jonah and the Whale" by Shepard Hardware Company, Buffalo, New York, patented July 16, 1890, National Gallery of Art, Index of American Design.

The whale's lower jaw comes up and snaps.

A.

B.

C.

D.

A. Penny bank, cast iron, "Independence Hall" 1876, American, National Gallery of Art, Index of American Design.

This was made to commemorate the "Centennial" celebration of 1876.

B. Toy church, rolled, tinned and painted iron, mid-19th c., American, 19 1/2" high, 10 1/2" wide, 14 1/8" deep, Herbert Schiffer Antiques.

Candles were apparently placed in these toy buildings, and they were used as Christmas decorations among the Pennsylvania Germans.

C. Toy house, rolled, tinned and painted iron, 19th c., Pennsylvania, Herbert Schiffer Antiques.

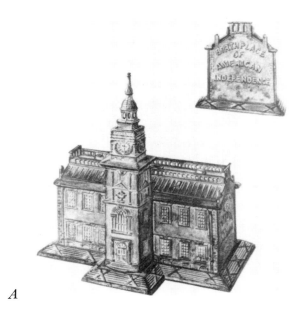

A

B.

C.

D.

E.

D. Doll's cradle, rolled and tinned iron, early 19th c., American, W. Himmelreich.

Many toys were made of tin. There is still some visible on the sides of this cradle.

E. Child's rattle, rolled and tinned iron, early 19th c., American, W. Himmelreich.

These rattles must have been made in large quantities. "For a Good Child" is stamped on the end and the sides have the alphabet in raised letters.

A.

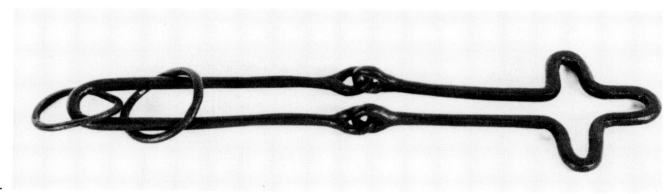

B.

C.

A. Child's kitchen dresser and dishes, rolled, tinned and painted iron, late 19th c., American.

Many doll house toys like this one were made of tin in the nineteenth century. The small dishes are charming, a nice supplement to the dresser.

B. Puzzle, wrought iron, late 19th c., American, 12" long, Pennsylvania Farm Museum of Landis Valley.

The object of this amusement is to remove the large ring. Blacksmiths made this sort of toy as a whimsey.

D.

C. Shooting gallery pig and rider, wrought iron, c. 1898, American.

A competent marksman could unseat the rider as the pig galloped across the range. Several types of shooting gallery birds and animals survive. Some of the birds were made of cast iron.

Friction toy, cast iron, Fowlows, late 19th c.

After this "friction" toy starts to move, the lady chases the goose with her stick. There is a weight in the box behind the lady.

A.

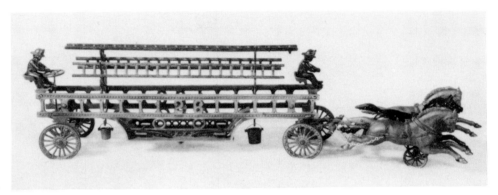

B.

C.

D.

E.

F.

A. *Toy Wilkins hose reel, cast iron, late 19th c., Wilkins Toy Works, Keene, New Hampshire, W. Himmelreich.*

B. *Toy hook and ladder, cast iron, c. 1910, American, W. Himmelreich.*

These laddlers hooked to the roofs, so the wagons that carried them were called "hooks and ladders."

C. *Toy Pumper, cast iron, Hublwey Manufacturing Company, Lancaster, Pennsylvania, c. 1900, W. Himmelreich.*

Here is a steam powered pump for raising water from ponds and low pressure hydrants to the tops of burning buildings.

D. *Toy ice wagon, cast iron, late 19th c., E. R. Ives, Bridgeport, Connecticut, W. Himmelriech.*

E. *Toy fire engine, sheet iron, early 19th c., American.*

This delightfully small fire fighting machine may have been a patent model. It is beautifully made and has all the hand pumping bars intact.

F. *Toy Horse and dray wagon, cast iron, early 19th c., American, W. Himmelreich.*

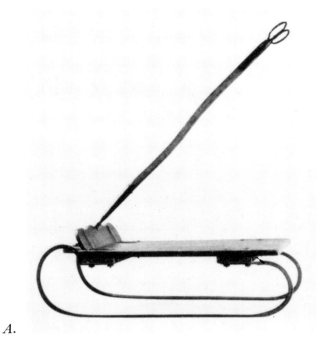

A.

B.

C.

B. Toy cannon, cast iron, late 19th c., American, National Gallery of Art, Index of American Design.

A. Child's sled, walnut and wrought iron, early 19th c., American, 28 1/4" long, Pennsylvania Farm Museum of Landis Valley.

Sturdy and durable, iron toys such as this child's sled, although made in the early nineteenth century, can still be used today.

C. Trackless clockwork locomotive, rolled, tinned and painted iron, cast iron and drawn wire, by E. R. Ives and Company, Bridgeport, Connecticut, c. 1870, National Gallery of Art, Index of American Design.

CHAPTER 16

Weathervanes

A.

B.

A. Weathervane, rolled sheet iron and wrought
iron, 17th c., American, National Gallery of
Art, Index of American Design.
This is one of America's earliest weathervanes,
made for the first church in Concord, Massachusetts
by a local blacksmith.

B. Weathervane, wrought iron, dated 1699,
American, Historical Society of Pennsylvania.
This fine, early weathervane was made for
a grist mill in Chester, Pennsylvania which
was owned in partnership by the three men
whose initials appear: William Penn, Samuel
Carpenter, and Caleb Pusey.

A.

A. Weathervane, hammered sheet iron and wrought iron, 19th c., American, 36" long, Ruth Troiani Antiques.

B. Weathervane, sheet iron, early 19th c., Pennsylvania, Mennonite, Guy and Diane Schum.

C. Weathervane, wrought iron, late 18th or early 19th c., American, James C. Sorber.

This is a small early type of weathervane that fastened to the gable.

B.

C.

A.

A. Weathervane, rolled iron, American, 1840, National Gallery of Art, Index of American Design.

An angel with a trumpet weathervane often was placed on public buildings and churches. This was made by Gould and Hazett of Boston in 1840.

B. Weathervane, sheet iron, end of the 19th c., American, National Gallery of Art, Index of American Design.

This bowling weathervane is a charming rarity.

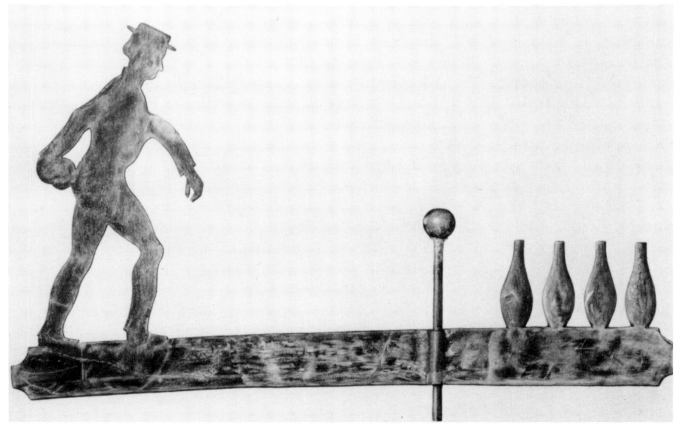

B.

B.

A.

C.

D.

A. *Weathervane, sheet iron, early 19th c., American, National Gallery of Art, Index of American Design.*

This amusing American weathervane shows Count Casimir Pulaski — a hero of the Revolutionary War.

B-C-E. Group of Indian Weathervanes, rolled iron, 19th c., American.

This group of Indians face their target, a deer weathervane. The Indian with two vertical supports may have been a shop sign.

D. *Weathervane, sheet iron, 19th c., American, W. Himmelreich.*

Indian weathervanes are rare and desirable and often display unique folk design. This one retains some of its original paint.

E.

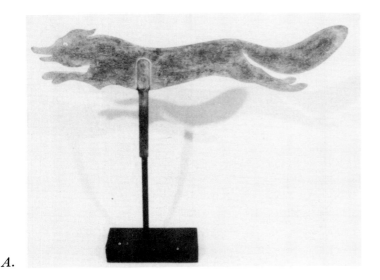

A.

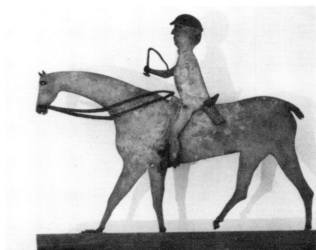

B.

C.

A. *Weathervane, rolled and tinned iron, 19th c., American*

B. *Weathervane, rolled iron, late 18th c., English.* This weathervane is an aristocratic fox hunter.

C. *Weathervane, rolled iron, early 19th c., American, W. Himmelreich.*

This rather ornate version of a trotting stallion may have advertised the availability of a stud horse. The exaggerated heavily crested neck is a design element often seen on weathervanes and posters for stud horses.

D. *Weathervane, sheet iron, c. 1841, 42" high, 53" long at base, Herbert Schiffer Antiques.*

This remarkable weathervane depicts a spotted Appaloosa horse. The wrought iron bracing bars riveted to the sheet metal were absolutely necessary to prevent the collapse of the large, rolled sheet iron plates.

D.

E. *Weathervane, rolled and tinned iron, 19th c., American, James C. Sorber.*

F. *Weathervane, rolled iron, 19th c., American, National Gallery of Art, Index of American Design.*

Men riding horses are rare subjects for weathervanes. This gentleman obviously will never make weight as a jockey.

G. *Weathervane, iron and wood, c. 1870, American.*

This weathervane of a trotting horse retains early paint. The iron bracing holds the wooden form which was a popular motif.

E.

F.

G.

A.

A. *Weathervane, sheet iron, mid-19th century, American.*

B. *Weathervane, sheet iron, late 19th century, American, Pennsylvania Farm Museum of Landis Valley.*

Fish weathervanes were common on barns in many locations in the late 19th and early 20th centuries and were said to represent shad.

B.

C.

D.

C. *Weathervane, rolled iron, 19th c., American, National Gallery of Art, Index of American Design.*

This cow has a painted surface. Cows did not appear on barns until late in the nineteenth century.

D. *Weathervane, rolled tin, 19th c., American, from Trexeltown, Lehigh County, Pennsylvania, W. Himmelreich.*

While most weathervanes of cows and steer are made of hollow copper hammered over a mold, some are made of flat tin, like this one which retains some of its rather amusing paint.

A.

A. Weathervane, sheet iron, 19th century, American, W. Himmelreich.

B.

B. Weathervane, sheet iron, 19th c., American, W. Himmelreich.

Rooster weathervanes were enormously popular and wonderful ones have survived. Bullet holes appear here as lighter colored areas.

C.

C. Weathervane, iron, 19th c., American, W. Himmelriech.

Dogs are a fairly common subject for weathervanes. This sorry looking animal was probably a favorite farm dog, perhaps a sheep dog. It retains some of its original paint.

D.

D. Weathervane, sheet iron, early 19th c., American, W. Himmelreich.

This early goat weathervane may be unique.

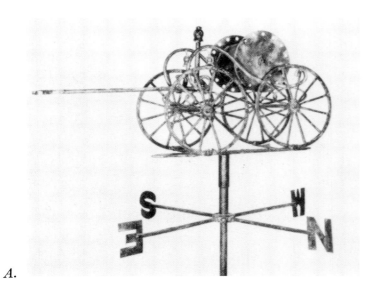

A. Weathervane, wrought iron, wood and brass, c. 1860, American, 22" long, 20" wide, 20" high, Insurance Company of North America.

This three-dimensional weathervane is a model of a four wheel crane-neck type hose reel. It has two lanterns and a lamp on the pole above the fore axel and four separate springs.

B. Weathervane, tinned, rolled iron and copper, 19th c., American, National Gallery of Art, Index of American Design.

Fire houses vied with each other for elegant details. A nineteenth century fire house was an important social club besides providing basic service. This large and complicated weathervane is one of about a dozen surviving fire house forms.

A.

B.

C.

C. Weathervane, sheet iron, 1830-1840, American (Philadelphia), 23 1/2" high, 50" long, Insurance Company of North America.

This weathervane is a model of a hand pulled and pumped end-stroke, double-deck, Philadelphia style fire engine showing a fireman with a horn standing beside the steering tongue. It is historically interesting as a weathervane, one of the best and most valuable.

Bibliography

American Firemarks. Philadelphia: Insurance Company of North America, no date.

American Institute of Metallurgical and Petroleum Engineers. *History of Steel Making in the United States.* New York: The Metallurgical Society,

Anglo-American Art Museum. *Louisiana Folk Art.* Baton Rouge: Louisiana State University, 1972.

Bining, Arthur Cecil. *Pennsylvania Iron Manufactured in the 18th Century.* Harrisburg: Pennsylvania Historical and Museum Commission, 1938.

Bining, Arthur Cecil. *British Regulation of the Colonial Iron Industry.* Philadelphia: University of Pennsylvania Press, 1933.

Brewington, M.V. and Dorothy. *Marine Paintings and Drawings in the Peabody Museum.* Salem: Peabody Museum of Salem, 1968.

Carlson, Stephen P. *Joseph Jenks: Colonial Toolmaker and Inventor.* Saugus Iron Works, 1975.

Christian, Marcus. *Negro Ironworkers of Louisiana, 1718-1900.* Gretna: Pelican Publishing Company, 1972.

Clarke, Mary Stetson. *Pioneer Iron Works.* Philadelphia: Chilton Book Company, 1968. Ontario: Thomas Nelson & Sons Ltd.

Coats Sewing Group. *Modern Spanish Blackwork Anchor Embroidery Book No. 755.* Glasgow: J.P. Coats Sewing Group, 1963.

Coffin, Margaret. *The History and Folklore of American Country Tinware 1700-1900.* New York: Galahad Books, 1968.

Colborn, Robert J. *Lamps in Eighteenth Century Philadelphia.* Independence National Historical Park, April, 1961.

The Colonial Williamsburg Foundation. *New Vistas to the Past.* Richmond: W.M. Brown.

Culiff, Robert. *The World of Toys.* Feltham: Hamlyn Publishing Group Limited, 1969.

Curtis, Will and Jane. *Antique Woodstoves.* Ashville: Cobblesmith, 1975.

Cushing, L.W. *Catalogue of Weathervanes.* Lincoln: Waltham Historical Society, 1974.

D'Allemagne, Henry Rene. *Decorative Antique Ironwork.* New York: Dover Publications Inc., 1968.

Fabian, Monroe H. *The Pennsylvania-German Decorated Chest.* New York: Universe Books, no date.

Fitzgerald, Ken. *Weathervanes and Whirligigs.* New York: Clarkson N. Potter Inc., 1967.

Geerlings, Gerald K. *Wrought Iron in Architecture.* New York: Bonanza Books, 1957.

Glissman, A.H. *The Evolution of the Sad-Iron.* Carlsbad: A.H. Glissman, 1970.

Goetzman, William H. *The Mountain Man.* Cody: Buffalo Bill Historical Center, 1978.

Gunnion, Vernon S. and Hopf, Carroll J. *The Blacksmith, Artisan Within the Early Community.* Harrisburg: Pennsylvania Historical and Museum Commission, 1976.

Hartley, E.N. *Ironwork on the Saugus.* Norman: University of Oklahoma Press, 1971.

Hornung, Clarence P. *Treasury of American Design. Vol. I & II.* New York: Harry N. Abrams Inc., 1950.

John, W.D. (with Simcox, Jacqueline). *English Decorated Trays 1550-1850.* Newport-Mon: The Ceramic Book Company, 1964.

Kauffman, Henry J. *American Axes.* Brattleboro: The Stephen Greene Press, 1972.

Kauffman, Henry J. *The American Fireplace.* Nashville: Thomas Nelson Inc., 1972.

Kauffman, Henry J. *Early American Ironware.* Rutland: Charles E. Tuttle Co., 1966.

Kelly, Alison. *The Book of English Fireplaces.* Feltham: The Hamlyn Publishing Group Limited, 1968.

Klamkin, Charles. *Weather Vanes.* New York: Hawthorn Books Inc., 1973.

Lea, Zilla Rider, ed. *The Ornamented Tray.* Rutland: Charles E. Tuttle Co., 1971.

Ledbetter. *Toys and Banks.* Phoenix: Ledbetter's Auction Gallery, 1973.

Lichten, Frances. *Folk Art of Rural Pennsylvania.* New York: Charles Scribner's Sons, 1946.

Lindsay, John Seymour. *An Anatomy of English Wrought Iron.* London: Portland Press Limited, 1964.

Lindsay, John Seymour. *Iron and Brass Implements of the English and American House.* Bass River: Carl Jacobs, 1964.

Lister, Raymond. *Decorative Cast Iron in Great Britain.* London: G. Bell & Sons Limited, 1960.

Matthews, Leslie G. *Antiques of the Pharmacy.* London: G. Bell and Sons Limited, 1971.

McCosker, M.J. *The Historical Collection of Insurance Company of North America 1792-1967.* Philadelphia: Insurance Company of North America, 1967.

Mercer, Henry C. *The Bible in Iron.* Narberth: Livingston Publishing Company, 1961.

Meyer, John D. *A Handbook of Old Mechanical Penny Banks.* Lancaster: Rudisill and Company, 1952.

Moore, G.M. *Seaport in Virginia: George Washington's Alexandria.* Richmond: Garrett and Massie, 1949.

Norwak, Mary. *Kitchen Antiques.* New York: Praeger Publishers, Inc., 1975.

Ottinger, Simon. *Old Saws Resharpened.* New York: Peter Pauper Press, 1972.

Owen, Michael. *Antique Cast Iron.* Dorset: Blandford Press Limited, 1977.

Pennsylvania Dutch Folk Art. Collection of Walter Himmelreich. Reading: Pennypacker Auction Center, 1971.

Pennsylvania Dutch Folk Art. Collection of Walter Himmelreich. Reading: Pennypacker Auction Center, 1973.

Perry, Evan. *Collecting Antique Metalware.* London: Hamlyn Publishing Group Limited, 1974.

Pierce, Arthur D. *Iron in the Pines.* New Brunswick: Rutgers University Press, 1957.

Poppeliers, John, ed. and Deborah Stevens. *Shaker Built.* Washington: National Park Service, Department of the Interior, 1974.

Revi, Albert Christian. *Antiques for Men.* Hanover: *Spinning Wheel Magazine*-Everybody's Press, Inc., 1973.

Revi, Albert Christian, ed. *Collectible Iron, Tin, Copper and Brass.* Hanover: *Spinning Wheel Magazine*-Everybody's Press, Inc., 1974, published under arrangement with Ottenheimer Publishers, Inc.

Robins, F.W. *The Story of the Lamp.* Bath: Kingsmead Reprints, 1970.

Savage, Robert H. *Pennsylvania German Wrought Iron-work, Vol. 10.* Plymouth Meeting: Mrs. C. Naaman Keyser, 1947.

Schiffer, Herbert F. *Early Pennsylvania Hardware.* Whitford: Whitford Press, 1966.

Smith, Elmer L. and photographs by Melvin J. Horst. *Early Iron Ware.* Lebanon: Applied Arts Publishers, 1976.

Smith, Elmer L. and photographs by Melvin J. Horst. *Early Lighting.* Lebanon: Applied Arts Publishers, 1975.

Sonn, Albert H. *Early American Wrought Iron, Vols. I, II, III.* New York: Charles Scribner and Sons, 1928.

Twopenny, William. *English Metal Work.* London: Archibald Constable and Co., Limited, 1904.

Victoria and Albert Museum. *English Wrought-Iron Work.* Her Majesty's Stationery Office, 1950.

Vince, John. *Old Farm Tools.* Aylesbury: Shire Publications, Limited, 1977.

Waite, John G. and Diane S. "Stovemakers of Troy, New York." *Antiques Magazine.* January, 1973.

Walker, Joseph E. *Hopewell Village.* Philadelphia: University of Pennsylvania Press, 1967.

Wallace, Philip B. *Colonial Ironwork in Old Philadelphia.* New York: Architectural Book Publishing Company, Inc., 1930.

Winterthur Newsletter, Vol. V, No. 9, November 27, 1959.

Winterthur Portfolio II, The Henry Francis du Pont Winterthur Museum, 1965.

Index